Flippi.

Flipping Teams

A Leader's Guide to Building
Top Performing Teams

Vernon Mason III

To order additional copies of this book, contact:
Xlibris
1-888-795-4274
www.Xlibris.com
Orders@Xlibris.com
811765

CONTENTS

I would like to honor and dedicate this to my father, who has given me the resilience, wisdom, motivation, and courage to strengthen my mind, body, and soul. Rest in peace. Now, I would like to give that same drive, devotion, and passion to help you grow. Thank you for your trust.

HAVE YOU EVER been turned down for a position that an outsider took? Or have you ever spoken to an outside hire that was being paid more than you even if you're in the same role, with more experience within that company? According to research made by Matthew Bidwell, a Wharton management professor, if someone was recruited from outside the company, on average, their salary was 18–20 percent more than those promoted from within. That's just average. My personal experience, I was paid over 35 percent more than those who were promoted from within. I discovered that businesses were willing to pay more in the short run in order to save and make more money in the long run. In other words, it could cost less in many scenarios to hire from outside than within.

You may be asking yourself, "Self, how is that?" An internal candidate only thinks about his/her salary, but in reality, the company's opportunity cost to develop them, such as development training (biggest expense and ongoing), compensation packages, paid bonuses, overtime, and additional benefits throughout their employment, is a costly process that doesn't truly yield a big return until years later, in most cases. Some team members don't even last that long in their roles. These expenses are seen as compensation and, therefore, considered in your salary, even if it's not reflected in your wallet. It's nothing personal. That is just how business is.

So when you're wondering why Jim from XYZ Company was just hired, getting paid ten thousand more than you, it's because they've developed under someone else's budget and your company was already invested into that concept. Your company already spent their thousands to develop you into your role. In addition, they hire outside prospects when the demand is necessary for broader experience or a stronger track record of success. Although they are paying them more in salary, they saved tens of thousands of dollars in opportunity costs since they didn't invest in their training. These reasons and more contribute to a higher salary offer, an opportunity for larger bonuses in the outsiders' pockets, and higher positions.

So if you're looking for a way to climb the corporate ladder faster *and* keep control of your career path and income, then pay attention. My guide and strategies not only help you develop into a stronger leader but also help teach you how to take advantage of this secret path. How? By teaching you how to take underperforming teams and developing them into top-performing teams. In other words, my guide teaches you how to flip teams, a solution that has been hiding right under you the whole time.

I've spent years trying to figure out how to climb the corporate ladder with multiple companies while maintaining an above-average salary. However, I've always found a barrier standing incredibly tall between me and those outside candidates. Of course, no one knew why because companies have created an uncomfortable culture where it's forbidden to discuss salaries. Pretty convenient, huh? Instead of a sign saying "Members only," it was "You can never enter!" It was even more unfortunate to see others who were less deserving of a role, hired, and pass you by with a smile. It's terrible, unbelievable, sometimes even unbearable. I would watch motivational movies where everything happens perfectly, and I would visualize my life as the plot in the story just to escape the predictable fortune of a mediocre life. As enjoyable as it may have been, it wasn't real. I couldn't get satisfaction or accomplishment out of these dreams. I couldn't become anybody by pretending to be somebody else.

Then one day, I accepted a position no one wanted that helped me discover a hidden path that not only led me to more successful positions but also allowed me to control when I moved up, how much I moved up for, and whom I moved up with. How many career paths do you know that put you in the driver seat to decline a 70k-salary job offer because you know you can get 80K+ somewhere else and actually *get* it? How many companies do you have lined up asking for *your* help and willing to pay your top dollar in mind for it? What I'm dedicated to do for you is to not only help open your eyes to the discovery of this secret career path but also teach you how to mold your own, how to walk it, and how to succeed as far as you want to go. I call this secret career path Flipping Teams.

The technique that you're about to learn is a well-developed and effective way to create top-performing teams from underperforming teams. In doing so, help you climb the corporate ladder wherever you choose. You can use it within your company if you are strongly loyal, but provide a strong position to negotiate a higher salary than average raises. Or you can use this guide across the industry to strongly reinforce your income and further your career getting recruited. This can be used in any retail environment with any team under any condition and even across multiple industries. My system trains you on how to develop underperforming teams into top-performing machines using five strong pillars as your foundation to build excellence. In addition, you'll discover that many of my strategies, tactics, and tips can be useful in any job position, sales or not. I will cover leadership, accountability, productive time management, salesmanship, training, branding, and the list goes on. In addition, to assist and reinforce your development, I will also share other insights for perspective and for you to improve yourself further through other resources.

Every time you flip a team, you will open the door for another opportunity, another team to flip and to climb the ladder. This guide not only helps you develop a top-performing team but also helps create a self-sufficient machine. In time, their performance can and will function without you, providing *you* an opportunity to move on to the next opportunity. In addition, you'll be developing team members into leaders of their own who will be promoted into stronger roles themselves. A win-win. The unique bonus that I will share with you is a faster and more efficient way to reach the top by using a career path that many have seen, but very few have noticed. Through my techniques, you will learn about networking, partnership, leadership, competitive advantage, team building, and much more. The only missing piece of the puzzle is one that only you control: execution.

Now before we move forward, I must say that this is not the perfect system to help only you close every deal you'll ever face. It does not have the perfect method that *you* can use in any way to get the results *always* in *your* favor. This system is about developing yourself *and* your team as one unit that also provides the best experience to your customers and clients. There are millions of variables in the world because of the extraordinary differences that you will encounter and cannot be predicted. However, I'm all about probability, which is why I've developed a system that will greatly increase your probability of success, regardless of the position you're in, sales or service, management or associate. In any situation, just remember that you can't control how people react, but you can certainly control how you respond. This is simply my system that I have developed over my career that has led to much success for myself and others in multiple industries and within multiple *Fortune 500* companies.

I encourage you to learn my system while continuing the development of your own skills through reading and other developmental opportunities. This is how the business world develops: learning and adding your personal, unique touch to an already existing system. I will tell you what I've been told before: "The best way to overcome inexperience is organization." My methods and strategies are your way to overcome the common challenges that you have or will face effectively. This system, as any other, relies on all the components operating simultaneously, like your phone or watch, none of which will operate daily unless all components work together simultaneously, harmoniously, and consistently.

This guide will also help you and your team members develop into a stronger person and a stronger leader. Like buying a home, you typically won't change the structure of it or its foundation, but you would certainly add your creative touch to make it look and feel like it's your unique home. Use my system as your foundation to become a strong leader and sales champion. Once you have mastered my guide, then you can mold, evolve, and even add your own unique style to it. In fact, I highly encourage it. That's how I was able to develop my system.

HISTORY

S INCE I WAS ten, I've always been what I believe to be a hard worker. I came to work on time. I followed policy. I wasn't afraid to roll up my sleeves. I was number one in sales and service. I've earned countless awards. Yet I was passed for promotions, lost internal interviews to lower-performing coworkers, and became close to invisible when corporate executives visited (outside of the obvious pat on the back for my performance). I felt like something wasn't right. I couldn't quite figure out what it was, but I knew if I continued, my performance would allow everyone else around me to move forward in their career. So I felt it was time for me to pay attention. I had to see why these individuals were chosen over my top performance record. My experience at a retail electronic store was where I had my first epiphany.

At this point, most people would probably look for another job or just quit their performance to see a reaction, but I knew that wouldn't do anything for my career. If I left for another business, I'd have to start over and might ultimately land in the same position. I couldn't quit. It's not in my DNA. Even if that was a choice, that is never the way to convince management that I'm worthy. The choice left was to continue working. This time, I began to observe like a kid at a museum, waiting for the figures to come to life. Every interaction I saw, I studied. I watched how particular individuals interacted with each other. Their body language, their tone of voice, and their responses all gave cues and clues to what I eventually discovered; within our work environment, we had subcultures. A few tight groups of similar personalities stuck together. They hung out during lunches. They took the time to wander into the others' department to have a quick chat or competitive banter or to talk about current events. Although I knew everyone in all the groups, I didn't have a home. I didn't have a particular identity where someone could look at me and say, "He's from that group."

That's when it hit me. That was what I was missing. I was missing a social identity. Everyone knew me as a top performer, but as a loner. I literally took the time to list all the teammates who'd been promoted or received merits. To my surprise, a majority came from some of these groups. Now it made sense. Those who received these accomplishments, even without the record or history, had an identity. Regardless of your achievements, they *can* go unnoticed without an identity. If I wanted to grow within the company, within my career, I needed an identity. Mark Zuckerberg created his identity when he chose to team up with a few Harvard colleagues and roommates, create a social network that connected campus students together on one platform, then took flight on his own to build an empire in the world we all know as Facebook. Larry Page walked the halls of Stanford for a tour to determine if he wanted to join the university, and met Sergey Brin, who was assigned to show him the campus grounds. Within three years, they started their own company on a new idea in a garage and earned a $100,000 check from an investor. Starting from a garage, they built one of the biggest tech companies in history, called Google. The list goes on for influential and innovative leaders, but the point that still exists is that all of the leaders you hear, see, and admire made a choice that forged their identity, an identity they wanted. Which group will help me succeed? What type of mentor could develop my path? Who could provide the opportunities I seek? These were the questions I needed to start asking. At that moment, it was time to choose what I wanted my identity to be.

In making my decision, I kept it simple, as I prefer to make most of my decisions. I looked at each group. To further illustrate my point, let's name these groups by mottos since each group had a unique style of behavior, demeanor, and motivation. I had three to choose from: Life Is Good, Work Is Great, Title Is Everything. Now, based off those mottos, I bet as you read each one, you immediately put yourself in a group. If you have already, that's the idea, but let's check for accuracy.

Life Is Good is a group who believed just that. I get a paycheck to pay for what I need, I have wonderful relationships, and I enjoy living life just as it is. This group knows how to have fun and live a stress-free life. For you analytics out there, this group has an 80 percent life, 20 percent work importance factor.

Work Is Great is the workaholic pool. These individuals are driven by staying constantly busy with work. They absolutely love what they do and are willing to shorten their personal experiences regardless of the outcome. They are proud to work hard and they do it well. This balance is the polar opposite, with 20 percent life, 80 percent work.

Title Is Everything has a unique curve. These individuals put success above all else, based on personal or professional goals. Accomplishing goals are their top priority, which means their reach is as high as the goal they set, and these individuals set multiple goals. For this reason, their balance can shift from 30/70 to 40/60. These individuals find efficient solutions to make life and/or work easier in order to accomplish their goal faster with minimal damage completely dependent on the goal they set.

Now that you've checked your answers, keep in mind that people change based off life experiences and could change from one group to the next, sometimes overnight. Nonetheless, as I mentioned earlier, to keep things simple, I looked at all three of these groups and compared them by the number individuals who received merits and promotions. The summary was this: Those within Life Is Good had the lowest amount of merits and promotions. It makes sense. Life is good, right? No need to overachieve or go beyond the job description. Those within Work Is Great had the highest amount of merits, but a low amount of promotions. They are so great at what they do that that is all they *can* do. Those within Title Is Everything had a low amount of merits, but the highest amount of promotions, typically because these individuals are socially linked to the decision-makers and make it well known that they are gunning for a management position. They are promoted because of their shares of ambitious attitudes mixed with their constant interaction with the managers. They typically skip the merit raise and go straight to promotions because they don't always perform at the level they should, even if management can't or doesn't want to see it. Here is a chart for you visual learners.

	LIG	WIG	TIE	?
Merits	-	+	-	+
Promotions	-	-	+	+

Makes sense, right? Now, I bet you have a bewildered look about that question mark. Who is the mystery group? I'll reveal the mystery group later. That group is only found at a certain level in your career path. However, to stay on point, I think you can at least agree for now that the results under these three groups make sense.

During that period, my main concern was getting promoted. So my obvious choice was to focus on developing my social status within the TIE group because at that time, I wanted to move up the ladder. Luckily, I had a great friend named John, who was already a part of this group. This made the transition easier than expected. However, at the time, I was in a department full of those within the WIG group and a few in the LIG group. I had to make a transfer. I learned it from firsthand experience that when you want to reach a goal, regardless of which group you're a part of, it is imperative that you surround yourself with those who have similar, if not already accomplished, goals. After one simple conversation with management, the transfer was complete.

That was a focal point in my life where I learned the emotional transition from caring for everyone to only caring for those who can assist my ambition, a very weird and emotional experience, but one very necessary to open my eyes. Think of it as a rite of passage. I had to earn my honor to be a part of this group. I had to develop their type of personality. And evolve I did.

After this transition, I took notes from all the moments spent leading groups, clubs, teams, etc., compiling all the successes and failures I had. Once collected, I started creating a system of dos and don'ts, then broke it into a simplistic strategy that could be used in any department, in any store within the company. My thought was this would reassure preparation and success for any available management position I take. I wasn't aiming for a specific management position, just that promotion.

After this development, I began to ascend the social status and performed remarkably. John and I became a powerhouse team. Our behaviors and actions were the envy of all within and, I'm sure, outside the group, enough to gain recognition when our supervisor was promoted out of the department. John's goal at the time was to be number one in sales. Mine didn't change. It was *my* time to achieve my goal. With my succession into management, there wasn't anyone else challenging John in sales. In a two-week period, he became number one, and I got my promotion. Win-win.

After taking my new position, I began testing my system. I learned a lot and I learned fast. My team flew through our sales goals, ranking in the top across multiple categories, and the recognition was coming in like crazy. The strategy worked. To develop my strategy, I took concepts that I used in college when I attended the Sam Walton Business College at the University of Arkansas and mixed them with my sales and management experience. At the time, the Sam Walton Business College was ranked twenty-third in the nation, so there were plenty of resources available from top professors to R&D business strategies. A plethora of information was at my fingertips in regards to team building, business management, marketing, finance, advertising, economics, category management, etc. Combined with my personal sales and management experience across all my positions, I felt that there had to be a system that I could use at any store and in any position and get the same results. Why would I want to make such a system? Well, I was the supervisor at a store where management stuck around for quite some time. My TIE mentality was turning gears, saying, "I don't want to stop here. I want a bigger title."

I hypothesized that the greater the challenge you face to turn a team upside down, the greater the recognition and opportunity for advancement will be. For instance, if I took a poor-performing team and trained them to be top performers, I could inherit such a strong reputation that other managers and companies would pay greatly to attract my skill set. If I took a team and just fired them until I hired new, motivated team members, then my skill set wouldn't be as desirable. Anyone can come into a team and turn over team members—easy.

However, if I took a poor-performing team and made *them* a top-performing team, then I would be known as a game changer. It can be tough to do, but plenty of opportunity if done right, especially when you're saving the company a great deal of money by minimizing turnover. That essentially puts more in my pocket. What I didn't understand at the time was the impact it would create in the team members' lives, by granting them a chance to excel themselves, as opposed to casting them to another company.

Let's look at this through supply and demand. Every company has many poor-performing teams and team members. Not *everybody* can change that. Therefore, demand is there, but the supply is short. What I failed to notice then was that there was a unique, hidden career path lying within this short supply chain. When demand is up and supply is low, what typically happens to the price of supply? It goes up. So it was easy for me to assume that if I could create a system that could consistently flip the poor performance (the supply), companies would be willing to pay me more than those promoted from within their store. I felt it was time to truly test my hypothesis and my system in a more distressed location, and I found the perfect location to test it. It was a location where the team had over three years of consistently poor performance and was twice the size of my current team. The controllable was still managing the same departments. It was a tough risk, but after a few phone calls, I made my last transfer.

Years later, my system had become an amazing formula to success that was developed and tested within multiple companies in industries including retail, hospitality, restaurant management, business management, and finance within major brand companies like Walmart, Fuddruckers, Embassy Suites, Best Buy, Wells Fargo, SunTrust Bank, and more. I created a way to use the modern-day corporate system in your favor by creating a new career path that develops a win-win relationship between every firm and *you*. Every firm wants strong leaders. They win because it puts more money in their pocket in the long run as you develop top-performing teams and future leaders. You win because you get promoted with higher potential of income than the average. Who doesn't want *that* business relationship?

Taking the poor performing teams, flipping them into top performers, and then earning your promotion through recruitment to move on to the next project, with an increase in salary, is what I'll teach you. Inside or outside the company, whoever wants you more—my system can improve any team. So why share my secret? I want to help as many people as I can become the best that they can be to improve our society. I'm a firm believer in progress, and I believe every one of you can contribute. Those who know me can confirm my passion to help others. A strong component in my management style is not allowing my team to perform less than what I believe they're capable of. And I believe everyone is an incredible asset to their company and are capable of great accomplishments. I just help pull the best out of them. I will teach you how to do the same for yourself and your teams.

I have found a career path that has plenty of room for millions at the top because every business secretly wants this career choice to flourish. Why? They need your help to increase production and minimize the costs in doing so. Like I said, the demand is always there, but the supply isn't. You can become their solution. My system can help you get there faster.

One of my goals is to help over 10,000 people become successful leaders. That's helping 10,000 people reach their goal. If you learn my five pillars, execute excellently, and never give up, you will win, and both of us will hit our goal. Win-win. Even if you choose not to follow this career path, you will still greatly improve your skill set to accomplish other passionate goals. I'm confident that my five pillars will help you be successful personally and professionally by increasing your skills in leadership, team development, sales, and more.

There are a lot of things in life that you will not be able to reach taking a step. That's why you have to learn how to leap. How else do you think great people reach the impossible?

This guide will teach you how to take leaps in management. Throughout my leadership studies and experience, I've developed a pillar system involving five crucial development skills that can be universally applied to any team. Anytime I would learn something new, I would want to incorporate it into my life. In many cases, I make visual reminders to make it real. For me to maintain the vision truly, I have to see it. So throughout my career, I've made sticky notes, posters, and printed pictures of the family and hung them all over my office. From impactful quotes to something I want to buy, it's hung on the wall to remind me every day why I do what I do. I understood that impact. Therefore, my guide will have essential visuals, real-life examples, and templates available throughout the pillars. I also encourage you to make notes, posters, or copies of your own from my guide to place throughout your office or on your desk to help reinforce what you've learned, even if it's just motivation. My five pillars consist of the following:

Pillar I: Leadership—This pillar expands on important factors such as the differences between a manager and a leader, the importance of leading from the front, motivating yourself and others, how to use my unique system called the Mason influential leadership model to identify performance levels and how to adjust your training to fit their specific needs, and much more.

Pillar II: Productive Time Management—This pillar will either help you develop a new basis for controlling your schedule or expand your current system by teaching you how to create effective priority lists and maintain all the unique benefits behind its execution, all for the purpose of maximizing your time for maximum performance.

Pillar III: Positive Accountability—This pillar emphasizes the misconceptions of accountability, the importance of having it in place, how to utilize it in a positive direction to encourage a passion to achieve within your team members, and how to create consistently scheduled one-on-ones for team development and strategic planning.

Pillar IV: Alpha Sales 101—Even if you and your team are not in a direct sales role, the behaviors of such roles are reflected in every position in every company within every interaction. In other words, this pillar is important for all roles to learn within any company. This pillar will help you understand how to provide exceptional service, strengthen your brand, learn how to identify key opportunities through assessment, and learn important behaviors and strategies that will maximize your business.

Pillar V: Building A Culture—This pillar puts all of what you've learned from the previous pillars into a training schedule. This pillar walks you through my one-hundred-day training program that you will execute to develop your team fully into performance machines. In other words, this is your action plan. Included, you will also learn important strategies such as how to observe interactions effectively, document interactions for coaching effectiveness, strategize with your team members for success, strategically analyze your community your business is within, and more.

The power of this system is not just what lies within these pillars, but how they're implemented by *you*. There is an old saying from Confucius that my father told me: "I hear and I forget. I see and I remember. I do and I understand." So if you study this guide, utilize the tools and resources provided, implement the action plan, and carry the confidence within yourself that I have in you to succeed, then you'll excel in any position.

TIP: It's extremely important to improve yourself and your career consistently. As humans, we were not meant to stay in one role forever, hence why we all have desires and goals. You must have progress. Otherwise, you go against nature and lose any desire to improve. That loss of desire invites depression and unwillingness to care; it destroys all career paths eventually. Both leaders and team members alike have to progress and grow in order to become and remain successful. This guide is for helping you *and* your team members improve your careers.

I have provided visual tools and resources to help enhance your learning experience throughout the pillars as mentioned before. In addition, you will see important tips and reminders throughout the guide that will help strengthen your behaviors. Along the way, I also provided real-life examples from my career as further illustration of real-life situations you may be able to compare to. Names have been altered out of professional courtesy.

If you're already a top-performing leader, my tactics and strategies can give you a leading edge over the ever-growing competition, making you a stronger leader. Either way, this conclusive guide will give you all the knowledge and tools to turn your career and your team members' careers into a complete success story of your own. When you master my system, you'll be capable of controlling where you want to work, how much you want to work for, and when you want to start. It's time to take the first step to flipping teams!

PILLAR I

Leadership

S O WHAT IS leadership? There are many very loose definitions in today's culture. It's not just about leading a project or managing a team or being the captain athlete. Leadership is not just a word or a position. It's a skill and arguably a behavior. I haven't seen anyone train leadership better than the United States military because they understand what is necessary to develop this skill set and why. If you have had experience within the United States military, you have a tremendous advantage and head start over the competition. However, regardless if you have military experience or not, it is a skill. You can learn it. Develop it. Grow it. And use it. Without consistent behaviors, without practice, you'll weaken your ability to lead.

This section is going to help you shape those behaviors and skills. It will strengthen your inner leadership capability. First, do you know what kind of leader you are? Although leadership is a behavior, there are many styles in performing that behavior, some of which are discovered through your personality traits. Care to find out what kind of leader you are? Then I recommend going out and buying the book *StandOut* by Marcus Buckingham, in my opinion, an easy guide and worth every penny. Take the *StandOut* leadership strength assessment code within and follow the instructions to take the assessment. This assessment helps you identify your strengths based off a set of scenarios and your decision on how to solve them. There are nine strengths in all: Advisor, Connector, Creator, Equalizer, Influencer, Pioneer, Provider, Stimulator, and Teacher. After determining your strengths, you'll have a stronger understanding of how to utilize my guide effectively, based on *your* specific characteristics. It's not necessary, but it is important to understand yourself and your styles before learning how to improve them. As I mentioned previously, I try to provide many tools and resources to strengthen your ability to succeed.

These days, business leaders focus on helping you find your opportunities for development, but what about your strengths? *If you focus entirely on building your lowest points to a medium, you'll never push your highest points to its maximum.* Your threshold is where you push your limits. That's where you do the impossible or unthinkable or unbelievable. That's where you make the biggest changes to you, those around you, and the world. Don't avoid learning your opportunities as it is a great benefit to be aware of them, but keep your biggest focus on mastering your strengths. Find your strengths and use this guide to assist the development and growth of your potential. We will dive more into this later in these pillars.

Another important factor about a leader is that a leader must never leave the classroom. It's not just a duty but a responsibility to evolve your knowledge base consistently in order to progress your skills and provide the best training to your teams. To get the best, you have to be the best—not the best at everything everyone else does, just the best you can be at being a leader. To provide the best, you have to become the pioneer of new tools, skills, behaviors, and knowledge to delegate back to your team and to encourage them to reflect the same behaviors. Knowledge will *always* be a competitive advantage. Don't stop at graduation! The best leaders in the world always continue their education. How do you think they remain the best? So let's start by learning how to master your 80 percent.

Mastering Your 80 Percent

Even though leadership is very crucial, the *right* leadership is most important. Your team members are links in a chain. The more links you have, the stronger the chain will be. As each team member is enlisted under your vision, the team gets stronger. You add links to your chain. However, no matter how long that chain gets, it is only as strong as the center link. That's *you*! Become the strongest bond that keeps the chain together, and you'll become the strongest willed team in the company. In this pillar, I'll teach you the importance of morale and its impacts, rules to help contain morale, how to use my Mason influential leadership model to identify their performance levels, and ultimately build the foundation to becoming a strong center link for your team.

However, before we start laying down the foundation for our first pillar, you must understand the difference between a leader and a manager. Everyone has leadership within them, but not everyone is a leader. Did I lose you? Remember, leadership is a behavior and a skill, something everyone is capable of developing. But just like any skill set, what's the point without a purpose? To have a purpose, you have to have a vision. Helen Keller was once asked, "What's worse than being blind?" Her response was "Having sight, but no vision."

In my experience, the most noticeable difference between a leader and manager is vision. As an example, if you or your manager show up to work, support team activities, participate in daily functions, and call it a good day, then you have a manager. If you or your manager show up to work, motivate the team to work together, help envision the greater good from daily contributions, and inspire all to be at their best for a common goal, then you have a leader.

As I mentioned, a vision. A goal. A destination. They typically see the bigger picture and make all attempts to fulfill it. A manager, simply put, is a leader without vision. A manager only sees the smaller picture and only works for the daily needs. They have leadership properties and may show great behaviors, but have a lack of passion for progression. They typically don't have vision to move beyond or impact more than expected of their role. Does this mean managers are not impactful on a business? Not at all. I've seen many managers who make huge impacts and contributions to their teams and businesses. Some of my friends who are impactful managers are some of the best in their respective areas. But do leaders make a bigger impact than managers? Absolutely! A single vision can change everything. Still don't understand what I mean by *vision*?

My favorite definition I've come across is "an experience of seeing someone or something in a dream or trance, or as a supernatural apparition." A supernatural apparition. Unlike the old English thought embedded with ghosts and spirits, an apparition can also mean something remarkable. Vision is the bigger picture, the main goal, the perfect ending to what drives an individual to excel. That can be achieving a million dollars or building a business or being number one. It's supernatural because it's foresight to what one believes he/she can or will accomplish. Your mentality has never felt more passion or drive than the anxiety of reaching what you've envisioned to be a perfect ending to your legacy. This single difference can alter everything within a business, a team, and even an individual. You must have a vision to be successfully using my system. You must see a bigger picture. Having a vision creates inspiration, which is one of the biggest attributes of a leader.

Sharing your vision with others encourages participation and self-motivation among other created attributes within a great team. Sharing your inspiration can encourage others to either create a vision for themselves, or adopt yours. In addition, as a leader, you need to have great courage not only to resist those who try to alter your influence negatively but also to face resistance courageously by either persuading or applying disciplinary action to encourage positive results. Either way, you're encouraging greater production by giving your team members purpose, a reason to exceed their daily expectations, a vision of something greater than just today.

TIP: If you don't have that vision, I invite you to put the book down and take the time to reflect on what you're going after. Deciding is the only obstacle. Reflect on what you want, how you want to impact yourself and the world, and when you want to do it. When you find it, write it down, and then return to this book. Once you have a vision, you have a goal. Once you have a goal, you have a purpose. Once you have a purpose, then you're ready to truly learn.

Effective Communication

This honestly wouldn't be a proper guide in leadership without referencing at least the importance of communication. We can go in all directions and list one important way of communicating after another, but the truth is, we'll cover this throughout the entire book in one form or another with a bigger emphasis on pillar IV. Therefore, I just want to address just how important it is here and the importance of constantly improving your communication skills. When we talk about effective communication, what do we mean? Typically, speaking loud and clear is mistakenly taken for effective communication. Effective communication is not just about speech, but how it is delivered. Remember this throughout this guide and career.

My daughter Anastasia, who was one and a half at the time, woke up in the middle of the night, crying. She asked for three things. First, she asked for milk. Once it was provided, she shook her head vigorously and said no. Then, she asked for her favorite toy. Once it was provided, she yet again shook her head vigorously and said no. Continuing, she cried, *"Mickey Mouse Clubhouse,"* indicating she wanted to watch her show. I turned it on my tablet, and once again, she pushed it away, saying no. Tears continued to fall. When those were provided, one by one, she would continue to cry while shaking her head no. That's when it occurred to me that she didn't know what it was called or even understand what it truly was, but she knew what she wanted. I didn't. She just didn't know how to communicate it. Or was it that I didn't know how to interpret it? Think about how many times people communicate like this on a daily basis (minus the crying). They want to communicate something but don't know how. So it comes out completely different, and the person who receives it doesn't respond properly. Ultimately, it can get frustrating for both.

Once I read her body language, I put together what all those things had in common. It made sense on what she was truly seeking. Comfort. Once I pulled her close for a warm snuggle, she calmed down and passed right out. All she wanted was to feel comfort from me after a bad dream. Although she asked for all those things, she was really asking for what they provided, but from me. The point here is as a leader, you have to read between the lines of speech. A team member may say they have everything understood, but maybe they are secretly asking for your help. As discussed previously, communication involves more than just words. Don't harbor on just what is said. Hear the tone. Read their body language. In some cases, you have to put pieces together. Only then will you receive the full message and deliver precisely what's really needed. Team members may not always be the bravest to say something up front, but there are certainly clues that you could help uncover it.

During the beginning of my communication studies, I studied Professor Albert Mehrabian's research studies completed in 1967 at the University of California. His research showed that 55 percent of all communication between people is expressed through body language, 38 percent is through the tone in their voice, and only 7 percent is conveyed through their words (the 7-38-55 rule). You may have heard this before as this isn't anything new, but if you haven't, definitely keep this with you. His discovery means that all this time, 93 percent of what anyone has been trying to say isn't even expressed in words. Yikes! Makes you realize why certain situations never went the way you expected in the past, right? As a student of communication, I certainly implore you to increase your proficiency in communication with emphasis on body language as the success of any strategy can literally hang in the balance on the effectiveness of your communication. Although we'll cover this in more detail throughout this guide, you should never stop learning how to strengthen your communication skills. This includes being able to listen and read others as well.

Morale

Morale is the most powerful weapon in leadership. Throughout my studies on stratagem, I've learned that it is a group's life force. If you deplete a team's morale, then the team dies (figuratively speaking) and any chance of your success. Assuming you've paid attention to history somewhere, you've learned stories of small armies that have conquered overwhelming odds and, in retrospect, larger armies that have fallen because of their capability or incapability to wield morale. If you've read *The Art of War* by Sun Tzu, you'll understand how morale in war and business has many of the same attributes, which is why soldiers are great candidates for sales, management, and retail. Vice versa, business leaders can be very effective military strategists. One of those similarities is the leader's capability of wielding morale.

I'm sure you've heard the expression that in order to be a champion, you have to act like a champion. The same concept applies to a team and even more so to a leader. Although a challenge that many sales leaders and managers face is turning loss into growth, they both handle this issue differently. In these situations, a manager immediately assumes it is poor execution from the team, only disregarding that their team is simply a reflection of his/her leadership. Champions don't play the blame game. Instead, a leader asks, "What can I do? How can I rally morale when sales are down?" More times than not, your sales are a direct reflection of the team's morale. It's not a secret.

Typically, companies are very reactive, so when the economy and/or a seasonal loss hit, it's too late to prevent the damage. The interesting thing to me is that the seasons never change and yet the results are always a surprise. A seasonal loss is a term I refer to when a company predicts a period of loss or minimum profit within the year. For example, if my company makes 50 percent of its profits during the summer, but only 10 percent during the winter, then winter is considered a seasonal loss for my business. Loss doesn't mean just profits. It can also mean other opportunity losses such as market share, growth, expansion, turnover, etc. Other examples can be January and February for retailers because everyone spent all their money during the holidays, or during the holidays for banks because everyone is spending their savings. These are where you see the job cuts, salary cuts, or budget cuts on benefits soon follow. A company that forecasts a seasonal loss would want to maximize marketing, inventory, and staffing during their peak seasons to take full advantage of their annual opportunities. Makes sense, right? Many companies say it's because of the market, but it is also because company managers as a whole run their teams like their predicted sales. If the first quarter is the lowest in sales, then they'll tell their teams, "This is the slowest part of the year, so do your best." This is where a leader says, "This is the competition's slowest time of the year, so let's take advantage." See the difference? One way accepts less than their best, and the other encourages it.

This "accepted loss" thought process was another motivator for me to find a way to outperform other teams proactively during these tough periods. By you understanding the importance behind morale, you can eliminate this type of thought process of planning for loss and encourage your team to supersede expectations. My proactive approach is heavily reliant on the morale of my team. So I'll teach you to follow three simple rules to nurture the morale of your team. The concept will evolve throughout this book, however. This pillar will teach you how to nurture it. Pillars II through IV will teach you how to build upon it. Pillar V will show you how to wield it for success. If any of these core rules aren't followed, you'll lose the team and your success plan. Keep in mind that morale is not easily swayed. These rules must always be reinforced, and you must frequently keep them nurtured because there are both predictable and unpredictable forces that impact your team's morale. The results will be based on *your* vision of success. So all that I request is that you use these techniques for the greater good and not self-preservation.

The Three Rules to Nurture Morale

Rule #1—One Dream

At all times, you must have 100 percent buy-in of your vision. More than one simple vision creates distractions and risks dividing the team. If they can't see it, you have to help them visualize it. Each member must understand their added value to accomplish this goal and accept it willingly. Once your team can see what you see, feel the passion that you feel, and believe in what you believe, you'll gain their commitment to work their best toward your vision. This rule is important because if one person doesn't see, feel, or believe in what you envision, I guarantee you'll have a broken team over time.

These individuals are what are referred to as cancers for their cancerous ability to start mutations within the team's morale by manipulating others with negativity, encouraging insubordination, and having zero accountability for their actions. I'm sure you've heard of the expression before. You can easily identify these individuals at your first team meeting, based on participation and body language. If you have an existing team, I bet you've already visualized them while reading this, if one exists. Every Charlie- and Bravo-performing team has one. We'll go into further discussion on that later in this pillar. If you've identified a cancer within your team, try the following:

> After your meeting, pull the individual(s) aside (individually if more than one. Never group them together. In addition, never address them in front of the team) and ask for their opinion on what you discussed with your team. Here is where you can find out underlying causes for their behavior that hopefully you can realign. Use a few of these questions below to help uncover more to their story.

- Why do you feel the way you do?
- How can I help you understand our vision/goal?
- How would you add more value?
- How could I add more value for you?
- What can I do to help you succeed with the team?
- Can you help me bring the team together?

TIP: All constructive feedback should always be given privately. Mostly negative outcomes result from public addresses.

If their verbal answers or body language are similar to "I don't know," "I don't care," or "Whatever," then the individual(s) do not wish to be a part of what you're trying to build. Further persuasion or disciplinary action will be necessary. Implementation and action plans for the unwilling will be covered in pillar III.

Rule #2—All-Inclusive

After rule #1, you have their buy-in and, therefore, commitment. Now, you need their loyalty. The most important piece here is participation. To earn that, you must encourage the team not just to play a part in your vision, but also to be a part of it. For example, if your vision is being the best team in the company, you have to illustrate to each team member how their actions can impact their success *and* the team's success in becoming number one. In other words, the team can't be number one without their individual contributions. Show the team how the best performs. Illustrate what the best teams in the business are doing and how they're doing it. If you're in the hotel business, you'll explain the importance of how the concierge (front desk) is the first and last face of the hotel to provide an optimal guest experience and therefore always be at your best. If you're in banking, you'll explain the importance of the teller and how they speak to 80 percent of the business, so they must encourage clients to speak to a banker and should, therefore, be at their best. If you're in retail, you'll explain the importance of utilizing each other's specialty from each department for cross-sell opportunities and therefore be at their best. You get the point.

TIP: If you're new to a company and you're unaware of what the best teams in that field are doing to win, here are some suggestions. Ask your teammates for names of those who are considered the best-performing teammates and write their names down. Ask peers or your manager for names of leaders and teams who are top performers and write them down. Now, either call or email these top performers, introduce yourself, let them know you were referred to speak to them because of their performance, and ask for their best practices. This is a perfect start to learning the game.

In reality, you don't just want them to see the vision; you need them to experience it. You want to encourage them to self-discover their value. Self-discovery is a very powerful tool for self-motivation. If you're the one who encourages them to self-discover their potential, you'll earn their loyalty. Make this journey inclusive. Help each member connect the dots between their success and the team's success. Here are a few example self-discovery questions you can ask your team members. Keep in mind that your goal is to help uncover their needs so you can find out how to make a win-win proposition to obtain yours.

- What would you like to achieve?
- Why do you want to achieve it?
- How do you see yourself achieving it?
- What do you need to achieve it faster?
- How can I help you succeed?

All these questions can help you find a link between your goals.

Rule # 3—Little Things *Do* Matter

When I say "little things," you may think of things such as saying "thank you" or buying a gift just because. Although these decisions can make an impact, I mean something more strategic. This is where I sharpen your guerrilla marketing skills. Under this rule, I'm referring to actions such as leading by example, encouraging independent decision-making, celebrating all successes, etc. As they say, this is where the rubber meets the road. Your job is to market your vision consistently by executing every behavior as you'd expect from your team and to encourage positivity. By doing so, you dramatically increase team morale and encourage top production as a result. This rule is ongoing. There are also other examples shared on how to maintain rule # 3 in the later pillars.

For an illustrative example, pretend you're an inventor. Once you've created a product to solve a problem (rule #1), you've decided to license your product to multiple manufacturers in order to work together to increase your chances for success (rule #2). However, does it stop there? Absolutely not! Now you have to do all you can to market your product, increase market awareness, and therefore, your market share (rule #3). Everything you do must be preplanned and executed. If you make a mistake during execution, own it and continue to follow through with the behavior. When you're molding the morale of your team, the wrong decision can set your team back greatly. Even worse, you can lose your team's passion to win, which results in losing your career.

When I make a decision on how to impact morale, I focus on two things: environmental impacts (the team's emotional state in the workplace) and competitive impact (the team's passion to win). In other words, when I need my team to feel confident and energized, I try to motivate these feelings with decisions that encourage positivity in the workplace and make it a competitive game to keep high spirits. Here are a few examples I've used that have been very successful with all my teams. We'll also cover these in greater detail later in this guide.

Environment influences
- If it's a team member's birthday, I buy their favorite cake for everyone to enjoy.
- Host at least one quarterly event for all to enjoy (bowling, picnic, social drink, dinner, etc.)
- Community service participation

Competitive influences
- Hold contests every quarter as needed
- Create a leaderboard (if one exists, then print it) and post publicly.

Although there are many ways to influence morale, the important tip to remember is to make sure what you're doing will create the result you need. In my examples above, I wanted to create a high-performing team that is motivated to come to work and produce their best as a team. To achieve that result, I knew I had to create an attractive work environment and maintain a fun, competitive spirit. Therefore, I focused on environmental and competitive influences. If you need to master operations, you may create a culture around minimizing loss and doing things right the first time. If you want to master customer service, you may incorporate a particular script that creates positive responses for all to master universally. In sales, I've found these two types of influences to be most impactful with my leadership style. Other types of morale impacts may also include attendance, tactfulness, demeanor, health, finance, and so forth. With all three of these rules followed, you'll be able to maintain your team's morale and, therefore, maintain their performance. Now let's make a bigger impact.

The Mason Influential Leadership Model (MIL Model)

You have a vision. You know the basics to influence morale. Now, let's learn the heart of pillar I and my performance model called the Mason influential leadership model. I have experienced, researched, and tested many different leadership styles and systems for years, some of which I'm sure you may have or are currently studying. The similarity I've found was that their processes or systems were too complicated in one form or the other. Either the system itself was complicated in some form, or the instructor made it complicated (meaning difficult to interpret, which equals complicated).

I remember hearing arguments with instructors and other students about which styles within these systems were right to use, when, and why. I saw a student at a seminar once that was so frustrated in trying to figure it out that he fought with the instructor in front of over fifty participants for twenty minutes. Although his approach could have been better, I understood and agreed with his reasoning, along with over twenty other people who expressed their confusion. It wasn't as simple as the instructors were paid to make it out to be. These systems either had too many steps or were missing steps—in many cases, only how to notice a situation, not how to handle it.

It reminded me of those security commercials. One of my favorite commercials was from LifeLock in 2017 when a group of bank robbers stormed into a bank and yelled for everyone to hit the floor. When they did, one of the customers asked the standing security guard still in his post to do something. With pretty epic music playing, it paused to hear him say, "Oh, I'm not a security guard. I'm a security monitor. I tell people when there is a robbery." He briefly looks up at the bewildered-looking robbers and back at the people. "There's a robbery."

When you're a leader, the expectation, responsibility, and accountability can bring enough of its own stress, so I aimed at molding a simpler and more accurate system that not only helps you recognize how to respond, but also when to respond and why. In addition, real-life examples and resources at your disposal truly help you take the field confidently and successfully. I created a sound, universal system because I wanted every team I developed to win regardless of where I went. Who would want to start all over with a new system every time you inherited a new team? As I was recruited to new teams, I needed a system that I could master easily and transfer promptly to help a new team win faster. In turn, I win.

My model will also help make micromanagement your best friend. "Wait, what?" You read it right. Micromanagement will be your best friend. Since I will use the term *micromanage* or *micromanagement* frequently, I will abbreviate it as M/M so your brain can register and retain more efficiently. M/M has a bad reputation. Probably as you read this, you cringe every time you hear yourself say M/M. That has become our culture. M/M became the evil spirit within management styles. If someone did it, they were feared or hated. However, this is a stigma.

I personally created two types of surveys with ten statements and gave them to three groups of employees during my career at a retail giant store to prove a point to another member of management. It was one of those agree/disagree-type surveys. The ten statements were the exact same on both surveys, except one survey had the word M/M in each statement and on the other, I replaced M/M with the activity or behavior, simply showing perspective. For example, one question asked, "I like to be M/M" on one survey, and the other stated, "I like my performance to be monitored by management." An astounding result: in group A, eighteen out of twenty selected "strongly disagree" about M/M, but nineteen of twenty selected "agree" or "strongly agree" on the other. Group B resulted in twenty out of twenty for the M/M survey and seventeen out of twenty for the behavior. Group C resulted in nineteen out of twenty strongly disagreeing about M/M and eighteen out of twenty agreeing or strongly agreeing to the behavior. Each survey had the same questions, but different ways of expressing it. Is that interesting, or what? What do you make of it? I saw team members who wanted the consistent attention and guidance of their managers, but not the negative stigma that has tarnished the management industry because of a distressed group of individuals. There is a better way.

M/M is a powerful weapon in management, and like any weapon in history, it is not the weapon that is dangerous, but how it's wielded (by the one wielding it). The problems that people face and the horror stories people hear are about those managers who excessively and obsessively M/M their team with negative intentions. I'm not saying it is done to impact the team purposefully in a negative way. I'm saying the negative intention is the manager not believing the team or team member could accomplish a task—no trust. That's negative thinking. What it really is, is an individual's lack of development in using this skill. How many classes have you seen that teach leaders how to train and develop their teams? How many books have you read that even reference M/M as a positive skill? For most, I bet this is the first you're seeing it referenced in a positive light. To better illustrate what happens in the average work environment under these underdeveloped managers, review the graph.

Micro Mngmt	Performance (short)	Performance (long)	Morale	Turnover
Up	Increase	Decrease	Decrease	Increase
Down	Varies	Decrease	Decrease	Increase

The average team member will either be M/M too much or not enough, regardless of their performance. As you can see, excessive M/M results in performance temporarily increasing, but declines in the long run. In addition, morale declines, leading to an increase in turnover. Makes sense, right? The opposite with minimal to no M/M results in variable performance for the short run because it is solely based on the team's drive (not the manager) and then decline over time (team members burning out doing all the work for the manager). Morale is typically higher as team members control their own activities, but turnover varies because these individuals are typically turned toward the Life Is Good mentality after the top performers were easily recruited to another company.

These detrimental examples are only one side of the spectrum. The other walks hand in hand with team development and increases production in the long run. Think of my example with the surveys. Team members want your support and consistent guidance. You just have to know when and how to apply it. We'll go into greater detail in pillar V on implementation, but for now, you'll learn how to recognize who needs how much of your time so you can plan accordingly. With the proper use of M/M, you can create the following results:

Micro Mngmt	Performance (short)	Performance (long)	Morale	Turnover
Up	Increase	N/A	Increase	Decrease
Down	N/A	Increase	Increase	Decrease

Notice something different? Not only does morale increase in both scenarios, but turnover decreases. That's huge. Now, you may be asking yourself, "Self, why is there N/A in each scenario?" That's because my system, and the proper use of M/M, transitions as the team member improves. Once you identify how much time the team member will need from you to develop, which you'll learn through the Mason influential leadership model, then you'll apply the right level of engagement. However, it won't last forever. After all, as the team member improves, doesn't it make sense that they'll be able to accomplish tasks on their own? Essentially, you'll start to M/M more from the beginning and then ease up over the training period as they improve. That's why. It's like the young developing into maturity.

As illustrated, when applying the right level of M/M, you'll get the desirable result. Performance increases in both the short run and long run. Morale hangs high utilizing what you've learned about influencing morale previously and a few additional strategies you'll learn later on. And because of that continuous success, the only turnover your team will experience are promotions decreasing your average turnover. This effective skill utilized with my system is how you will impact your teams everywhere, every day.

My model consists of three levels: Alpha, Bravo, and Charlie. Although I do come from a military family, that wasn't my only influence. I named these levels as such because of their meaning. In the Greek alphabet, Alpha is first or number one. In nature, Alpha identifies the dominant leader. In the military, the Alpha squad is considered the elite. Even in school, you're given an A, B, or C to judge your intelligence on a certain subject. Simply said, my system teaches you how to take a C or Charlie-performing team (or team member) and make them an Alpha performer.

One of the things I've always told my teams is that only they can become Alpha performers because they've always had that ability within them. All I can do is show them how. They will need to act. Before you use this system, you must believe that everyone has the potential to become Alpha performers. Greatness is not a unique and rare gift. It truly exists in everyone around you, including yourself. They just need your help learning how to unleash it. The only thing that prevents an individual from becoming an Alpha performer is themselves. It is their *will* to improve. Their *will* to become great. Without it, no matter the level of skill one possesses, they will fail. Help them find it.

Negative willpower is the only *real* challenge you'll face, but I will show you how to minimize these situations proactively and how to confront those uncontrollable moments when you *can't* avoid them later on in pillar III. Since you truly believe in everyone, then we can get started by first identifying one's current level of performance. Although their performance level is obvious, it's not about identifying the best and the worst. My system is not about segregating the top from the bottom. It's not about who's first or last. Remember, we're developing a team—a top-performing team, an Alpha team. Given different goals, you are all different in your choices and results, but united under one vision, *your* vision, you are all the same. You are one. So in this system, it's about who can you improve and how.

The MIL Model

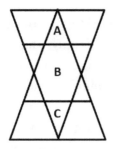

- Green

- Yellow

- Red

Since some leaders are colorblind and others cannot visualize color in their minds, I left the model colorless, but labeled. Try to picture this however you can, or use color pencils to fill in accordingly. Trust me—this will help. I coordinated each level with the colors red, yellow, and green. Red requires your utmost attention (or influence) for development but results in the least amount of production. Yellow requires a moderate level of your time, resulting in a balanced outcome in production. Green requires the least amount of your time while receiving the most out of production. However, at no point in your leadership do you take your eye off any team member's performance. You just simply shift your focus as illustrated in the previous M/M chart.

I've always said winners keep score. A great saying I've heard from many other great leaders as well, but I'll give the credit to whom I heard it from first, my old football coach Steve Ensminger. They all say it because it's true. An effective leader will always be aware of his/her surroundings, including performance so they can proactively adjust their strategy before it's too late. If you want to win, you have to adapt during the game, not afterward. Being reactive loses opportunities. You must adapt in the moment. This model helps you adapt accordingly.

This is the full view of the Mason influential leadership model, in other words, the final product. My MIL model, which I also refer to as the hourglass model, will be your most impactful tool. Think of this model as a summary model that will remind you of what you're about to learn in one simple glance. We'll revisit this model after our breakdown. I gave it the nickname Hourglass not just because of the shape, but as a reminder that this model takes time to master. Practice doesn't make perfect. Practice makes better. Perfect practice makes perfect. This is not an algebraic equation you can memorize and then look like a genius when solving a problem because you remembered how to plug it in. The model reflects the respect to the most important asset all living things have in life: time. So utilizing the MIL model coupled with the five pillars helps you maximize every minute to your best advantage. Do so, and you'll master your own destiny within any company.

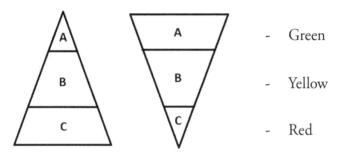

- Green

- Yellow

- Red

The MIL model is simply two pyramid-style sub-models complimented into one. We have our performance sub-model (figure 1) and our IL (influential leadership) sub-model (figure 2). The performance sub-model measures the team and/or team member's performance level. The IL sub-model measures the approximate amount of influence necessary for development. By influence, I mean a combination of what you're learning in this guide: your time, knowledge, encouragement, coaching, etc. Now, earlier I mentioned the three-color schemes and the three performance levels: Alpha, Bravo, and Charlie. Hopefully, you retained that information, but if not, don't worry. We'll revisit it more shortly. For now, I want you to recognize the similarities between both models. What do you see?

Although I gave it away prior to asking, you should have noticed that both models have the same amount of levels with the same label on each corresponding level. In addition, they are colored in the same pattern from top to bottom: green, orange, and red. Is it starting to come together?

The only difference is that the performance model pyramid is inverted. You'll learn momentarily why these models have an indirect relationship that can complement each other. The basic concept of the MIL model is to match the influential leadership level with the corresponding level of performance. A C performer should be paired with a C level of influence. Let's break down the performance sub-model first.

Performance Sub-Model

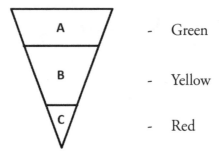

As referenced, our performance sub-model helps you identify the level of their current performance, which will help guide you later to establish the respective level of influence. Each level is referred to as a level of performance. You will discover their current level using multiple measurements already available to you. If you manage a think group, you would measure participation. If you managed factory members, you would measure production. If you lead a squad or a sports team, you would measure accomplishments. Whatever it's called in your industry, you are measuring performance. Since the term *performance* is a sales metric and it's more accepted across all industries, *performance* is what I'll use in these examples. However, I would like you to use the language in your field to make this model more real for you.

The pyramid is inverted to reflect the respectable production of the team member or team to the overall performance. If their performance is below the average standard in your industry, then they are not contributing enough to themselves or their team—therefore, on the Charlie level, the smallest level reflecting the lowest amount of contribution, or production. We have Alpha, Bravo, and Charlie from the performance sub-model broken down below.

(Charlie piece). Charlie is represented in red because of the opportunity for development that lies within it. Unless you're playing American football, a member in the red zone is not a good thing. This zone indicates a team member is in desperate need of your leadership, your guidance, and your time. The size of this level reflects the level of performance, typically reflects inconsistent behaviors and minimum task completion with low levels of succession. A low level of performance indicates a red zone member (a Charlie performer), which should trigger the corresponding influential leadership level. In other words, match C with C for stronger improvement, which was referenced previously.

(Bravo piece). Bravo is represented in orange because of an improvement in performance: good but not great, typically reflected with inconsistent behavior and tasks not being fulfilled at their best, but are fulfilled. An ideal position here is to bring all your Charlie performers into the Bravo level. Bravo performance indicates skill, but would need specific development—in other words, motivated to carry conversations with customers, but fails to complete expected behaviors consistently, like completing an assessment or asking required questions and so forth.

(Alpha piece). Alpha is represented in green for reasons you've already concluded: top performance, elite. The size of this level reflects it, typically reflected with consistent behaviors and fulfilling tasks at their best. We want to match Alpha performers to an Alpha influential leadership response to keep their success engulfed with passion. Their success is what makes you successful. The ideal position here is to have all of your Bravo performers reach the Alpha level. At the very least, you want to maintain two to three Alpha performers on your team at all times. These performers make up 80 percent of your production.

Influential Leadership Sub-Model

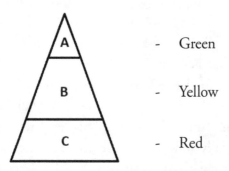

- Green

- Yellow

- Red

The IL sub-model is divided into three levels as mentioned before, but these levels are referred to as the levels of influence. Here, the colors indicate the amount of influence. For a stronger perspective, how much M/M will be required for each respected level of performance? As referenced previously, the objective is after you identify their level of performance, you will match the appropriate level of influence to help them learn, develop, and grow into the best they can be. Each level of performance has a different mentality. I'm sure just by reading these descriptors, you may already have a few people in mind who would fit into these levels and immediately notice the difference in attitude and skill. That is why there are different levels of influence. Each level responds differently. Therefore, they are influenced differently. It's very important to match up each performance level with the respective level of influence. Otherwise, you'll influence the wrong behaviors. Here are the corresponding levels of influence broken down.

(Charlie piece). Just as the performance sub-model, the Charlie level of influence is in red, but not because of performance. Here, the red indicates the amount of influence this team member requires, influence again meaning more of your time to coach, observe, and motivate. The size of the level represents the relative amount of M/M that will be required. Obviously, the more you M/M, the more time you will have to spend doing it. As a leader, you want to free up as much time as possible because your time is your most valuable asset. It's more valuable because your time has the greatest impact on the whole team. We'll go into greater detail in pillar II, productive time management.

(Bravo piece). The Bravo level of influence is represented in orange because this level of influence doesn't require as much M/M as the Charlie level, hence the decreased size of this level. The more they learn, the more trust you will have in their abilities to perform, therefore freeing up more of your time to focus on other tasks or to develop Charlie performers. However, they still need a little more of your influence than Alpha performers to become the best they can be.

(Alpha piece). The Alpha level of influence is represented in green because they only need a fraction of your time. The complementary size indicates very little M/M necessary. All you do at this level of influence is to keep Alpha performers passionate, and they'll do the rest. For some, that can be as simple as recognition and saying, "Great job." This is the ideal position, freeing up more time for developing Bravo and Charlie performers, completing tasks, and increasing your business.

Putting It All Together

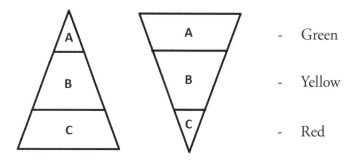

- Green

- Yellow

- Red

Now that you have a better understanding of each sub-model, this side-by-side view should make more sense. Again, this model helps you match the right level of influence based on their performance. So let's put our Mason influential leadership model back together piece by piece. This will help put each level into perspective and explain how you can determine which level your team member should begin in.

Although some may seem obvious in behaviors, they are not always the case until you match up with metrics.

TIP: Never assume a team member's performance level based on only behaviors or performance metrics. This will lead to mismatching influence, which becomes a breakdown in communication. Always look at the whole picture and include both their behaviors and performance metrics before deciding the best placement.

Charlie Level of Mason Influential Leadership

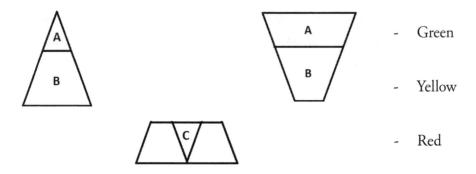

- Green

- Yellow

- Red

Once you identify a team member's performance through your reports and observations, and you identify a Charlie performer, then we are looking at the Charlie level of influence to complement their opportunities. As a reminder, in these scenarios, we are assuming that these team members have a will to learn, improve, and grow. Those without a will to improve will be covered in pillar III, positive accountability. Here are a couple of ways to identify Charlie performers:

- If a performance report is available, these are team members who are less than 80 percent to goal (or 25 percent or more behind pace).

- Observation: Observe their behaviors like body language, tone of voice, and how they uncover opportunities (if they can at all). These team members typically have minimum participation during team events and meetings, tend to avoid eye contact during conversations, will seem insecure about themselves and their ability, will not have a sales process with customers or clients, consistent with only being disengaged, and/or in some cases, have a negative outlook.

- Other examples of typical behaviors reflected: unorganized or seemingly won't care, consistently late, misses deadlines, easily distracted, fails to follow instructions, timid, poor tactfulness, and poor communication.

Once you've identified a Charlie performer, you can utilize the Charlie level of influence. How to execute these levels of influence in greater detail is shared in pillar V: Build a Culture. This pillar focuses on the concept of this model to help your understanding first. I want you to get familiarized with the concept of what to expect within these levels of leadership to build a strong foundation to this five-pillar system.

Charlie performers will require much of your time. Why? Because they need your vision. They need your guidance. They need you to lead by example. They need your confidence to help them discover their passion. All these take time. In addition, they will require a higher amount of M/M than the average team member because these individuals need to build a new process or rebuild an efficient process. These team members can range from someone new to a position to an experienced team member who is experiencing a change in their daily process (new technology, new product lines, mergers and acquisitions, change in roles, etc.). M/M is extremely important at this level because this is your team member's foundation. If you don't help them learn, plan, and execute efficiently and effectively at the beginning, then you've already allowed them to fail.

Think of this stage like the foundation to a house. I own a duplex that is over 100 years old. When I purchased it, I purchased it as a 3,000-square-foot single-family home. I found more value in it by converting it into a duplex and renting both units out, plus cashing out all the equity I could. However, it was a century old and needed renovations. I had one contractor who was ready to jump into the project. After my due diligence, I found out the contractor didn't have any experience dealing with a century-old home. If I said yes, rushed in there, made a quick conversion, and put two families in there, I guarantee you that their lives and my business would have been at major risk. If you're a contractor or in the real estate business, you may have already figured out why. If not, here is why. The experienced contractor brought this to my attention. Any modifications I would have done would have been completed using updated materials—materials that are much different from what homes were made out of over 100 years ago. There would definitely be a risk of those modifications not being compatible with the foundation of the home, which would increase the weight on the foundation. That additional weight would cause the property to sink and possibly collapse. Many lives would be at stake, and my business and personal life could have been destroyed. Instead, I took the time to find an experienced contractor, inspect the foundation, uncover the opportunities, make the proper repairs and improvements to bear the weight, and then build upon it. Now it is a successfully strong rental property, and all my tenants and their families are happy to call it home. Don't underestimate the power of a strong foundation.

This is the foundation you would need to lay here for Charlie performers. Do not be concerned about the level of M/M required. That team member will appreciate every second of it one way or another. Think back to my example with the surveys. Focus on how they responded to the second survey. They agreed to "I like it when management monitors my performance." This should remind you that they are acceptable and appreciative of your time. With one of my banking teams, I shared the same survey with similar results. Not even weeks later, that same bank ran their own internal survey and discovered that team members abroad responded positively to the idea of more management involvement. The participants even asked for it. So with the support of these examples, believe in M/M. Although we'll cover this more later, here are a few examples of how you will M/M at this level (illustrated examples and tools in pillar V):

- Daily morning check-ins and/or debriefs (one-on-ones held at the end of the day or after client/customer interactions) five to ten minutes
- Four to five documented in-action observations weekly with role-play demonstrations
- Weekly documented role plays
- Daily performance tracking
- Performance reporting (held weekly)
- Milestone celebrations

During this process, it is important to help your team member self discover that they can accomplish anything if they put their mind to it. Self-discovery is when one finds one's own meaning, something you can certainly assist with. All they have to do is follow your guidance. Self-discovery will always have the biggest impact. They must believe in themselves. Simply telling someone what to do never works out in the long run. And I'm pretty confident to say "never" there. Just follow up on your history.

On the other side of the spectrum, you have to be careful about giving too much motivation to a team member this early in the process. Think back to my duplex. Overconfidence (like the first contractor) before setting a proper foundation will lead to many mistakes and eventually lead to starting over or worse. In some cases, you can't go back. It is a step-by-step learning process. So you want them to stay encouraged in practicing their role but also be encouraged to come to you for further development at every necessary moment in between daily activities. I'll let you define *necessary*. Here are a few tips when influencing Charlie performers:

- Always use encouraging phrases, such as "You can do this," "Keep up the good work," "I believe in you," or "Don't give up."
- Always keep good eye contact when listening. This helps the team member to develop trust and encourages your brain to respond and retain accurately.

- Make a development plan (also called an action plan) and execute flawlessly (consistently). This helps build structure and makes it easier for both of you to set and follow through with expectations.

Bravo Level of Mason Influential Leadership

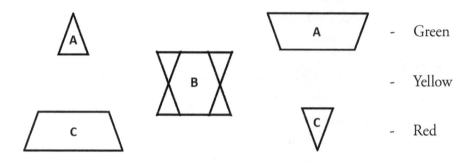

- Green

- Yellow

- Red

Once we identify a Bravo performer, we want to use the Bravo Level of Influence to make the appropriate impact. These team members are those who show great motivation and passion to help others but may lack structure. In other words, they may hit up to 100 percent of their goal or have great conversations with clients, but their behaviors or results are not consistent. Unlike Charlie performers, who will need a step-by-step process, these team members already understand the basics in their expectations. At this level, they're learning the details of perfecting their craft. These can be experienced team members within the company or industry whose performance varies or is gradually developing. Here are some pointers on how to identify a Bravo performer:

- If a performance report is available, these are team members who are performing between 80 percent and 100 percent or greater than 25 percent behind pace. Hits 100 percent of goal occasionally.

- Observation: As mentioned above, our Bravo performers are perfecting their craft, so what you're looking for are inconsistencies. They typically have moderate participation (more so if called upon), keep eye contact (but can still get distracted), are unorganized (but open for improvement), inconsistent with behaviors (but only because of being unorganized), and/or always willing to improve. Observe their process and their engagement skills. They may do an assessment for one customer but fail to do so with the next, maybe not on purpose. They just don't have the behavior mastered yet to perform predictable experiences.

- Other examples of typical behaviors reflected: eager to learn, engages customers with positivity, eager to take on new responsibilities, confident, impatient, easily motivated, and ambitious.

Listen to their tone of voice and body language with different clients. These team members can typically allow exterior factors and emotions to reflect in their performance more often than not. That can be a good thing and a bad thing. For example, if they're excited, they may speak to clients faster and louder, which could lead to miscommunication. Or if a team member is feeling insecure about a subject or specific behavior, they may only feel comfortable speaking to clients they can relate to. These can lead to unintentional discrimination and an unpredictable experience. Vice versa, if they are feeling great, these members can have very engaging interactions with consumers. That's the side you want to develop.

Why are they this way? Just nature. Think of a middle child with an older and younger sibling, and you might see why. A majority of your attention will go to the Charlie performers, and the Alpha performers are the best of the best. Some will want all your time and expertise. Others will feel that they can figure it out because they are *just as* good as the Alpha performers. It's important to have them understand that although they certainly have the ability to be an Alpha performer, it takes perfect practice to perfect their craft. Either way, you can't let their emotions deviate them from their development plan. Patience is a huge virtue on this level, and your team member doesn't know it yet, but they're relying on your help in teaching this.

TIP: Interact frequently with Bravo performers. Your interactions do not always have to be performance related. At this stage, your presence and interactions impact these individuals more greatly than any other-level performers. That's because they are beginning to see your vision come together and how you are helping them grow. They are seeing their development in action and starting to believe in themselves entirely, thanks to you.

Remember: Not matter what you discuss, keep the interaction work-related. Remember they display emotions through their interactions because they are still learning. They will soon learn to control it, but not if you keep bringing up unrelated topics.

REAL LIFE

I had an experienced team member at a branch I took over in the banking industry. She had the skills in place to succeed at her job, but she was only consistent in showing up for work. Some months, she would hit her goals, but YTD (year to date) she was at 70 percent and we were in November. Based on her performance reports and behaviors, even though she was experienced, I certainly placed her on the Charlie level of performance because of her inconsistent and rebellious behavior. In addition, she performed less than 80 percent.

After putting a development plan together and a heart-to-heart one-on-one to help her align her goals with my vision, she began to really take off. Her behaviors were improved into a consistent machine, and thus, so did her results. She was developing incredibly fast. During that development, I hired a new team member (Charlie performer), and I graduated her into an Alpha performer, easing off her development plan. In essence, I started M/M her like an Alpha performer. Within three weeks, her performance started going backward. My observation discovered inconsistency. When I pulled her to the side, she said it was her fault because she started deviating off the plan, but I knew it was my fault and I owned it. It was my fault because I didn't use the proper level of influence. She was still developing, and I graduated her from the Charlie level to the Alpha level. I used the Alpha level of influence on a Bravo performer, thus not enough M/M she required to continue her development. I had to be patient. Luckily, I caught on to this early, but imagine if I hadn't. Her performance immediately turned around once I aligned the proper influence, and within a couple of weeks, she truly became an Alpha performer.

It can seem difficult to identify when a Bravo performer graduates into the Alpha level of performance, but the important factor is patience. Between your observations and their performance report, you'll know exactly when they have graduated. That is, if they don't tell you first. With that said, here are a few examples of how to M/M a Bravo performer:

- Two to three check-ins a week and/or debriefs
- Two to four documented in-action observations weekly
- Daily performance tracking
- Performance reporting (weekly)
- Role-play at least twice a week during observation debriefs
- Milestone celebrations

From the examples above compared to the Charlie level, you'll notice that your time is beginning to free up. These performers have earned more trust and therefore will require less attention. However, as I've learned, don't move faster than their development plan. As they develop and strengthen their opportunities, these performers will become consistent. Eventually, your coaching will turn into encouraging, and that encouragement will become motivation. That motivation will push your team member across their limits to become an Alpha performer.

Alpha Level of Mason Influential Leadership

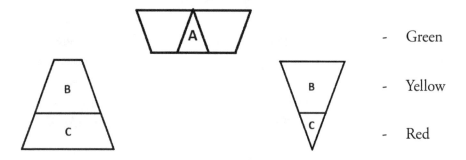

- Green
- Yellow
- Red

It is really easy to identify these elite individuals among any team. They are competitive at heart, energetic, self-motivated, positive, and typically very engaging. When a goal is hit, the world knows about it. Once you identify these Alpha performers, you need to use our Alpha level of influence to keep these top performers at the top of their game. At this level, 80 percent of your time spent with your Alpha team member is mainly to motivate and support. Only 20 percent will be spent on training, coaching, and so forth. M/M is at a minimum because these team members already know the right steps to take and the best path of execution. Here are some ways you can identify Alpha performers:

- If a performance report is available, these are team members at or above goal (100 percent +) or typically ahead of pace, consistently over 100 percent of goal. These are experienced salesmen and women.

- Observation: Alpha performers have perfected *their* process. These team members can be seen consistently engaged, eager to assist the next customer or client, recognized using scripts, assessments, or other resources consistently, and typically display positivity and a passion to win.

- Other examples of typical behaviors reflected: self-motivated, very active, observant, detailed oriented, goal oriented, fast talkers, expressive with body language, competitive, sometimes over confident, and/or loyal.

You must be very careful at this level. I'm sure you may be thinking, what could possibly go wrong with Alpha performers? But that answer is you. Don't make the same mistake that even top-performing managers make with these team members. That mistake is ignoring or neglecting them. It is very easy to be so confident in a team member's ability that your natural reaction may be to trust that team member fully to complete all tasks independently, allowing you to focus all your time on other team members or tasks. In addition, sometimes these team members may use their performance to their advantage and influence you to make those types of decisions. To be proactive and to help your top performers remain at their best, you want to avoid this neglecting behavior. Although M/M is minimal with these performers, it is still just as important as with each of the previous levels. I'm sure you've heard "Trust, but verify." That is what you're doing on this level of performance. We still want to give our team members space to perform at their best, but you have to check in to remind them that you are still there for support. Your presence subconsciously reminds them that they must abide by the same standards of operations as everyone else on the team because that is what you all are—one team.

As I mentioned earlier about proactivity, these check-ins can also avoid behaviors that appear as favoritism, which can lead to HR issues, demoralization, and unethical behavior. These behaviors are leading contributors to the dismantling of top-performing teams across the United States. Now, what does that 20 percent of M/M look like? More detail will still be outlined in pillar V, but here are some examples of what M/M at this level will look like:

- One to two weekly check-ins and/or debriefs
- One to two documented in-action observations weekly
- Daily performance tracking

- Performance reporting (weekly)
- Role play only when necessary or requested
- Milestone celebrations

This level is the true meaning of having fun while being the best. When your team's performance collectively has reached Alpha performance, the team's morale, loyalty, and passion to win are highly visible. From here, the sky is not the limit, but only the beginning. The energy Alpha performers have is very addictive, infectious, and incredibly powerful. All the energy is reflected through you. These team members inspire Bravo performers to continue their development. Utilize this. Keep your Alpha performers motivated and engaged in front of your Bravo performers, and you'll see a tremendous impact. Remember, Bravo performers already think they are better than Alpha performers. Watching Alpha members perform will encourage many Bravo performers to outperform. Keep your Alpha performers engaged and motivated. They live for the thrill of sweet victory in achieving their goals and the team's goal.

REMEMBER: Never neglect your Alpha performers or place too much responsibility on their shoulders. These team members still need your attention, guidance, and support, especially when they win. Always celebrate their success and keep them motivated through contests.

The Secret Formula

During the development of my system, I have also discovered a secret formula to measure your success. I call it the 10/80/10 formula. If you can *at least* maintain this formula, you'll guarantee your success. The key is to maintain this formula at minimum or better: 10 percent Alpha performers, 80 percent Bravo performers, and 10 percent Charlie performers. You want always to have at minimum 10 percent or more of your team members on the Alpha level of performance and at most 10 percent or less on the Charlie level of performance. Your Bravo performers should only rise because a Charlie performer graduated or should only fall when a team member graduates into the Alpha performance level. In other words, all team members should only go up on the MIL model. But you knew that. As long as you maintain the 10/80/10 formula, you and your teams will exceed your goals, launching you up the corporate ladder.

For example, if you had a team of ten members, to successfully flip a team's performance, you want to have *at least* one Alpha performer and can only afford one Charlie performer at all times. Minimum you want. The additional eight need to be at least on the Bravo performance level. There is one exception to maintain the balance of success. For every Charlie performer you have, you will need an Alpha performer to complement. Makes sense, right? Charlie performers typically are still learning their role and will have very little impact on the team's performance. As a matter of fact, these team members typically impact less than 8 percent of your total goal. However, the more Charlie performers you have, the more time you have to give up. You only have so much time in your day, right? The only team members who are experienced and motivated enough to make up for this gap are your Alpha performers because they've mastered their role well enough to balance this challenge, hence why you need an Alpha performer for each Charlie performer to balance the lost performance. Essentially, the more Charlie performers you have, the harder it gets, which is why you want to aim at maintaining the 10/80/10 formula or better.

Here is how you can use this formula to your advantage. Let's say you take over an underperforming team with ten members, to make the math easier. After reviewing the performance reports and making your observations, you discovered that you have one Alpha performer, six Bravo performers, and three Charlie performers. Where would you start to focus your efforts on development? Although you have the MIL model to identify and develop any level of performance, you'll need the 10/80/10 formula to help determine where to start, or who to start with. Here are a couple of ways to construct or illustrate your formula:

10/60/30 (10% A, 60% B, 30% C or 1/10 A, 6/10 B, 3/10 C)

Or

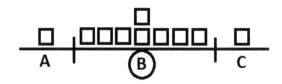

High
Performance

Low
Performance

Now compare your current formula to the 10/80/10 formula:

10/80/10 (10% A, 80% B, 10% C)

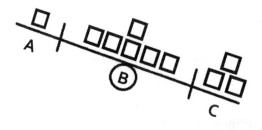

10/60/30 (10% A, 60% B, 30% C)

You'll notice that you have two Charlie performers more than the maximum allowed under the secret 10/80/10 formula. In addition, with respect to the exception rule, you only have one Alpha performer, which can't balance your three current Charlie performers. Where should you start? You have two choices. You can either start your focus on developing at least two Bravo performers to become Alpha performers. Or you can start your focus on developing at least two Charlie performers to become Bravo performers. Whichever you chose to start, the end result is, at the very least, a balanced formula for success: the exception rule.

This doesn't mean if you chose to develop Bravo performers first, you'll neglect all other team members, or vice versa, starting with Charlie performers. Those respective M/M strategies are still necessary for every level and every team member. This formula is simply a proactive measurement for you to identify where to start turning your team around. The goal is to get all team members into the Alpha stage, while at least maintaining this balance of your Charlie performers.

Again, the formula displays the minimum you'll need for success represented in the center. Success illustrated here is at least a balanced beam (10/80/10 formula) with the goal of shifting your weights to the left. Through this illustration, you can see that you want the weight of your performance to favor the left side of the balance scale to maximize performance. Everyone has to become Alpha performers. The best way to do that is either minimize the number of your Charlie performers and/or maximize the number of your Alpha performers. Are you starting to understand?

I hope you're getting excited to use this secret formula. You should. This is the secret tool to guarantee your team flipping success. The 10/80/10 formula is for you to keep your eye on the balance of success. Knowing your formula will help you strategically adjust and align your development plans to impact the team's overall performance greatly. Control your formula, and you'll control your success. Once your scale is at least balanced, now you can coordinate your time strategically to tip the scale to the left, increasing your performance.

REMEMBER: You need an Alpha performer for every Charlie performer you have. If you only have one Alpha performer but you have three Charlie performers, strategically plan on which team members are the easiest to develop into the next performance

level in order to balance your scale. Once balanced, you can focus maximizing your team's performance.

The Effects of Mismatching

To keep this model realistic, I'm going to share three personal examples that will demonstrate the effects of the following situations: (1) not having this model in place, (2) mismatching the levels of influence to the performance levels, and (3) when you pair a perfect match. I want you to accept that mistakes will happen and failure somewhere is inevitable. However, you are not defined by these moments. In order to succeed, you have to learn from them as all champions and historical individuals have done.

This is a process of development, and like any process, it will take time and practice. But the examples I'll give will help you understand why you want to have my system in place and, when in place, how redirecting your influence appropriately can make just as big of an impact as if you've made the perfect match the first time. Of course, I wouldn't be honoring my principles around development if I didn't check for your understanding. So after each example are some review questions I'd like you to answer. For a greater impact, while you're reading these examples, I'd like you to think of a few things, and I encourage you to write them, as your responses may change throughout the story. I would like you to think about what performance level the employees are on, the level of influence I used, and what you would have done differently (or continued doing) if you were in that role.

First Example:

I led an electronics team where I was promoted from within. After I was promoted, I knew I had to find a way to replace my performance since I was one of two Alpha performers and one of the two only "Title is everything" motto-driven team members in that department. Working with all the team members who used to be coworkers wasn't too difficult since they were the ones to encourage me to take that role, but I did want to be fair. Based on our company's focus of the month,

I rallied the team around a new metric and service we offered. We measured its success by attachment rate, and our GM wanted to be number one. Therefore, so did I.

After a meeting, my team began execution immediately, and it was beautiful. I observed several team members using the benefit of this service in their presentation and asking for the sale. Tracking the attachment that day seemed relatively easy, until I heard this one particular presentation. Johnathan gave a great presentation on a loaded package, comparing a home theater system, plasma and LED TVs, bundled HD accessories, and installation services. As he smoothly transitioned into closing the sale, he checked for objections while entering the products and services into the register. When his customers arrived at their budgeted limit, the customers were torn between two services we offered, both of which were amazing deals and recommended services, but they could only afford one at the moment. As you may already speculate, one of those services was our new installation service. As the customer was talking himself out of this service, John accepted his objection and pursued the other service of calibrating his TV.

Although a calibration is an excellent service, John didn't rebut what I thought was a simple objection for a better solution. After the sale, I approached John to discuss how surprised and disappointed I was about him missing a perfect attachment opportunity. Our conversation got heated quickly as he fired back to defend his decision. Regardless of what I said and how calmly I said it, John continued to argue about his choice and how he was against the new metric. We were clearly not seeing eye to eye. We ended up arguing two different points with two different perceptions about one solution.

Frustrated, John stormed off and stepped out of the store. It was very important to me that we solve this difference immediately so we could continue to take care of our customers. My approach was that we were still friends and that I respected his input, so I encouraged him to tell me what was going on. That's when John helped me realize that I had it all wrong. What John's explanation told me was that he didn't understand the importance of the metric and how it impacted customers. In addition, after he explained his assessment with his customer, he determined that the best service for the customer and for the company was the calibration. His point was that although we did not have the attachment in that transaction, we still made more profit and the customer was satisfied. In other words, even though he didn't understand that service and its impacts, he still made the best decisions he could for the customer and the company based on what he knew. Even if John understood the service and its impacts, turns out that what I thought was best for the customer was actually just best for the report. John said, "You need to trust me."

I discovered my dilemma. As a top performer, I assumed John knew and understood it all. I assumed he had it all figured out as I did. However, I failed to realize that it was my responsibility to check in and help him understand changes. I also didn't have the trust in John that he deserved. Since I didn't have a system in place, I was blinded by his achievements and didn't see that he still needed guidance. I M/M John like the rest of the team because I wanted to be fair. I had a team with a majority as Bravo performers, but John was an Alpha performer. Turns out it wasn't fair after all. Not having this system in place put too much pressure on John to make quick decisions and resulted in making him feel that I didn't trust him. His performance, if it wasn't for my pursuit to resolve it, could have declined. After my apology and promise to put more faith in his abilities, that's when I realized that I didn't have any way to avoid a scenario like that. I didn't have or know a system that could. This was the moment that sparked my effort to create a system that would help me proactively avoid those frustrating situations and keep my team committed to being their best *while* having fun.

> **Review** (feel free to refer to the previous sections):
> Based on the influential leadership model, what would John's performance level be?
> What was my level of influence?
> What was my dilemma?
> What were the effects of this dilemma?
> If I had my system then, which level of influence would I have used?

Why is it important to have my system in place?

Conclusion:

Based on my model, John was an Alpha performer. Although I didn't have a system yet, I treated everyone alike and since I mentioned that a majority were equivalent to a Bravo performer, I used a Bravo level of influence with an Alpha performer. Not having a system in place was the reason I couldn't proactively identify the best influence for my team members or be able to redirect appropriately before our situation escalated. That situation could have easily been worse. The best level of influence to use with John would have been the Alpha level, considering that he was an Alpha performer. Besides this obvious example, it is very important to have my system in place to influence your team proactively to excel. More importantly, shorten the time it takes to reach the next level of performance. This system will become the heart of your success.

Second Example:

I was given the honor to acquire a struggling team in the banking industry that didn't achieve their goals in the past two years (reporting only allowed to view the past two years). The team suffered from massive turnover with six out of nine team members being fired or quitting, including management. One of the bankers, named Rebecca, was one of the three who survived the turnover virus, as I refer to those drastic turnover events. She still had fond memories of the managers before me and wasn't welcoming change. This created communication breakdowns and even a few challenging conversations about willpower. She was not used to having a leader therefore, one who encouraged her development to become great herself.

Since Rebecca was not used to my form of M/M, every step to help develop her was passively ignored. Soon, her performance was in the mid-70s percentile, and her behaviors were not reflecting what we agreed upon. Not only was her performance not improving, but our clients' experience was unpredictable and her performance was negatively impacting our brand awareness. Her body language was aggressive, her tone of voice was taken offensively at times, and conversations were almost unnoticeable with only two to three sentences ever spoken. I began to suspect her will to improve was absent in her efforts. Under that observation, I brought her into an office with my assistant manager to have my "A or B" conversation. This conversation is a powerful tool to utilize under these situations, and this tool has worked 100 percent of the time. We will cover the details of this tool in pillar III.

After our talk, we put an action plan into place. To impact her improvement effectively, I needed an action plan in place that reflected the appropriate level of influence. It was outlined with three morning check-ins, three to four observations I needed to complete, and two to three coaching sessions (one-on-ones to develop sales techniques) per week. Her newfound enthusiasm took off. The very next day seemed like a new beginning.

For two weeks, Rebecca really tried to improve her behaviors, but her performance was barely impacted. During an observation I made, I noticed that Rebecca missed key opportunities with her client—more specifically, missed opportunities to ask more open-ended questions, a chance to rebuttal a typical objection, and the perfect moment to offer a unique solution of ours. Although her enthusiasm was contagious, her body language was comfortable, and she did a great job building rapport with the client, I noticed her performance report was at 68 percent.

I felt I was missing something. My observations reflected that she was a Bravo performer and our plan was a direct reflection of the Bravo level of influence. However, her performance report reflected otherwise. It turned out I created an action plan that reflected the Bravo level of influence when she was actually a Charlie performer. I discovered that each of her interactions was very inconsistent and yet her attitude was very positive and engaging. I brought her back into my office to ask a few to questions to confirm my suspicion, and sure enough, she knew what was required, but she didn't know how to accomplish it.

After confirmation, we updated our action plan to reflect a more effective M/M style on the Charlie level of influence by outlining daily check-ins, four to five observations, and at least three coaching sessions per week. Proudly, Rebecca accepted the terms and was thankful for spending more time on her development. A week later, she improved dramatically. Her interactions became consistent, and her performance soared, obtaining her most successful quarter and receiving consistent quarterly bonuses thereafter.

This taught me to look at the bigger picture. If all you can measure is either the performance report or your observation (industries that may be restricted to only one form to measure), then you have to start somewhere. However, if you can compare both measurements, seek to do so. By comparing both your observations and their performance report, you'll have a more accurate view of their performance level. A good rule to remember here is if you identify two different performance levels, then that team member needs to be identified as the lower level of the two. In this example, Rebecca's performance report reflected a Charlie performer, while through observation, she was a Bravo performer. Therefore, Rebecca was truly a Charlie performer. Note that she willingly and enthusiastically accepted a higher M/M style and greatly improved after the realignment.

Review:

> What performance level did I give Rebecca?
> How did I determine her first performance level?
> What was Rebecca's true performance level?
> How did I identify her true performance level?
> What's a good rule to remember when measuring a team member's level of performance?

Conclusion:

After measuring Rebecca's observations, I was positive she was a Bravo performer. From that perspective, I figured our action plan was a perfect fit using the Bravo level of influence. However, after recognizing her performance reports and her consistent struggle to gain traction, I realized that she was truly a Charlie performer. I didn't see the bigger picture. Once I had a full understanding of her performance, I redirected using the Charlie level of influence and updated our action plan. As a result, Rebecca increased her performance and her career, eventually moving to the department she desired to join, after achieving the most production in three consistent quarters.

Third Example:

Recruited, I had the honor of taking over another banking team with a competitor bank. Their performance overall ranged from the 80th to 90th percentile and at least reviewing back two years. They had never had a successful quarter where all team members achieved their goals. Among the team, I had a team member on the teller line named Joanne. At the time, she was ranked in the top 7 percent of the company, which was recognized as gold status. She had four consecutive months achieving over 120 percent of her goal. She had a great, positive attitude, believed in what she offered, and remained consistent in her conversations.

As her new leader, it was my responsibility to not only help her continue her success but to help her improve and excel to the best of her ability. A leader can't forget that responsibility. After several observations, I discovered opportunities to help her improve. The way I viewed it, if she was doing this great with the opportunities I identified, she was capable of far more greatness. The level of influence I knew I had to use was the Alpha level, to help continue her drive but to also encourage her to become her best. At this point, Joanne felt that she was already at her best.

Joanne was a proud individual who would modestly say she didn't need any attention, but secretly, it motivated her to keep performing. I made sure to take time out of my day to always converse about her day, life, or her most recent achievements. When she did something great, I always recognized her enthusiastically. The energy in my recognition fueled her energy to continue. At this level, M/M is minimal with only one to two observations a week and a weekly check-in because I can trust this team member to continue her performance with little supervision. However, as I mentioned previously in this section, I still have to check in. As I noted, my energy and enthusiasm for her achievements were contagious to her. With that kind of positive reinforcement, Joanne was excelling in her career of thirteen years with the business.

There were a few opportunities that even Joanne encountered such as negative history with coworkers that presented problems from time to time, some of her interactions perceived as aggressive by some clients, and difficulty she had relying on her bankers to assist with closing her referrals (bankers were relatively new). Together, we were able to bring closure to past transgressions, identify how to avoid negative perceptions through body language and tone with clients, and create multiple activities that would encourage trust and workmanship between her and the bankers. With our aligned strategy, Joanne learned from her opportunities and not only continued her performance remarkably, but she was able to drive herself to rank in the top 2 percent in the division, referred to as platinum, by the end of the year. As her award, she was given an all-paid trip to Miami to celebrate. Upon her return, she brought the team pins from the Platinum Award ceremony that I proudly wore for her achievements and the honor she brought to our team.

Review:

> What was Joanne's performance level?
> How did I determine her level of performance?
> What was my level of influence?
> What were the opportunities Joanne had?
> What was the outcome of aligning her performance level with the correct level of influence?

Conclusion:

After comparing both her performance report and my observations, I determined Joanne was an Alpha performer, matching her performance with the Alpha level of influence. This example goes to show that even Alpha performers have opportunities to improve, which is why you never want to remove yourself from their daily routine. This is why M/M is still critical, regardless of their level of performance. You just need to apply the appropriate level of M/M (influence). With the Alpha M/M strategy, I was still able to determine that she had some negative history with existing team members, found it difficult to know who to send her referrals to (in most cases, they came to me over the bankers), and her approach to offering solutions may have been perceived as aggressive. All these were affecting her performance, even when she didn't see it. However, the best part about Alpha performers is their competitive and enthusiastic behavior to improve and succeed. With that said, Joanne helped herself improve in all those opportunities, which helped excel her performance to the highest she had achieved. She truly became her best and continued that success.

Putting It All Together

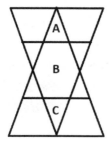

After the breakdown, I hope you feel more comfortable with how to utilize this model. Now you can recognize which level of influence, or M/M, is required for each team member on each level of performance. You should at least understand the basics of identifying and managing opportunities within each level. Don't be concerned if you must revisit this section. Take the small quiz below to test your understanding. If you don't get all of them correct, I recommend reviewing this pillar one more time before moving on to the next four. This first pillar is the heart of my five-pillar Flipping Teams strategy because this leadership model helps you identify how to effectively influence your team to improve and develop them at their best.

CHECK YOUR UNDERSTANDING

1. During your observation, you identify that your team member is very consistent with their behaviors and seems very proactive. Currently, they are 20 percent ahead of pace. What level of performance is this team member on? Why?
2. During your observation, you discovered that your team member doesn't seem to have a strong process in place and tends to avoid eye contact when engaged. Their current performance report said they were 68 percent to goal. What level of performance is this team member on? Why?
3. Your team member's current performance is at 102 percent. During your observation, you noticed only a few inconsistencies. What level of performance is this team member on? Why?
4. A team member's current performance is at 85 percent, but observations have shown dramatic improvement in their process. Your team member is not shy about telling you how well they have improved. What level of performance is this team member on? Why?

To minimize the chances of your eyes instinctively wandering for the answer, I've answered your questions within this paragraph. As we have discussed previously, if you have a team member that is consistent in their behaviors and is ahead of pace, you are observing an Alpha performer at work. During your observation, if you ever discover behaviors such as avoiding eye contact or being very inconsistent, you are typically observing a Charlie performing. The current report reflects 68 percent to goal, which strengthens your observation. The third one was a little tricky. Although you have a team member performing over 100 percent, you noticed inconsistencies. Remember my rule about conflicting results between your observation and their performance report? Their performance level is reflected in the lower result of the two: 102 percent clearly says Alpha level of performance, but the few inconsistencies reflect the Bravo level of performance. Therefore, this team member is still a Bravo performer. Remember that an Alpha performer reflects a strong process and is very consistent. The last should have been a home run. Their current performance is 85 percent and they have shown great improvement, which they weren't shy about sharing. Remember that Bravo performers are typically overconfident (not a bad thing). This team member is a Bravo performer as well.

How did you do? As I shared before, if you missed one or more, I recommend reviewing this pillar, or at least the MIL model, one more time. Don't be concerned about not getting 100 percent the first time. Remember, this guide is about development, not acing exams. This path requires patience, development, and willpower to evolve your skill set constantly. Start here by mastering pillar I. If you got them all, great job!

As I mentioned previously, the MIL model is not about identifying and only praising top performers. This model is about creating top performers by influencing and developing behaviors identified on their present level of performance. The industries I've worked in were extremely competitive, and I had to create a competitive advantage. I had to outperform the competition within and outside of business for sales and upcoming leadership roles. However, the longer it took to improve my team, the harder it was to accomplish it. Think of the bigger picture here. If you plan to flip teams because your goal is to move up the corporate ladder or to move up the salary grade, then you'll face two very difficult challenges. First are existing top-performing teams. Not only do these teams have the experience and perceptive power (regardless of a single event, everyone perceives a team as being one of the best under any circumstance based on brand history), but these teams are typically more motivated by competition in which you're creating. Second is the "other" you. You'll be fooling yourself to believe that you're the only one with your ambitions to reach goals and move up the chain. This is the most overlooked competitor out there, and they can sneak up and steal your dream if you don't at least acknowledge their presence. These are individuals that you typically don't know about until you apply for a new role and they swoop in to take it. They're going after the same thing you are, which turns your career path into a racetrack. Use my system to gain a competitive advantage over these competitors, and you'll win the race. You'll be capable of doing what some with over ten years' experience do, within your first one hundred days. Talk about leveling the playing field.

Rushing was a little too unpredictable for me in business, so I searched for a better way to take the lead. My thought was not how to just drive faster than the competition, but how to get the jump-start. I created this strategy to help myself and future leaders within my teams get the jump-start on the competition by identifying these opportunities and responding more effectively. Taking on a new team can be very challenging and especially time-consuming if you don't have a strategy in place. This is a strategy that helped me continuously create top-performing teams in the most efficient time, within the most competitive industries. Companies typically expect approximately six to twelve months to master your expectations and to outperform others competitively, assuming there is a will to improve. Depending on the leadership, it could be even longer. My system will help you conquer these challenges within six months. As a matter of fact, with flawless execution, you will accomplish this within one hundred days using my effective one-hundred-day strategy covered in pillar V. I know because I've succeeded these timelines and I believe you can too. However, you must be realistic. Each team and each company present their own unique challenges. This means if it takes a little longer than one hundred days, don't give up. That is not necessarily a bad thing. If the extra time is needed, then it is necessary. As long as you stick to my five-pillar strategy and follow the Mason influential leadership model for effective execution, you'll reach your goal twice as fast as you would have without it. Even better, you'll surpass the competition right off the line, and any professional racer would tell you that it's easier to maintain the lead than catch up to it.

Now that you know how to reference the MIL model to identify your team members' performance level, you can effectively M/M each respective level. However, before you can provide your time toward team development, you have to take control of your time on the clock. Let's develop your time management skills and learn how to effectively control the clock.

PILLAR II

Productive Time Management

How You Define Time

You better have a plan to run your day because it already has a plan to run you.

D O ME A favor and see what time it is. Depending on when you're reading this, if you've checked the time on your watch, then you *typically* try to control your time because it's always by your side. This is due to your belief that time is a higher commodity over other values. If you've checked your phone or another mobile device, then time may not be as important as convenience, style, or money. For example, keeping track of time on a phone may be more convenient because it's a clock and phone rolled into one, cost-effective because you don't have to buy two devices to do the same thing, or it's more stylish in the tech world. These individuals typically find the value of time about equal to other values. If you had to work a little harder to find the time, such as asking someone else or peeking around the corner for the nearest clock, then time may not be as relevant compared to other values. My point here is about how you value time. There is time management, which everyone does one way or another, depending on how one values one's time. And then there's productive time management. If you're about efficiency, you probably already know the basics, and this pillar will help strengthen what you already know with a few additional tricks. If you're still learning, you'll see how to be more effective with your time throughout this pillar. Where you start is believing that the most preciously rare commodity you own is time. Why? Because it's not *just* rare—it's one of a kind.

Your life is a clock ticking backward. If you ever want to make the most of your life, you have to know how much time you have in it. Therefore, you have to control the clock. All the champions of the world know how to control the clock. The best football, basketball, and soccer teams typically have the highest times of possession because that dramatically increases their chance to win. Professional fighters use the clock to wear down their opponents by controlling their breathing and practicing techniques prior to fights to endure extended periods of time. Top sales performers have a system to accomplish their sales goals because they know they only have forty hours in a week to achieve them. The best soldiers keep to their word on completing a mission within a certain period of time because it can be a matter of life and death, and in almost all cases, they only have one shot at it.

Now when I say "control time," what do I mean? I don't mean use a time machine to travel through time. You don't have to use a special remote to rewind, pause, or fast-forward time. You don't have to jump in a whirlpool or a black hole to see if it can alter time, none of that. However, you *can* control time all the same, but with much less effort and lower risk of your life (or looking like a fool for trying). Controlling time is about perception. Although we can't control the life clock itself, we can control how we effectively manage the time left in it. That's what I mean: creatively and effectively managing the most efficient way to accomplish more in less time.

Maybe this example will hit home for you. If you were given $100,000 to spend, how would you spend it? Think about having this money added to your current situation. Would you go straight to pay off debt? Or would you buy a car? If I turned around and said that's all you can have for the rest of your life and you aren't allowed to earn more, how would you spend it? Do you think your choices of what to buy and when to buy it would change? Do you think your perception of the $100,000 will become more valuable to you after finding out there isn't more available to get? Absolutely! Basic economics such as supply and demand apply to time. What happens when supply is low, but demand is high? The price goes up. In this case, as high as priceless. This is just a monetary example of time, but this is how you need to see time because that *is* what it is. To get a really great concept, check out the 2011 film *In Time* staring Justin Timberlake and Olivia Wilde along with a great cast of other actors and actresses. This movie depicts the replacement of currency with time and how your use of time really defines who you are as a person and your place in society.

You only have a set amount of years to accomplish whatever it is you need to accomplish, and there isn't a way in this world you can replenish it, refill it, purchase more of it, or make it. Time is your most valuable asset because of this, and to use it most effectively is heavily dependent on your perception of it. So if you want to make this system work and accomplish what you want to accomplish faster, you have to get serious about how you use your time. Wearing a watch would be a good start, but learning how to prioritize would be even better.

Master the Basics of Productive Time Management

REMEMBER: Just like any skill, you can't just say you're going to be proactive, do one thing, and stop. It's a developing skill. You have to practice being proactive in order to become proactive innately.

The Art of the List

I once heard Warren Buffett say, "My brain is not a general-purpose brain that works marvelously in all situations." From someone as brilliant as Warren Buffett, it is a testament that one person can't do everything. However, managing your time effectively can help you accomplish more than the average person. Productive time management is what can help you accomplish great things. It's an essential part of becoming great yourself. And nothing is more effective in managing your time than utilizing a priority list.

If you're unfamiliar with the use of any list to accomplish tasks, don't be concerned. In many cases, it's not your fault. Organizing your time using lists is a skill highly used with certain personality traits. That's right! You may not be born programmed to rely innately on this tool, but just with anything else, you can *still* program yourself to learn now.

I recommend starting by making a list of smaller tasks to accomplish. Keep it simple! For example, a grocery list, an errand list, a shopping list, etc. Starting here for minor tasks will help develop your memory and your innate behavior to use it when fulfilling bigger tasks in the future. Consistent practice using smaller lists will help you develop a routine. Once you start to master the basic use of a list, you'll be able to learn truly how to utilize a priority list properly. You'll also learn fun techniques that could help you accomplish multiple tasks that serve to fulfill one bigger task or goal, called sub-listing. It's a more effective way to complete more difficult priorities efficiently. This will be illustrated a little later in this pillar. If you dive into making a priority list without practicing these types of applications, you'll only delay your progress and possibly frustrate yourself through the gate—not a great start. It's not impossible to do, but it could just slow your learning curve. With that said, let's move forward. If you feel you need more practice with using lists, then great job identifying that opportunity. I encourage you to do so before continuing.

From To-Do List to Priority List

Times have changed. We are no longer referring to a to-do list. These lists are just a form of unorganized tasks that one wishes to accomplish in a given period. As a leader, you need to learn how to use and effectively manage a priority list. A priority list is a specific and strategically organized list of tasks that are prioritized based on their direct impact on your goal. When you're looking at what to put on your priority list, you need to think of your priorities first. By priorities, I mean start with the tasks that will make the greatest impact on your goal. These should be related to your overall goal. For example, if you're in sales, then your priority list might consist of some of the following:

- Set three appointments
- Close $1,000 in phone sales
- Onsite business presentation

If your goals were to hit your daily goal and set up your next day, then each of these examples is directly related to the overall goal. Setting three appointments will allow you to hit your goal. Closing $1,000 in phone sales contributes to your daily sales goal. The onsite business presentation is expecting to product additional sold products, which contribute to your daily sales goal. These tasks will help reach the daily sales goal and proactively set up the next day for success. However, reality will tell you that there are more ways to achieve sales than direct sales. There are some tasks that indirectly impact your sales goals. In many industries, it's called pipeline management, behaviors that could set up future sales. Some of those may look like these:

- Make ten follow-up calls
- Confirm next-day appointments
- Call finance department about client approval

By completing these tasks, I will still impact my sales goal. Follow-up calls can turn into additional products and services. Confirming next-day appointments will help prepare for the next day. If a client changes the appointment, then a new appointment has to be made to close that gap. Calling the finance department relies on a third party to help get your client approved for the purchase of a product resulting in a sale. These indirect tasks are also necessary to achieve goals, so indirect tasks like these should be listed as well. However, there are also operational tasks that will have to be completed in order to complete your daily expectations. Those tasks may look like the following:

- Call to reset password to POS system
- Count inventory
- Attend sales meeting

These tasks won't have a direct or indirect impact on a sales goal, but they still have an impact one way or another on your direct and indirect tasks. Some of these tasks may consist of things that if not completed, will prevent you from doing your job efficiently. For example, if you don't reset your password, you don't access your POS (point of sale) system. You can still make sales; you just can't personally ring them out—could be a good thing in some cases, could be a bad thing in others. That is up to you to determine.

Now, let's take a look at our daily list in its entirety.

- Set three appointments
- Close $1,000 in phone sales
- Onsite business presentation
- Make ten follow-up calls
- Confirm next-day appointments
- Call finance departments about client approval
- Call to reset password to system
- Count inventory
- Attend sales meeting

This list just turned a nine-hour workday into nine tasks. That's one task per hour. Sounds easier to fulfill, doesn't it? The point of a list *is* to make life easier. Your life is easier when you're making your day more efficient. However, I think you would agree that only in a perfect world will you be able to accomplish your one-task-per-hour list 100 percent of the time, every time. As this is not a perfect world, here is a very important tip to learn early on when utilizing your lists.

TIP: The list is never complete, but that's how it's supposed to work.

That's right. You make a list to accomplish as much as you can within a given time, but the list will never be complete. In other words, you'll never accomplish everything on your list. Why? Because this is real life. Unless you keep your list real short, you will continuously add to it. That's a good thing! The main reason why I don't like to use the term *daily list* because it should realistically be ongoing. The better name for it would be everyday list. Or I prefer to call it a priority list.

Although you have nine tasks on your list (if this was your list), you still have incoming calls to answer, the boss asking you to do a specific task unrelated to your list, there may be a family emergency in your family or a coworker's, and the list goes on for uncontrollable variables that can and will throw your day off balance with additional, unpredicted tasks. That is why you should absorb this truth. This way, it is no surprise that you didn't complete 100 percent of your list and avoid depleting yourself for not doing so.

However, now that you know your day can have unpredictable impacts on your list, then you can plan for it, right? How can you plan for it? It's in the name. Prioritize. If an unpredicted event occurs, having tasks prioritized will have you already accomplishing the most important or highest impacted tasks for the day first. Like an investment, if you know you're going to lose money, you'll work to minimize the loss until you can make a change. If you know you're not going to complete your list, then you'd want to complete the highest priorities first. "Self, how do I prioritize my list?" I thought you'd never ask.

Let's revisit our list from earlier. We'll pretend that this is the list you've constructed. I'll guide you on how to organize your list into an efficient tool step by step, but first, you'll want to construct your list with whatever you feel needs to be accomplished. Don't worry about the order right now. Let's just say you've constructed the following list in this order:

- Call finance department about approving client
- Set three appointments
- Reset password to system
- Attend sales meeting
- Close $1,000 in phone sales
- Confirm next-day appointments
- Count inventory
- Onsite business presentation
- Make ten follow-up calls
- Ask Ryan to cover Saturday shift

To make math easier, I added one more task because we are going to apply the 80/20 rule again. Applied to your list, 20 percent of your list is responsible for 80 percent of your production. If you let that sink in, you'll understand why someone (maybe you) can accomplish so much in a day, yet make such a small impact toward your goal. It's because the typical manager doesn't prioritize their daily tasks. They usually stop short of making a list, if that, and that typically leads to managers focusing on 80 percent easy-to-do items that contribute to only 20 percent of their overall production. However, you are or are becoming a leader, and a leader has to be strategic. That means you have to prioritize these activities. So looking at your list, pretend your main goal is to achieve your sales goal by the end of the day. Based on what you see, what would be your 20 percent focus, or top two tasks that you feel would have the greatest impact and no matter what the day throws at you, you must accomplish?

The top two tasks that had the highest impact on the daily goal referenced were "Close $1,000 in phone sales" and the onsite business presentation. Both of these tasks can result in closing business that day, which directly contributes to the main goal. So let's choose these two and call these tasks our top-priority tasks, or Alpha tasks. Alpha-priority tasks are the top 20 percent of your tasks that must be completed above all else. These tasks have the greatest (direct) impact on accomplishing your set goal. Now we need to label our top two priority tasks. There are multiple ways to label your priority tasks: numerically, alphabetically, or a hybrid method. Since my system uses the Alpha, Bravo, and Charlie levels of performance and influence, I use the same ideology for my priority lists. Therefore, I recommend using the same method for simplicity and faster development.

In this example, we'll label our priorities with identifiers such as A, B, and C, followed by a numeric value. A represents the Alpha task, a task that directly impacts your goal and carries the highest importance to achieving your goal. B represents the Bravo task, a task that indirectly impacts your goal. C represents a Charlie task; this is any additional task that impacts your daily functions such as operational. The numeric value following the task identifier simply represents which task should come first in the event you have multiple tasks listed under a single identifier (which you will). For example, a task labeled A-1 and A-2 should be completed as soon as possible, but task A-1 should be completed before task A-2. The numeric value is measured by your perception of importance. If the business presentation was scheduled at 9:00 a.m., then you would label the presentation as A-1 and making your phone sales calls A-2. If the presentation was scheduled at 2:00 p.m., then you would label the calls as A-1 and the presentation as A-2. Again, your perception. For this example, let's say the onsite presentation is at 2:00 p.m. Now that you have identified and labeled your top two priority tasks, you can label the following tasks that directly impact your main goal with the Alpha identifier. The list could be labeled as the following:

- Call finance department about approving client
- Set three appointments
- Reset password to system
- Prepare for sales meeting
- A-1 Close $1,000 in phone sales
- Confirm next-day appointments
- Count inventory
- A-2 Onsite business presentation
- Make ten follow-up calls
- Ask Ryan to cover Saturday shift

Identifying your top-priority tasks is crucial. Once they are identified and labeled, you can apply more Alpha identifiers, if applicable, and your Bravo identifiers. It is very important to identify your top 20 percent first before moving forward. This helps your brain register your top priorities independently from other tasks, which will make it easier to remember among the daily turmoil. Based on your goal, I have labeled the following:

- A-3 Call finance department about approving client
- B-1 Set three appointments
- Reset password to system

- Prepare for sales meeting
- A-1 Close $1,000 in phone sales
- B-2 Confirm next-day appointments
- Count inventory
- A-2 Onsite business presentation
- B-3 Make ten follow-up calls
- Ask Ryan to cover Saturday shift

These items are identified as Bravo tasks because based on the goal set, these tasks don't directly impact the goal for this day, but indirectly since they impact the goal tomorrow. Bravo tasks are necessary tasks to complete right after your Alpha-priority tasks. All that's left are the daily functions to identify and then placing the list in their respective order.

- A-1 Close $1,000 in phone sales
- A-2 Onsite business presentation
- A-3 Call finance department about approving client
- B-1 Set three appointments
- B-2 Confirm next-day appointments
- B-3 Make ten follow-up calls
- C-1 Prepare for sales meeting
- C-2 Count inventory
- C-3 Ask Ryan to cover Saturday shift
- C-4 Reset password to system

Your priority list is complete. If you are more prone to proactive thinking and your goal was to set up success for the following day, your Alpha and Bravo tasks may be swapped or mixed. However, we'll cover more about proactive vs. reactive thinking in pillars IV and V. You now have to take action and remain focused on your list in the order you've prioritized.

Distractions and those in-the-moment added tasks will sprout up throughout your day. Before altering your list, you have to evaluate how the newly added task will impact your goal, then list it according to the level of importance. For example, based on your goal, let's say you received a phone call from a customer who wanted to make a purchase over the phone. Which priority would you list this call? Alpha, Bravo, or Charlie? Since this unexpected opportunity has a direct impact on your goal, you would classify it as an Alpha task. Regardless of what you're working on, this would be an acceptable task to complete immediately.

Instead of a call for a sales purchase, let's say the customer was calling to request copies of receipts. How would you classify this requested task? Evaluating the urgency, you will find that the task doesn't directly impact your goal, nor does it impact tomorrow's goal. For those two reasons, you should label this task as a Charlie priority. This doesn't mean you don't accomplish it. You're only acknowledging that you have higher-priority tasks to complete first. At this time, you would simply give the client a timeline to fulfill their request (by the end of the day, by noon tomorrow, etc.) and jump back on your top priority. If you haven't noticed it already, these events will happen *every day* and at any moment, which is why you need to prioritize: to keep you focused on the goal at hand. Having a list will develop the behavior to recognize strategically how tasks will impact your day. It will help you remember to use your best judgment always when altering your list and remain aligned with your goal. As mentioned previously, your list will never be completed. By accepting that, you'll avoid anxiety and remain focused on accomplishing your Alpha-priority tasks first, followed by your Bravo tasks. The good news is there are still a few more tricks to help make your priority list even more efficient and more effective.

How to Manage Your Charlie Tasks

Charlie tasks can impact your time the most, but not in a good way for two reasons: First, these tasks can magically take up all of your time to complete because no matter how many you complete in a single day, these tasks continue to sprout up. These tasks can easily suck you into believing you are being productive because of the amount of Charlie tasks you can accomplish in a given time, but there are always more Charlie tasks to be added. Second, no matter how many or how big you knock out, these tasks will produce absolutely *zero* results toward your goals.

Now, you may be asking yourself, "Self, why would I worry about Charlie tasks if they never end and they don't help me achieve my goal?" One word—function. These tasks are necessary for your day to function. Failure to complete these tasks in a timely manner could throw your day, week, or month into disarray. Charlie tasks are typically those that impact your daily process in one form or another, the same daily process you need to flow smoothly to achieve your goals. The natural response to these tedious tasks is to ignore, procrastinate, or forget them. Sound familiar? After all, they are, for the most part, boring, unexciting, and unimpressive. However, if you think about it, these tasks are usually the ones that make the most noise in the world if neglected. Since they are typically tedious, each Charlie task triggers a negative, emotional response that can paralyze your critical thinking. For example, I've illustrated typical responses for the Charlie tasks listed previously.

C-1 Prepare for sales meeting	"I have plenty of time." (It's 9:50 a.m. meeting is at 10:00 a.m.)
C-2 Count inventory	"I'll do this first so I'll have more time later."
C-3 Ask Ryan to cover Saturday shift	"Ryan is here in ten minutes. I'll just wait for him."
C-4 Reset passwords to POS systems	"This won't take long. I'll just knock it out now."

Everyone at some point, in some form, has used these or similar excuses for similar tasks. You may have chuckled at yourself saying something similar. I know I wasn't immune to it before. Unfortunately, it's human nature to underestimate situations, particularly because we don't take the time to analyze the possible outcomes. These are typical responses. To clarify the detriments, let's look at a fallacy within each response.

C-1. I'm sure there have been several moments in your life when you told yourself that something was so simple that you pushed it off all the way until it was due. That's procrastination at its best. In this case, it's easy to underestimate the task because you assume the task is so simple that a large amount of time isn't necessary to complete it. Although it may be true, it's not the required time to complete it that's the challenge. It's the "What if?" What if you don't have the expected time before the meeting to prepare? What if what was required to help accomplish the task was no longer available? You have to take "what if" into consideration because if the task isn't completed in a timely manner or you're left unprepared for issues you can't predict, you'll have two dilemmas: (1) You replace a top-priority task with preparing for a sales meeting, which can negatively impact your goal. (2) You'll miss the deadline and have to face consequences, if any.

C-2. You may have heard time and time again that knocking out the big projects or hardest tasks first will free up time in the future to do more. This is very false, especially if the task doesn't contribute to your goal. If the task at hand is time-consuming *and* it doesn't rank at the top of your list, you're wasting a lot of valuable time. Don't let the idea that completing bigger tasks just because they're big will always yield the highest reward. Analyze your outcomes from completing a task. Compare the impact to your goal. Then decide. Two dilemmas can happen here: (1) You have replaced your top priority, which will negatively impact your goal. (2) You will lose a lot of time and accomplish very little.

C-3. Although everyone falls into this trap, you must remember that the little things will keep your time on hold, which distracts you from your top-priority tasks. As mentioned previously, you also need to factor in the what-ifs. What if he can't answer your question immediately? Or what if he runs late unexpectedly? All of which waste more valuable time. Always minimize the distractions, especially the ones you control. There are two dilemmas that you will run into: (1) You have replaced your top priority, which will negatively impact your goal. (2) If you're working on a top-priority task, you will constantly distract yourself looking out for Ryan, which will minimize your production.

C-4. This is the ultimate fallacy people tend to tell themselves: "This won't take long." If anyone else was telling you that, you know the first thing that comes to mind is probably "Yeah right." That's because, culturally, we tend to miscalculate opportunity costs in completing a task, especially if it doesn't take long to say. Funny, huh? As humans, we tend to assume that things which are easy to say are easy to do. In this case, the thought of changing a password sounds really easy. However, we tend to underestimate the procedures required to do so in the real business world. Changing a password on a business system on an employer's network tends to involve logging out of a system entirely, then authenticating yourself to change, and logging back in. Depending on your network, that will take your time. Or if you're calling a service department, forget about it. There may be holding periods, listening to the menu for the right number to press, and an operator may request to provide personal and/or professional information to identify yourself before transferring. Finally, you get a service representative who will have to use the same resources as you to look up procedures, reset your password, and walk you through the process. Everything described just took thirty to forty-five minutes for one "easy" task. Two dilemmas you'll experience: (1) You have replaced your top priority, which will negatively impact your goal. (2) A ton of your priceless time has gone right out the window.

After reviewing each of these common fallacies, what was a similar dilemma? Replacing your top priority. So that should tell you to teach yourself and your team to focus always on your top priorities first. It's easy to see where our time can be lost throughout the day and why. Using discipline to stick to your top-priority tasks first is crucial for production and efficiency. At times, even hearing the Charlie task out loud can create a difficult urge to complete them prior to top-priority tasks on your list. The typical manager will fall for this fallacy almost every time, but you're not a typical manager anymore, are you? Avoid the thought that you will save time and produce more evading or postponing top priorities. The point is that before you jump into a Charlie task, be sure to really analyze the possible outcome of fulfilling it in respect to your time and that you don't replace a Charlie task with a top-priority task (whichever task is first on your list at the time).

Now of course, Charlie tasks must be completed before they cause an even bigger issue. Otherwise, you won't be able to function throughout your day. For example, missed important information at the meeting, forget to order inventory to sell, didn't get your shift covered and now put the team in a tough position, or you got locked out of your system, which requires back office to solve it. No one wants that. So you might be back asking yourself, "Self, if the Charlie tasks must be completed so I can function throughout my day, but I can't stop working on my top priorities first, how on earth am I supposed to complete Charlie tasks?" Glad you asked. Here is how you can manage to complete Charlie tasks and still maintain your top priorities.

1- Strategic Procrastination

I bet you've been told a thousand times never to procrastinate. Now that's funny. You can't avoid an innate behavior naturally instilled in all of us. Neither can the person saying that. It's an emotional response. What should be said is for you not to overestimate procrastination. The truth is, you can't avoid it. It is an innate behavior triggered from an emotional response given from how you feel about the task needed to be complete. If you feel it's not important, you'll put it off until it becomes a bigger problem than it initially was. Overestimating procrastination can cause one to believe that one can accomplish anything without preparation and/or there is always plenty of time to do so, a fallacy that dramatically increases your chances to fail. Everyone procrastinates in one form or another. It's the how and the when that really make the difference between making a right choice and a wrong choice to procrastinate. You read it right. There is a right choice and a wrong choice to procrastinate. Here is an example of how I fell into this fallacy of overestimating procrastination during my school years.

REAL LIFE

I was a master of procrastination as a student, but not in the greatest sense. In high school, I believe I had one of the best chemistry and physics teachers out there—Mr. Gordon. He created very elaborate and inventive projects. One of those projects involved building a rocket. However, we had to insert an egg that couldn't break upon impact. We had to build creatively a rocket that would fly as high as it could but land safely enough to keep the egg in its best condition. We were graded on two variables: the vertical height from liftoff and the condition of the egg after landing (or after impact for most). Forty percent of the grade was on the height reached from launch, and 60 percent on the egg's condition. We were given two weeks to complete the project. I spent the last night designing and building it. To provide more time to do what I wanted to do, therefore, I designed my rocket based on the expectation of a failed landing. Instead of spending weeks designing and building a rocket that had landing gear, some form of parachute-dispensing mechanism, and hours of testing, I spent the few hours I had designing the rocket to suspend the egg within the rocket casing. Knowing that my rocket was going to plummet, I focused on reinforcing the frame surrounding the egg and its suspension within to absorb the energy of the crash. My rocket was one of the highest in the sky and certainly crashed the hardest. The rocket was in pieces, but the egg was in perfect condition.

In college, I was able to stay up late playing video games, watching movies, or hanging out with friends, and the very next morning, crunch my studies within a couple of hours to prepare for the test. I was so experienced that I created a unique way of studying just right to increase my chances of receiving a B or higher with only an hour and a half or two to study. My strategy was so specific that if I knew it was multiple choice, fill in the blank, math, or essay, I had a unique way to remember material under each circumstance. I didn't have special powers. I didn't have photographic memory (otherwise, I wouldn't be writing this guide).

I aced both the project and the test. I only stressed for less than half a day. I figured something out. My emotions said, "Don't be like the other stress freaks in school, and have fun." That emotional response triggered these procrastinating behaviors.

Procrastination can be useful, but I started to notice a challenge in the long run with my strategy. You can't always avoid procrastination, but you can certainly be strategic on when and how to use it. What do I mean? Take these examples for example. The advantage with my strategy back in school was that all the other students were stressed out while I got an opportunity to do whatever I wanted, whenever I wanted. During those times, it was just more time to play.

People assumed I was really creative or had photographic memory, but it was just a strategy all along. I couldn't stop procrastinating for these types of situations because it consistently worked and it allowed me to have fun. I felt that procrastination was the answer to being able to do anything and still pass through life. However, I learned a hard lesson later in life.

The disadvantage I discovered when it mattered most was short-term memory. The first two years of college didn't matter to me as I was just knocking out a bulk of my electives and core curriculum. However, starting my junior year made a difference when I was taking career-driven courses that I felt had more importance. In addition, working full-time with two jobs to pay, I was beginning to use some of those studies in real life. Or I wanted to. Yet I couldn't remember all that information from my crunch studies. Worst of all, I lost almost all memory from previous courses that would have been useful, making learning a little more difficult. That's when I realized I was overestimating procrastination.

I thought it would solve everything with a due date. Turns out it was only a solution for what I needed at the moment, not the long run. It was not the solution for everything. If I wanted to improve my critical thinking skills and compete with some of the real geniuses in the class, I had to change how I procrastinated. My priority changed. I was the only one who aced these tests but couldn't retain the information. I was the only student who aced the rocket project that crashed his rocket. I achieved my short-term goals, but it created challenges in the long run. I had to learn how to improve this behavior if possible. Turns out it was the why I used it that held me back. My goal was to play. So why would I need to retain information if all I wanted to do was play? I misunderstood how procrastination worked.

You're always going to procrastinate in something. The key I learned is to redirect why and when to use procrastination, hence strategic procrastination. Procrastination is a natural tool or behavior in life. It is a byproduct of an emotional response when you feel something else is more important than the task at hand. Read that sentence again and relate it back to your priority list. The difference between knowledge and wisdom *here* is using procrastination on the tasks that are least important—Charlie tasks, for example. That's the right use of procrastination. If you must procrastinate because of a constraint on time, procrastinate on the tasks that don't have a high priority. Perhaps changing a password didn't involve multiple steps. Just log in, select settings, and log off. However, we all tell ourselves it takes seconds when we know it can take minutes. Instead of pushing back lead calls, you push this task to the end of your day. That would be making the right choice to procrastinate because you're focusing on the top priorities that will help you achieve your goal first. If you procrastinate on a follow-up call, someone else will get the sale, and you could fall short on your goal. That would be the wrong use of procrastination. If a soldier procrastinated in providing intel to allies behind enemy lines, that soldier may have forfeited their life. If I procrastinated on writing this book, you could have been seeking help from a more complex system. Making sense? Don't avoid procrastination because it will eventually lead you to procrastinating on the wrong task at the wrong time. Redirect its use instead. Be strategic on when to use it. It isn't a one-size-fits-all solution, but using this tool on some of your lower-priority tasks can buy you more time to accomplish your top priorities.

REMEMBER: If you must procrastinate, strategically procrastinate on the priorities that have the least amount of impact on your goal.

NOTE: Procrastinating on all your Charlie tasks is not strategic. Avoid using this method as a means to ignore Charlie tasks. The goal is to avoid putting Charlie tasks ahead of higher tasks when time is scarce. With due dates, even Charlie tasks can become Alpha tasks.

2. Delegate, delegate, delegate!

Do what you do best and delegate the rest.
—Anonymous

In my opinion as a leader, this is the ultimate tool, which is way underused and yet is the most powerful tool to free up your time. By delegating, you provide team development, mentorship, accountability, teamwork, responsibility, motivation, growth, and the list goes on, which is why it is truly the ultimate tool for a leader. The most important provision is your time. As a leader, you delegate to generate more time to accomplish your top-priority tasks first. Delegation, however, is a form of art. It isn't about finding anyone to fulfill the task. This use could lead to setting up team members and yourself to fail. You must be willing to trust those you delegate to and make sure their skill set and motivation match the task entrusted to them to fulfill. In addition, you must set aside your pride or your "do it right, do it yourself" mentality.

Once you follow those two steps, delegating is easy. Any manager can point to a task and have a team member complete it. The unfortunate part is, managers take advantage of it, like other tools, and make team members fulfill tasks that may not impact their skill set or complement their skill set, which results in incomplete tasks or unsatisfactory work. As a result, the manager(s) usually place the blame on the teammate. *Or* a manager delegates a task just to free up their time to do nothing. As a leader, you must be strategic in your delegating technique in order to support growth, balance morale, and help you focus time toward higher priorities. Here are a few questions I ask myself when I'm figuring out which team member to delegate a Bravo or Charlie task to:

- Will the team member learn anything new?
- Is there a team member enthusiastic about fulfilling this task?
- Is there a team member who is an expert at this task?
- Is there a team member who has a skill set that complements the task?
- Can this task help develop any skills for the team member?
- Does this task have a specific timeline?

This is pretty basic, but don't stop with these questions. These types of questions are just examples of what you want to ask yourself when identifying whom you should delegate to. Think of it this way. If someone asked you to do something for them, wouldn't you appreciate the task more or be more willing to fulfill it if you had an opportunity to learn from it? Absolutely. And if you were more enthusiastic about the task given, do you think you would be motivated to complete the task satisfactorily or better? Absolutely. Whatever task you plan to delegate, try to tie it into a team member's development. This will assure the task gets done in a timely, willing, and enthusiastic manner—a win-win.

REAL LIFE

I even delegate to my family. During the holiday season, when it's time to set up our tree, we have three sub-tasks to complete: I unpack and construct it, my wife fluffs the branches, and my children decorate it. Although it sounds like a typical family tradition, I have time-efficient and team-development reasoning behind it. The project is completed faster if we work as a team, and I create more time to fulfill other, higher-priority tasks. I delegated each task based on their skill level and their desire to do it. I'm used to constructing, and I have the most knowledge around doing so; therefore, I knew I could complete this task most efficiently. Although my wife may have not volunteered, one year, she filled in for me to fluff the tree, and she was amazing. It looked authentic. Since she did a great job, she was nominated to take the responsibility. And my kids—well, they just love hanging those ornaments. It could take a thousand ornaments, and they would still be enthusiastic from the first ornament to the last. They had a serious passion behind this task, so I allowed them to unleash it. My wife and I just did a touch-up during the final inspection. The result was a beautiful tree every year. This annual delegating tradition frees up my time to put up lights, create a fun learning environment for the family, and develop teamwork skills for everyone. The best part is that no one notices it.

This is what you can do every day for your team. Matching up the right task with the right team member(s) most times can create a bigger impact than if you were to fulfill it. In most cases, team members would be so enthusiastic to help that there will be a point where no matter what task is given, a team member will complete it in a timely, satisfactory manner. It's been proven that a team with delegated tasks has the strongest teamwork ethic and is the most productive as a unit. Don't hold back from allowing your team members to have a bigger role in your team development and certainly gain more time to make a bigger impact on your goal.

Leadership is the art of getting someone else to do something you want done because he wants to do it.
—Gen. Dwight Eisenhower

Delegation is an extremely powerful tool that you need to master to control the time you have in fulfilling your top priorities. If it was my task to count inventory, but I had a team member who was very analytical and detail-oriented, this would be a perfect task to delegate to him or her, which could ultimately free up a couple of hours while developing their skill set. This will undoubtedly be the most powerful tool to use in managing your Charlie tasks, as it should. All the greatest leaders have mastered this technique. It's your turn!

REMEMBER: My reference to top priorities refers to the top priorities at the top of the list in the following respective order to be completed: Alpha tasks, Bravo tasks, and Charlie tasks.

3. Sub-listing

Sub-listing is a unique way to organize your bigger priorities by creating a secondary priority list under a particular task. Specifically, you want to create a sub-list for tasks that would require additional tasks to complete, called sub-tasks. If you want to delegate a larger task, then you have a sub-list to refer to for that team member to complete. If there are specific sub-tasks that require your time to complete, then a sub-list will work perfectly. Use my previous story about my family Christmas tree as a simple example. The task was setting up the tree. My sub-tasks were construction, fluffing, and decorating, where I was still responsible for constructing the tree, but delegating the two other tasks to my family who were more skillful and motivated to fulfill those.

Let's say that I have a team member named Sarah who can assist because of her inventory experience, but I am responsible to submit the count online because that requires my access information. My list will look like the following, with a combination of a sub-list and delegation. I also added additional examples to illustrate further the use of sub-lists.

A-1 Close $1,000 in phone sales
A-2 Onsite business presentation
    1. Collect assessment sheets
    2. Print handouts
    3. Upload presentation. Test for response.
A-3 Call finance department about approving client
B-1 Set three appointments
B-2 Confirm next-day appointments
B-3 Make ten follow-up calls
    1. Clients from Sept. 1–7
    2. Clients from Sept. 8–15
C-1 Prepare for sales meeting

C-2 Count inventory
1. Complete prep log   - Sarah
2. Scan inventory   - Sarah
3. Confirm count   - Sarah
4. Approve and submit log - Me
C-3 Ask Ryan to cover Saturday shift
C-4 Reset password to system

Since counting inventory is a Charlie priority, very time-consuming, and has a deadline approaching, you can choose to delegate the task to free up time for higher priorities. In this case, it was Sarah. Although you still have responsibilities such as approving and submitting the inventory log, you can still save time delegating the bulk of your sub-tasks. As you're working on your top priorities, Sarah can check in when her tasks are completed. If you are the only one permitted to complete the task, then your list would simply look like the others:

C-2 Count inventory
1. Complete prep log
2. Scan inventory
3. Confirm count
4. Approve and submit log

Here's another way to understand how impactful utilizing delegation and sub-listing can be. Think back to my goal of changing the lives of over 10,000 managers and leaders. Imagine if that was a priority on my priority list instead of a goal. Do you think a sub-list would be necessary to tackle it? Definitely. The priority is too big. It would need additional tasks to complete and take up much of my time by myself. In addition, I still had other priorities to fulfill. If I wanted to complete my priorities faster and effectively, I need to come up with a creative solution and generate a sub-list to delegate. That solution, let's say, is this book. My dilemma, however, is that I also run multiple businesses. So I have to create a sub-list accordingly. By doing so, I'll help organize and coordinate this priority and accomplish it faster and more effectively.

Thinking about what tasks are needed, I somehow have to generate copies of the book, distribute them, learn the legal processes, market to my target audience, and create events to generate buzz, like signings and seminars. Now that's a lot of work, but also a lot of time. So I'll choose to delegate a majority of those tasks within my sub-list to a publisher who will take care of publication and distribution, an attorney for legal protection, and a marketing team, which will save me days or even weeks of time in research. In the end, I'll be capable of reaching millions of people across the United States with the help of my team and, in return, increase my chances of changing the lives of 10,000 managers and leaders. If I didn't delegate this task to those experts, this could have taken years.

A leader's ability to accomplish larger goals and priorities is measured by their capabilities of effectively using their time *and* their team simultaneously. By working with these experts, I was able to increase my chances of reaching 10,000 managers exponentially in a fraction of the time. Sub-listing is an essential tool to organize a busy priority list. Delegation is an essential tool for team development and efficiency, saving time and accomplishing multiple tasks simultaneously. Master the use of both skills, and you'll truly master time management. As a result, you'll become a more productive and more effective leader.

4 - Control Your Environment

I don't mean harvesting your inner power to alter weather patterns and the earth around you. I mean control the environment *you* surround yourself with—people, settings, culture, etc. Although the world is full of books regarding the impact those around you have, I'm only going to discuss how it can impact your ability to develop these new skills. There's a reason why the rich only socialize with the rich, top executives only socialize with top executives, and top performers only socialize with top performers a majority of their day. It's because nature has a secret rule: You're a product of your environment.

To truly unleash *your* greatness, you have to be surrounded by those who have already done so or are doing it now. To become a great leader, you have to be surrounded by great leaders. Wherever you want to take yourself, you have to be around those who are or were already there, whenever you can. I believe that it is a crucial part of learning, adapting, and utilizing new skills. Surrounding yourself with those leaders in your industry who use the same vocabulary will help reinforce your memory and your skill set.

These days, you won't find people standing around to discuss how they manage their time, or how much fun it is to organize their priority list. If I ever came across one, I'd probably pass out in the nearest chair. So while around these leaders at social events or meetings, listen closely to how they talk about their achievements. If you listen closely enough, you'll hear how those leaders use time management effectively. You may hear how they had to delegate to another team member, had to choose which task they had to drop and why, or had to organize a project in order to help accomplish their goal. They are making the same decisions you are going to make during your career. Without noticing, they'll tell you exactly how they organize their time to accomplish their top priorities. After reading this guide, there shouldn't be any surprises as to how, just assurance that the best utilize these methods in some form.

Just as you would surround yourself with like minds and experienced leaders, you also don't want to surround yourself with clutter. Just like people, if you surround your bedroom, your home, or your office with clutter and disorganization, then you yourself become cluttered and disorganized. Eighty percent of the employees out there don't realize that they induce their own stress at the start of their day simply because of the mess they've left in their workplace. It generates stress because it is the first thing you see at the beginning of the day, which doesn't generate any positive reinforcement, not to mention it puts lower priorities ahead of your top priorities to avoid embarrassment. Just the "Oh great. I forgot I have to clean this up." You can also lose or trash something important during those rushed moments of cleaning. So always clean your work environment, or what I call home, at the end of your day, with your priority list out to assure a smooth transition the next day.

The Time Is Now

Leaders are put in place to take decisive action for the best of the team. Where others will not be able to analyze a situation like you can, it's imperative for you to make those decisions for others. It will require courage to drop pride and delegate a task if you need additional time elsewhere, or to decide to skip or erase a task for the same result. I've had many encounters with upper management asking why a particularly useless task wasn't completed. After I explained that I felt it was imperative to adjust the priorities at hand in order to accomplish a goal, they usually supported my decision. In the presence of other leaders, hearing these examples will encourage you to remain consistent with managing your own time effectively. So be sure to identify these leaders and take advantage of their time, like a mentorship. Learn all you can when you can, but more importantly, keep yourself surrounded with like minds. Others will learn from you, and you will learn from them, which will only make you more successful.

Remember, like building a house, my guide is your foundation, and the pillars are your framework. This time management model and the skills and behaviors you've learned will help you manage your time efficiently and effectively, which provides you optimum time to accomplish your top priorities. "Practice makes better. Perfect practice makes perfect," my old football coach used to say. He meant focus on building and mastering the basics. Over time, you'll develop new mastery skills that will allow you to master your style truly. It's an art. It's a form, something you must consistently practice. Utilizing your priority list with the three priority markers (Alpha, Bravo, and Charlie) in combination with the four additional advanced skills (targeted procrastination, delegation, sub-listing, and environmental control), you'll immediately become three times as productive as the competition, the same competition that still checks one item off at a time without direction or purpose other than to complete a list they aren't aware will never end. Following this guide will allow you to develop and accomplish beyond what you thought you were capable of. In addition, you become the ultimate brand of leadership in the industry, the rarest of all: a leader that not only produces top performers, but also generates and develops future leaders.

TIP: At the end of your day, take thirty minutes to clear your desk and create your priority list for the following day, using the structure you've just learned from pillar II. Upon completing it, leave it right in front of your computer or in the center of your desk. With a clean desk and only your priority list waiting for you, the next day you come in, you'll feel energized with less stress, less distraction, and your planed day waiting for you. Already starting your day ahead of 80 percent of the competition—now that's a good start!

PILLAR III

Positive Accountability

ACCOUNTABILITY IS ONE of the most highly anticipated behaviors upper management expects from your leadership. Yet it is also rarely discussed and one of the most underdeveloped skills in management. Why is that? Throughout my career in multiple *Fortune* 500 companies, I've never had a manager teach me how to hold my team members accountable properly. Only the whys were explained, but never the hows, outside of using some form of documentation. This was just about as useful as reading one of those columns from a business magazine listing the "top five manager traits" or something similar, with accountability being on the list. Even those lists reference the importance of accountability and do not discuss how.

I began to notice that managers were not trained on how to hold team members accountable themselves, which is typically hard to notice until you are in the hot seat yourself. Most have winged it. Some have learned and adapted. I have seen managers say, "This is what you did and why you are getting a warning. The next time will result in a formal warning. Sign here." It began making sense as to why this is an avoided topic. It's an awkward conversation no one wants to have until it's absolutely necessary. The managers want to avoid it, and the team members want to avoid it. That equation always equals disaster followed by miscommunication and resulting in a negative experience, an unfortunate situation that must change.

Accountability, to sum up how I've heard it, has always been as a negative response to a negative behavior. In my first few attempts to hold team members accountable without training or guidance, the responses I received didn't seem to provide the outcome I desired. I felt something wasn't right. It is almost used as a fear tactic more than anything, simply because everyone left its meaning loose for interpretation. The meetings I'd attended shadowing other managers seemed to feel like an interrogation. Whenever I was on the receiving end during my youth, I felt the same way. It felt very dim, bleak, and discouraging. Notice that HR policies always word it as a "warning." Verbal, informal, or formal warning, to be specific. This is HR's fault. This just became a business custom to view such a situation as something negative when it *can* be the complete opposite. That's right! Accountability *can* be a positive thing.

Warnings are useful in avoiding danger, right? Warning: Don't swim here. Warning: Thin ice. Warning: Pedestrians crossing. Signs like these help avoid possible dangers. Although I've never seen one that said, "Warning: You'll lose your job," that doesn't mean some places wouldn't benefit from it. As I'm sure HR would love to have those signs up throughout the workplace, the truth is, that would create a negative atmosphere. However, people make mistakes. Again, we are assuming that the issue we face isn't *will* related. When one makes a mistake, one shouldn't be shamed for doing so. If mistakes were really perceived this way, we wouldn't have the hundreds of thousands of successful businesses and stories we hear today. To become great, you have to learn from your mistakes. When they told Thomas Edison that he failed to make a light bulb, he said, "I didn't fail. I just found 2,000 ways not to make a light bulb; I only needed to find one way to make it work." From this perspective, you can see why accountability is a positive thing. This is a moment to help a team member reference a mistake they've made, work with them to learn from it and become a stronger team member, all because of your guidance. It's a perfect time to reconnect with a team member and help them redirect their behavior in the right direction, which is up, not out. This is another way you will make a major impact on your team member's performance and, ultimately, their life.

REAL LIFE

One day, my manager wanted me to hold a team member accountable as their supervisor, because of their performance. So I had a thought. Like an equation, when having those conversations, if there was more negativity than positivity stimuli, then the outcome would be negative. My idea was reversing the presentation. What if I held a team member accountable, but in a positive way? Keep them motivated to improve, rather than fearing to make a mistake. Could I expect a positive impact? Mathematically, it made sense, so why not in this case?

I collected all necessary documentation and prepared to have a conversation, not an interrogation. I also changed the language by dropping the "warning" and calling it a conversation. Again, it's about perception, right? During our discussion, I asked open-ended questions to uncover any barriers or objections that may have existed. In doing so, I uncovered an unfortunate matter that was weighing heavily on the team member's mind, directly impacting his performance. I positioned the team member's impact on the team under his current performance and reinforced how I knew and believed he was capable of far greater performance and to fight through his personal challenges. Sticking to the guideline I created prior to our meeting, we were able to create a strong action plan to assist his recovery, and more importantly, he left the office smiling with encouragement to improve. Three months later, he was the second-highest producing team member. I knew I'd discovered the right way to have those accountability conversations. I shared this process with my management team, and the responses in their departments were incredible: simultaneous lift in performance and minimal turnover.

To help you prepare and hold a meaningful, impactful, and encouraging accountability conversation, I have provided a detailed outline in this pillar to teach what others, for whatever reason, cannot. It's very important to utilize accountability meetings as a tool of development, focused on encouraging, motivating, and in more cases than not, assisting the team member to envision their success. Absolutely avoid interrogations. As a reminder, we are still assuming that the team member is willing to improve. Later in this section, we'll cover the unwilling team member. First, you have to prepare.

By failing to prepare, you are preparing to fail.
—Benjamin Franklin

Boy, was he right. Let me show you how to prepare to hold a meaningful, impactful, and encouraging accountability conversation (used during sessions with action plans).

Preparation

Preparation will always be a key to success. If it weren't for having a strategy, you wouldn't see the country you live in today. You must be strategic and focused to be as successful as you want to be. We discussed the effects of overestimating procrastination and how to direct your procrastinating nature toward other lower-priority tasks through strategic procrastination. This is something you want to make sure you are creating thoughtful time to complete. Preparing to have these conversations is essential for you, your teammate, and the team. You want to anticipate the most likely scenarios that could take place so you will be prepared to respond in a professional manner. Typically, these conversations turn south quickly because the manager or leader was not prepared to receive a response. Taking the response personally and turning the conversation into a confrontation—this can all be avoided by preparation. Just like any priority, you want to have a main goal to reach, in this case, an objective, something that will keep you and the team member focused on the topic at hand. Identify any possible objections and create proper responses. Collect all necessary documentation prior to the meeting and support your position with analytical data: reports, charts, attendance records, etc. Next, we'll cover all four steps broken down:

1. Objective

As stated, we want to have an objective for this conversation, not just "Provide warning and document response." An objective is what will ultimately unite or realign your team members' vision with yours.

Objectives need to set like SMART goals—specific, measurable, achievable, realistic, and timely. You don't want to create one simple objective like "My objective is to identify why John is not performing." Why? Because it ultimately carries no value to anyone but yourself. These meetings aren't about you. It's about the team member. If that was your objective, John may say he is not performing because his mom passed away. He may not be performing because he doesn't understand how to close the sale. Or he may not be performing because he hates Mondays. In any case, if this was your objective, then once you have the why, you've met *your* objective. Therefore, you don't need to continue your conversation. That's an objective for an interrogation. The objective needs to be the focus point on the action plan that should follow. We'll cover more later on action plans.

Although the why is very important, don't let that be the only reason you're having the conversation. Your objective needs to add value to your team member. That's how you impact lives, gain loyalty, and display leadership. Typical objectives may be simple four to eight-word sentences, but it needs to have three elements to truly provide clarity in becoming successful. You need to discover why the wrong behavior was made, what action plan needs to take place to progress, and how to measure success. You should set an objective similar to the following examples:

1. Identify why John is behind pace by 30 percent, create a thirty-day action plan to realign John's daily behaviors to maximize opportunities, and achieve over 10 percent of pace by day 31.
2. Discover why Jane did not complete her part of the presentation, create a two-week plan to observe and coach, and complete her presentation by the end of January.
3. Seek why Joe was late four out of the past seven shifts, create a seven-day plan to support his reason for late attendance, and achieve a consistent thirty-day tardy-free goal.

Notice each objective carried the same three elements. This is not where you will outline the details. That comes later. Also, remember that you can't provide specifics to a problem not yet identified. Again, this objective is to give you a focus point for the conversation. During your conversation, you'll make sure you're fixing the right problem. For now, your focus, or the objective, should only be one sentence with three elements: Find the why, create the how, and what success looks like.

2. Identify possible objections and responses

> **You can't control how people react, but**
> **you can control how you respond.**
> **—Commander Shepard**

It will only benefit you to anticipate reactions and objections. In doing so, you can create professional responses. The benefit for you to have these responses in place is to control your emotions and to respond appropriately, which in turn helps the team member control their emotions. Emotions tend to send conversations deep into HR territory because when your emotions get involved, you then take offense and defend your point of view (ironically, a view that no longer pertains to the original objection). We want to avoid these situations. Chemically, I don't have whatever it is that helps you react the best to surprises, like expecting a job or a conversation to go one way, but it somehow goes way out the other end, the kind that catches you off guard with a "How in the heck . . ." only not as nice. Since those situations definitely happen a lot in business, I had to take the time to create anticipated reactions and objections so I could handle those responses appropriately. Or at least be a heck of a lot more prepared to respond appropriately. Of course, you can't plan for every situation, but you'll be more prepared if you create a few appropriate responses. I would predict their reactions based on what I've learned from their body language, personality, verbal communication, and how they socialized with other team members throughout their time on the team. Basically, you can identify these reactions just by remaining observant of their daily behaviors and personality traits. Here are a couple examples of what you may encounter and how to respond:

1. May react offensively. Typically reacts offensively to criticism.
   Example Responses: This is only an opportunity for improvement from my observations.

   Let me show you where I see an opportunity to improve and tell me what you think.

   I don't mean to offend you. As your leader, I want to help you succeed and overcome obstacles such as these. What barriers, if any, are you experiencing?

2. May not agree with the opportunity identified. May have a habit of not accepting the opinion of others.
   Example Responses: It's okay to disagree, but let me show you where I see the opportunity and you tell me what you see.

   I appreciate your honesty. Can you tell me why you believe this isn't an opportunity to improve?

Now, with your responses created, you won't be surprised if the team member reacts offensively or standoffish. You can now respond appropriately and professionally. Looking at my example responses, what similarities do you see? I hope you noticed that I made it interactive. In each response, I left a moment for the team member to respond. This is a conversation, so invite the team member to interact. Keeping communication open with allow the team member to be more receptive to your point of view and open the door to self-improvement. Be prepared so you can keep control of the moment and create encouragement. Your team members will respond positively, you'll gain additional trust, and they'll appreciate your leadership.

REMEMBER: This is a conversation, not an interrogation. Open communication for both sides by encouraging their input.

3. Documentation

I know that any HR manager or leader would be praising me for this section, but I can't stress enough about the importance of documentation. This isn't new, but this is still a huge problem for managers and leaders. Since the '90s, it has been proven that anyone can sue for anything. Not to mention, there are so many distractions in the world, team members, including yourself, will forget everything discussed the second you change the subject. For the sake of protecting you, your company, and the team member under both situations, be sure to document everything you do. I will provide additional tools on how to document performance in pillar V: Team Development. Nonetheless, the most important part about documentation is that it will help you and the team member stay committed to your plan. Like a contract, an action plan is an agreement and will naturally help the both of you remain committed to the objective. If anything were to happen, such as forgetting or misunderstanding, you'll have a reference to help get you both back on track. Documents you would want to have prepared prior to your conversation are as follows, but are not limited to:

a. Action plan (We'll cover the action plan in more detail later in this section.)
b. Previous observations and/or coaching logs
c. Current and/or previous performance reports (preferably related to the opportunity identified)
d. A verbal informal or formal document (whichever is necessary, typically provided by your organization within the HR department)—If you don't have one, there are many easily accessible online.
e. Any additional supporting documentation *relevant* to the objective, such as supportive analytics.

4. Supportive analytics

Mathematics is known as the language of the universe and it always speaks the truth. This is a culture you have to create, and during these accountability meetings, you want to help incorporate that into your meetings. Providing analytical proof will put any doubter in a position of acceptance, those *willing* to accept and improve, that is. You can have someone argue all day about how they are truly the best, but it will only take one report to show that they're tenth to change their tune. However, with that in mind, depending on your approach, utilizing these numbers can become demotivating. So when you're referencing performance reports, keep in mind that you want to have an encouraging conversation. You want to show them what their opportunity is and how they can turn it around. Supportive analytics are strictly performance reports. These documents should always go hand in hand when analyzing a team member's performance, as referenced in pillar I, when you were analyzing your team members' performance level to match the appropriate influential leadership level. Here are a few examples of performance reports to reference:

1. WTD (week to date)/MTD/QTD/YTD sales results
2. Customer experience survey results
3. Reports reflecting completed transactions (attachment rates, cross sales, etc.)

To Converse, Not to Interrogate

Now that we are prepared, now we hold our accountability meeting. This conversation should be all about self-discovery. Self-discovery is when you find that a-ha truth identified within yourself to improve with the guidance of another. In other words, instead of giving a team member all the answers, you help direct them to find the answers for themselves, by using a series of directed questions. We'll cover more about this technique in pillar V. It is a very crucial part of this conversation because it's your responsibility to encourage, inspire, and motivate the team member to succeed. This conversation is a moment where you could help that team member define themselves and truly turn their performance around. To maximize this outcome, you want the team member to feel as though they are directing the conversation. This is their moment to talk to you, not the other way around. So make sure to ask the appropriate questions to guide them, listen, and then respond appropriately. You want to help the team member connect the dots, by asking open-ended questions about what they see, how they feel, and what they think is the solution. Remember that coming into this conversation, you already planned for multiple outcomes and you created an objective. You are utilizing your questions to help them realize that the action plan you've created is the best thing for their improvement. You have documentation of their behaviors and their performance records. Utilize these resources while asking your questions. These resources make words tangible. And to human nature, tangible is real. Make this real. Make them see that their success can be real. With your help, they'll succeed. If you truly believe that, they truly believe you. Here are a couple of quick pointers on what to remember during this conversation to make sure you get the necessary outcome.

1. Stick to the objective—Stay on point. Don't allow the conversation to fall off topic. It can prove difficult to find your way back or you could drive the team in the wrong direction with the wrong motives.

2. Avoid making it personal—If their objection has to do with what you do or don't do, listen and respond. A part of leadership is to adapt. If a team member identified an opportunity for you to improve your leadership skills, you should feel lucky for someone to address it to you. Think of the courage it may have taken for the team member to say something. You may have a future leader in front of you. Develop that.

3. Motivate through encouragement—When a team member doesn't believe in themselves, you need to rebut every time, reminding them that you believe in them. In more cases than not, they don't feel others believe in them.

4. Make sure the impact is team related, not individually related—It's easy not to care about something you own because the outcome only affects you. The second something impacts someone else, team members will begin to hesitate making selfish decisions like not offering a product. It's our natural instinct not to let others down because it's a survival mechanism that we developed through evolution, telling us that we have to work together. Use this to your advantage. Let that team member know that their performance impacts the team more than themselves and tell them how.

5. Gain acknowledgment and commitment—Before moving forward with specifics, like their action plan, make sure that you hear them acknowledge what their opportunity is and their commitment to improve. Only accept their commitment to improve, not to try. These moments always remind me of one of my favorite quotes from Star Wars by the great Yoda: "Do. Or do not. There is no try." You can't allow your team members to perform less than what you believe they're capable of.

6. Action plan—If you work for a company with an HR department, there is already an action plan guide or form available to complete that reflects the guidelines of your organization. However, if you don't have one, or you feel the one you have is not adequate, I have an example of an action plan I would recommend in the resource section at the end of this guide. Below is a rough outline that you want to make sure your action plan references:

   a. State the objective (goal or what success looks like)
   b. Reason for the action plan (opportunity)
   c. Steps to improve
   d. Timeline for completion
   e. Expectations from leadership
   f. Follow through

TIP: When asking follow-through questions, there are two ways to ask. One way gives the perception that you didn't expect or don't believe the task was fulfilled, i.e., "Did you get those documents delivered?" The other way gives the perception that you believe they did, i.e., "How did the delivery go?" Just this slight change in your communication can make a massive difference in how your team member(s) react and respond. Regardless if you know they did or did not, you create a positive environment, which will generate more positive outcomes in your meetings when you always ask as if they did the task, reinforcing trust, confidence, and motivation to excel. Start this immediately!

Performance Follow-Through

This last section of the action plan deserves its own section because this is the most important part of the action plan in my opinion. Without a follow-through, there is no development, no opportunity for improvement, and no success. As with any plan, to make it successful, you must have execution. You have to have a follow-through. In order to confirm the steps toward improvement are being taken, you have to have a good follow-through. The second you don't follow through, the team member will notice, and the impact you made during the conversation will fall to ruin. Following through is a crucial part of leading from the front. When you stick to your commitment, your team member will be encouraged to stick to theirs. As I stated previously, it's human nature not to want to let people down.

When you lay out your timeline and your follow-through plan, be sure to set reminders. Your daily priorities can and will distract you from these opportunities. Also, to encourage development and assure you're both following through, create weekly debriefs where both of you meet one-on-one to discuss progress. I call these meetings checkpoints for success. Checkpoints are used to measure your team member's development. Every time you hear the term *checkpoint*, regardless if in racing, in the military, or in a movie, it is always represented as a point of progress. Your follow-through plan should have checkpoints established, where the team member and you will debrief from the last checkpoint to measure progress, resolve any barriers together, and review upcoming expectations. These points will help establish a strong communication link between both of you and your objective. In addition, it strengthens the relationship between you both. This is another powerful way trust and loyalty can develop between a leader and a team member.

When to establish these dates will depend on their level of performance. As we mentioned in pillar I, you don't want to schedule weekly checkpoints if they are an Alpha performer, and you don't want to establish monthly checkpoints for Charlie performers. Refer back to the Mason influential leadership model to determine the best course of action for your follow-through.

The biggest factor is executing the plan as discussed with the team member. Your reputation and that team member's success depend on it. Please refer to the resource section to view an example of a follow-through plan as a reference. Although it seems simple, this is the most difficult part of the action plan. Out of sight, out of mind, right? People tend to forget what's not in front of them in today's extremely fast-paced world, hence why we develop priority lists. Make sure this priority is a part of your list when that checkpoint date comes around.

Developmental Necessity

As we discussed earlier, accountability is typically referenced negatively because it's seen as an action. An action, as I reference it, is a necessary way or process to fulfill at a certain point in time, like strategy, to achieve a goal. You act in order to execute successfully. Accountability cannot be an action. To see it positively, it can't be something that has to be done at a certain point in time. It is a behavior. This is why it is misconceived. A behavior is a consistent way in which someone acts or conducts oneself. Accountability is simply assisting the correction of a behavior, not a disciplinary action. Although disciplinary action can be given during this conversation, managers fail to realize that it's not about disciplinary action. It's about behavioral development.

This negative perception will die with you. It doesn't matter what you've experienced or heard or seen. It is absolutely critical that any negative reference to accountability is ignored. You have the ability to make it a cultural behavior, and once you do, your team members will embrace it. Eventually, they'll hold each other accountable. This is called peer accountability. And to a leader, it's a beautiful sight because this is where you can see your team members becoming leaders. If you've experienced the negative use of accountability, understand that it may have been a very misguided situation. Without a doubt, that individual who held your one-on-one was either not trained to handle those conversations or misguided by those who were under the same misfortunes during their time of development. Don't be like them. This is your education. This is a very powerful developmental skill for your team members. This behavior is a developmental necessity.

If you're still unsure or in doubt about this, look at it this way. There are two sides to everything, right? There is good and evil, right and wrong, yes and no, high and low, heads and tails. There are even analogies that reference this balance, like "There are only two kinds of people: hammer and nails, wolves and sheep," etc. Well, knowing that, you have to know that there is another way of having these types of conversations. There has to be a balance, right? So if there is the negative perception of accountability, then there is a positive one. The positive way helps on multiple levels. We know that holding disciplinary meetings aggressively utilizes fear and intimidation, which may be beneficial in some cases, but only to a manager. It doesn't do anything for the team member. Leaders don't want that. Leaders don't do that. It's supposed to be a win-win. As a reminder, we are only considering those team members who display a will to succeed. We'll cover the unwilling soon.

With the positive approach, we are allowing the team member to self-discover their own opportunities. In doing so, will allow the team members' eyes to open wider to how much they impact the team. In addition, increase their self-drive and self-motivation to progress with your guidance. When they have their vision of success aligned with yours, they turn the heat up instinctively. It's necessary as leaders to find this passion inside our team members and help them unleash it. Help them unleash the greatness within them as you are harnessing during your development. So in many cases and for many different people, accountability conversations can act as a second motivator. To put it in another way, the worst case from this is that your team member will discover that they may not be in the role they desire. Because of the belief you've instilled in them, they may discover a different passion they wish to pursue. If that were the case, you still changed their lives even when they may no longer be a part of your team. A passion they wouldn't have found without your guidance—that's still a win-win.

The aggressive results will only yield more damage than good. You will still put a new flame under 20 percent that will turn around and perform just to spite you, but that's not how you develop leaders. The other 80 percent will become defeated, demoralized, and disconnected, only furthering their failure and your disappointment. One hundred percent of them will resent you in some form. I have been in those situations on both ends. It is a terrible experience to be in, on either side. I listened sharply to the feedback from my team members and learned that this wasn't the right way. Luckily, a small few were brave enough to let me know. I was appreciative and found a stronger way to unite their passion with my vision—again, holding a conversation, not an interrogation.

Accountability Coaching (Daily Accountability)

What we've been covering was the one-on-one accountability conversation when you're dealing with situations requiring the implementation of an action plan. We'll soon discuss how to handle those situations where using a level of disciplinary action is necessary. However, what about the daily routine? I share this prior to discussing the disciplinary steps because I'm about proactivity. Holding team members accountable routinely, either daily, weekly, or monthly, is a very proactive way to avoid a disciplinary situation. Use the Mason influential leadership model to determine the best course of action for each team member or the team at hand when determining if a daily, weekly, or monthly check-in is necessary. Here is an example of a morning (daily) check-in sheet:

Date: ___March 7th___

Team Member: _____Jennifer_____   Goal: ___$1,500 Revenue___

Appts Today: ___2___   Expected Closed Sales: ___$1,000___

Appts Set Tomorrow: ___1___   How many calls: ___20___

New Appts Goal: ___2___

Notes:

Date: ___March 7th___

Team Member: _____James_____   Goal: ___$800 Revenue___

Appts Today: ___1___   Expected Closed Sales: ___$500___

Appts Set Tomorrow: ___1___   How many calls: ___25___

New Appts Goal: ___2___

Notes:

Possibly two appointments. One did not confirm yesterday, but still in books.

Date: ___March 7th___

Team Member: _____Jake_____   Goal: ___$1,000 Revenue___

Appts Today: ___0___   Expected Closed Sales: ___$0___

Appts Set Tomorrow: ___2___   How many calls: ___20___

New Appts Goal: ___3___

Notes:

Have to leave earlier today. Focusing on appointment setting and follow up calls.

Like my previous examples in pillar I, I've used daily, weekly, and monthly check-ins based on their level of performance. In some cases, you may determine a fixed amount of check-ins as required by your manager or leader. As you've experienced in the past, or perhaps currently, each team member knows their manager's expectations on how they contribute to the daily team goal. However, there are often many distractions and obstacles that can derail the team member from accomplishing it. This is where your leadership can assist throughout the day, not only to hold team members accountable to their daily commitment but to help remove obstacles and distractions prior to derailment or a crash.

As a leader, it's your responsibility to keep your team focused on the task, priority, or goal at hand. I know to some that may sound crazy, but you are. When I hear managers blame their team's performance on team members, I just hear a terrible case of denial. *You* are fully responsible for the team. Your team reflects *your* leadership. *You* control the momentum of your team. If and when production is low, you have to assess the situation and redirect behaviors. You'll only be capable of holding your team members accountable and redirecting their momentum if you make yourself present with the team on the front lines. When necessary, you must also be available to lead from the front to encourage reflective behavior. Either way, that is your team. Own it.

Regardless of which industry I was in, I've always had pulse checks. Winners keep score, right? Pulse checks are what I call those pass-by check-ins to discuss how their day is going. In other words, a friendly way of proactively checking on their production. However, I was also helping my team members keep to their commitments. Those pulse checks were reminders that I inspect what I expect. I hold them accountable to the goals they or I set. I've always created a form of some sort as a best practice to document all team member commitments, as our daily priorities can and will cause us to forget as I provided. Create one if you don't have one and rely on referring to it during your check-ins and pulse checks. As another best practice, it helps to keep this sheet on you throughout the day. This will keep your process consistent and keep your team members aligned with their own commitments. Team members will have priorities that may cause them to forget their commitment if they didn't record it themselves. Having that commitment documented where the team member can see will also encourage self-accountability. Remember, this makes it tangible. In addition, this behavior will also encourage peer accountability (competitiveness). I've had multiple team members ask to look at how another team member is performing just to assure they win the day. This is another guerrilla leadership tactic. You're covertly helping the team member become more productive and aware of their priorities at hand to accomplish their goal.

Now, these pulse checks throughout the day I'm referring to are just for keeping score, and all team members participate. Not to be confused with check-ins that were set based on individual performance, such as a Charlie performer for whom I scheduled a check-in at the beginning of a shift and a debrief at the end. I will still hold my commitment to that particular performer, to help develop their needs in addition to my pulse checks throughout the day. These pulse checks provide many other benefits. They can help team members remain motivated knowing that you'll check on their progress and celebrate when necessary. No one likes to say zero during those check-ins or pulse checks. In addition, team members are also motivated when seeing their leader get involved in their daily activities. It's physical proof you care about their progress. Pulse checks can also help you identify opportunities for your team members to improve during their shift, greatly increasing their probability of success, as opposed to a reactive method, which is at the end of the day. Many hours of improvement wasted.

Accountability coaching is a great proactive tactic. In the long run, this will encourage team members to become loyal, effective, and productive. This daily activity will also encourage team members to hold each other accountable. As we all know, peer accountability can play a big role in team development, courage, and leadership. Now, what if we have to step into the disciplinary role?

Developmental Accountability: Understanding the Levels of Discipline

Have you asked yourself, "Self, what does this conversation look like during a verbal/informal, written/formal, final, or termination situation?" That would be a great question. Typically, if you're encountering a skill issue with a team member, it is uncommon to see disciplinary action take place further than informal—rare to see it develop over formal (written) if their *will* to perform is *not* a factor. Anything involving final and up to termination is a conflict with willpower. Willpower is very difficult to influence if negative habits have developed prior to your leadership, but is not impossible to turn around. You will encounter these scenarios often through your career when inheriting a new team. However, remember that this isn't the only way you'll encounter this. If you don't consistently use these pillars and follow the Mason influential leadership model, you'll create a setting where this problematic position could develop. Team members could feel left out, you could over/under-micromanage, or you could also forget about a commitment; all scenarios and more can cause frustration. In jest, I know Yoda himself would say something like "Frustration leads to resentment. Resentment leads to anger. Anger leads to hate. And hate is the path to the dark side." Using this foundation helps prevent these possible outcomes and keeps you ahead of any negatively altering behaviors.

Nonetheless, it is a force you will face in your career. Therefore, I will introduce you to multiple techniques up to my A/B ultimatum that has benefitted greatly to help struggling team members facing a decision that will either generate a serious passion to succeed or end their negativity. Before we reach that point, let's briefly cover the informal and formal stages of discipline. As I referenced previously, accountability is usually referenced as a disciplinary source to force action. I hope you've learned that it can be a very positive tool and great benefit when you were learning Accountable Coaching. Here, I will show you how accountability can continue as a positive tool even under a disciplinary context. To begin differentiating disciplinary action and development, I call this accountability tool developmental accountability.

However, before we get into these conversations, you have to remember the golden rule when having any level of these conversations. Here's a hint: we discussed this under preparation, number 3. I know all your HR team members out there know exactly what the rule is, so I may earn some brownie points here referencing it again. Leaders, you have to make sure that you document *everything* and document with time stamps. These conversations are very sensitive and, in some cases will have very undesirable results: rumors, false accusations, unprofessional emotional responses, etc. Although my techniques will help significantly limit these situations, each opportunity has its own unique risk of being created, and each leader will have different responses. I always quote a phrase I picked up from Commander Shepard I referenced earlier. "Although you can't control how people react, you can control how you respond." Everyone you speak with will give you a different reaction and a different experience. How you handle it, following my technique, will help limit your chances of creating a hostile conversation. As a sub-rule to this, try your best to include another party in the conversation, preferably someone in a management or supervisor role. Don't ever include another team member on the same level as the one receiving the discipline. Although you may not always have a witness available, you're going to want one if you can, especially if the opposite sex is involved. This step can protect both parties from the same scenarios mentioned. Regardless of having assistance from a third party or not, documentation alone, even on verbal warnings, will help with five very important factors:

1. **Keeping the conversation honest**
   If both team members have a copy and accept all the terms, then instincts will tell us that all went as planned and all in agreement to improve and how; thus, helping to avoid confusion and turmoil.

2. **Role clarity**
   The document should always outline an action plan, and the team member should have a copy, but let's be honest. There are too many daily activities and distractions that prevent remembering everything from a single conversation. Having a document to revisit will help maintain clear expectations. Even if something may throw a team member off course, they'll know their role and expectation to follow it.

3. **Making the conversation real or tangible**
   Now, I can sit here all day writing books, but if I don't network, go out, or hold seminars, then I'm not being effective. If you read every book you own but don't put any of that knowledge into practice, you won't be effective. The point here is, if you just have words, words can be forgotten. If you just show body language to an untrained eye, the message can be misread. A document complements the discussion. It makes everything

discussed real enough to touch. You need that team member to connect, and there is no better way than to appeal to the sense of touch by documenting the conversation.

4. **Generating motivation through accountability**

For some team members, accountability isn't real to them until a punishment of some sort is proven—a very simple nursery rule that every cause has an effect, or karma. Notice I didn't say given, but proven. For some people, observing others being disciplined is more than enough motivation to avoid a similar outcome for themselves—makes it tangible. Sun Tzu shared an extreme but very effective example of just that in *The Art of War* when Sun Tzu was challenged to prove that he could create an effective army out of anyone, in this example, the emperor's concubines. Through a brutal example of discipline, he proved that anyone from anywhere, with any background, can become an effective army. His strategy: people are motivated to avoid one path when they witness the negative result of another who didn't.

5. **Creating a genuine track record**

In the event of a negative or positive outcome, you have a track record to refer to. If something great transpired, you'd want to reference what worked and how. This can help you repeat future successes with other team members. If something negative transpired, you'll have documentation available that can shield you from retaliation or false claims about the whys or hows. In addition, it could help you learn how not to approach in future discussions. As discussed with the first factor, it keeps the situation honest, and your HR partner will appreciate you making their lives much easier during the investigation. It doesn't take a genius to know that the last person whose life you want to make difficult is the same person running an investigation you're a part of.

In the scenarios that follow, I'll describe my course of action and then follow through with a real-life example. If you have any questions, feel free to raise your hand. (I'm sure someone around you would be entertained to see that.)

Informal

The thing about an informal is that it's just that—an informal. Some managers tend to use this step as a formal, or written, approach—meaning they tend to be too aggressive during this initial step. That's too much. This step is really in place to show that mistakes do happen and you can forgive them and team members can learn from them as a first offense. This is the time to help encourage team members to change or that it's okay to make mistakes as long as you learn from them and continue to grow. These moments are perfect opportunities to uncover any underlying or unperceived obstacles the team member may be experiencing, an opportunity to nip particularly unhealthy behaviors in the bud with a coaching follow-through. Take advantage of it.

Informals are usually to the point. Unless it was a unique action that could've resulted in something worse, these conversations aren't usually longer than five to ten minutes. Once the issue is addressed, always follow through with a coaching session such as a role-play or some self-discovery questions, whichever will make the greater impact, in your opinion. Remember to still follow the steps we outlined earlier about preparation. Have your objective outlined and documentation ready. Although this can sometimes be referenced as a verbal, we still want documentation for the reasons mentioned previously. See how I introduce this concept in the example below.

TIP: After you have prepared your paperwork for an informal/ verbal conversation, be sure to keep your documentation out of sight. As you can imagine, a team member called into your office

and noticing papers neatly stacked between you two can create negative perception, which can lead to confrontation. This meeting is about encouraging. You don't want to incite this type of reaction during any informal warnings. Keep the documents out of sight until the appropriate time.

REAL LIFE

I had a team member who was typically a Bravo performer averaging between 90 and 100 percent to goal, had great behaviors, and was improving his performance. However, I noticed a downward trend developing in his performance. After two unusual performance days, we held a check-in to review his performance. When asked about his performance, he said he was doing great, but clients were just not saying yes. "No problem," he said. "I'll start falling back into yeses soon enough. Just a rough week." After two observations, I discovered that he was no longer following the appropriate behaviors consistently. In fact, it appeared he purposely didn't offer products or services and avoided customers. Although it was nothing serious yet, it can and will lead to greater issues. Therefore, a verbal or informal warning was necessary to help the team member redirect his behavior. Just enough to add urgency, but not necessary to put this behavior on record. Besides, we don't know why yet.

When I brought him into the office, my desk was clean and my body was sitting at a forty-five-degree angle to look more relaxed and less confrontational. Sitting at ninety degrees straight up or leaning forward will give a more aggressive tone in the office. Sitting back, I explained that I noticed his change in behavior recently and was concerned about how it would impact his progress and his team members' progress. I did not ask about his day or ask about how he was feeling because I wanted to stick to my objective and help my team member correct his behavior. These conversations are very easily misinterpreted and miscommunicated. So be sure to cut straight to the objective and share why you're having the conversation, but in a professional and empathetic manner. I brought him to discuss why I observed Jay not offering prime services that are expected to be offered with every client. However, I didn't discuss everything I observed yet, like not using his assessment or keeping eye contact. I found it more impactful allowing the team member to identify their own opportunities through self-discovery. There are times where they are aligned, and there are times when they're not. It's a good thing if the team member identified something you have not—makes a great opportunity to cover both opportunities.

Anyhow, Jay went on to explain some complications he was having in his personal life and how he apologized for allowing those matters to reflect in his job. It's important to avoid pulling personal matters into business. When emotions get involved, you risk the chance of creating irrational behavior. So to avoid such a situation, I empathized about how difficult it is to balance personal and professional lifestyles; however, I encouraged him to remember what his goal was and to believe in his ability to triumph over such difficult times. Since he was improving his performance, I motivated him to see it as a testament to what he can overcome. To reassure his confidence, I offered to assist in any way I can to minimize any stress at work during this transition.

Encouraged, Jay responded by apologizing for not offering our services to every client and providing mixed experiences. He also admitted to avoiding clients and not using the required assessments (which I will cover more about in pillar IV) because of his distractions. He immediately followed up by confidently admitting that he can certainly overcome his current situation, recognizing what he has accomplished at work, and continue to support the team. Soon after, I asked for a commitment of improvement, and we set a date for a follow-through. At that moment, I presented the documented informal like this: "Thanks, Jay. I really appreciate your commitment to improve the lives of our clients, commit to supporting the team, and how you're willing to accept the challenge of overcoming your situation. Of course, I will always be a resource to help you on your journey. Now that we set our commitments, I have here our commitment sheet that also gives an overview of the reason why we're here. The action plan attached will help remind us of our commitments and outline how we'll succeed together. Once you sign here, I'll have a copy for you and we'll meet back up to review this during our progress check Friday. Sounds good?"

TIP: Developmental accountability conversations will go much easier if you share with your team this process prior to their first experience—for instance, a reference during your introduction to the team or a point where you explain how you help develop your teams, whenever an opportunity presents itself. When anyone is in a predictable position, it will always be handled more professionally.

I presented the informal document along with the action plan (sticking with the principles we discussed in preparation) after I gained his commitment. This is the best time to present documentation because by this point, you've eased the tension, established stronger rapport, and earned their commitment to improve. In addition, presenting as I did, not an informal but a commitment sheet to help both parties stay committed, creates loyalty, encourages improvement, generates motivation and leadership development. As always, make sure to stick to your commitments in the action plan. Leading from the front by keeping your commitment will encourage them to fulfill their part.

Formal

A formal warning is a misunderstood level of discipline. Typically, when someone mentions a formal warning, someone else cringes. Morale sinks, rumors spread, and the atmosphere changes. For many, it becomes a career nightmare—for some, a career killer. It doesn't have to be any of those things. As a matter of fact, it shouldn't be. Unfortunately, in the business world, if you do get a formal warning, this may impair your ability to move up in the company for a specific time. As I said, that's unfortunate. In most cases, when a situation results in a formal warning, it is due to a mistake made unaware against a policy or procedure. It's more uncommon than you think that it is a result of a repeated offense unless the teammate has displayed a lack of will. For this case, we are still referring to team members who are willing to improve. Again, we'll cover the unwilling shortly. In any event, the key word was *mistake*.

I never understood why most corporate policies include one that prevents a team member from progressing in their career if they are placed on a formal. That's like telling a student, "You better get straight A's all year, or you will get held back." Talk about being afraid of making a mistake. If life was truly that way, I don't think Thomas Edison, the Wright Brothers, or Benjamin Franklin would have made the strides they made in history, if making mistakes were punishable (assuming legal—I always have to add that line). For example, I've worked for companies that would bar you from promotions for at least a year. Others would deny bonuses or prevent raises for a period of time. This is the unfortunate truth that I have always disagreed with. I have seen many situations where strong leaders, and even some who were my friends, get punished for what looked like an honest mistake. Some of them had an amazing history in performance. The end result for many was moving on to another company. Another reason for this guide is to help you find the right position for your career, no matter where it's at.

Unfortunately, when working for a corporation, in many cases, you won't have a choice but to file a formal. Such policies were put into place for many reasons. I would absolutely encourage you to view all angles and policies, including teaming up with your HR partner prior to providing a formal warning. In some cases, situations can qualify as an informal on record. Since it is on their permanent record, you want to be sure there aren't other options, especially if it was truly a mistake. No matter what, *do not* disregard your policy. If the policy states that it's the necessary step to take, then you must take it. However, you can control how it impacts the team member. Remember, you're talking to a willing team member who made a mistake. Here is an example of a team member I coached, unfortunately bound to policy, whose unfortunate mistake had to result in a formal warning. My approach wasn't a punishment. It was an opportunity to encourage development.

REAL LIFE

Lisa was a banker with already two years of experience who was written up by the previous manager, but only as an informal (first warning), for not following expected behaviors. Now, this was prior to my establishment. That manager moved on to another company, and I was recruited to take over the team. This branch had been unable to achieve their goals in over two years, hence why I was requested to be assigned there.

To learn about my team, I was looking at the previous employee records, and I noticed that Lisa was documented for failing to ask the required questions in order to identify further opportunities, a pretty important behavior necessary to provide quality service and generate top performance. As I was learning the processes and expectations of the company and my team, my district manager visited to observe the progress and check in with the team. Unfortunately for Lisa, she also observed a couple of her interactions. Evidently, my DM remembered the previous documentation very well, and it appeared her supported visit was actually a follow-up on Lisa's progress. Lisa failed. At the end of my DM's visit, she referenced the previous documented offense and pressed for pursuing the next course of action, with the expectation for me to carry it out as her new manager—a formal, written warning.

I'm sure as you're reading this, you're thinking that doesn't seem right. Well, that's how I felt. I called HR and searched links to review policy and the impacts on disciplinary offenses. Unfortunately, it had to go to a formal warning, but when I saw the impact it held against Lisa (at least six months of probation, unable to apply to a different position or acquire a raise), I had to run it by the DM once more. That conversation was rather short. I requested to give Lisa another chance under my leadership, but my DM insisted she knew Lisa didn't want to be a part of the company and only worked enough not to get fired. Unfortunately, I had to move forward.

That following Monday, I held the meeting with my assistant manager Sally to act as a mediator and witness. Lisa came into the back room, sat down, and immediately said, "What did I do now?"

Taken back, but wanting to get to the root cause of her question, I asked, "Why do you think we're here?"

She replied about how there was always something that she was being "targeted" for and she never had a chance to just do her job.

From her body language and tone, I could tell she had mixed emotions like anger, embarrassment, nervousness, and sadness. From my experience, I knew it was a matter of time before she would feel overwhelmed and begin to break down. Unfortunately, this was that moment she did. I immediately knew that a big piece of the story was missing, so I bluntly asked, "Why are you crying?"

I didn't ask to play good cop, bad cop. I didn't ask because I like to intimidate others. I asked because I genuinely cared. In my experience, anyone who cries about something other than physical pain just shows me passion behind something, and from what my DM explained the previous week, Lisa supposedly didn't have it. It turned out that Lisa *was* very passionate about being successful at her job. As a matter of fact, she really wanted to move into another role on the corporate side. Although she knew the basics of how, she was never developed on how to build the appropriate behaviors or how to execute. So as you can imagine, she was devastated to know that she couldn't qualify for the position with a formal on her record. Even though her probation was over in six months, everyone looking to hire her would see it.

We took this time to visit why she was here. What motivated her to wake up and rush to get here on time? What was truly the end result of everything she put into this role? Once we created a common ground of why both of us were here, I established why I was brought to her team and how I was going to help her succeed. I promised her that although this was a permanent document on her record, I would personally write a letter of recommendation should she not only achieve her goals for two consecutive quarters but also show the same passion to succeed, as her tears displayed in the room. Following up with the action plan I put together for her to improve, she enthusiastically agreed.

This is how I presented the formal: "From what it sounds like, Lisa, this document right here is just going to be our staging point for progress. Although it does define a moment, it does not define you.

Although it reflects on your record, upon completion of your action plan, you will have two successful quarters and have my word that I will do everything it takes to help you succeed in any role you wish to reach. Let this only serve as the motivation you need to move in the right direction and to prove to everyone who doubted you that they were wrong. The future you want has to start now. Are you ready?"

Imagine this impact. This team member enthusiastically signed a formal warning with confidence that it was only the staging point of her improvement. She signed willingly, knowing that it only served as the day she turned it all around to reach her goal. She was motivated and ready to improve. That is the impact you can create versus the ever-common interrogation tactic of accountability and disciplinary action.

Every circumstance involving the delivery of any disciplinary document is different from the next. Although I kept it short, it was all but that. As you saw, she was prepared for a confrontation because of previous experiences. This happens often when taking over new teams. However, notice that I didn't allow it to throw me off my objective, which was to discover the root cause of Lisa's underperformance, help her make a commitment to an action plan, and assist her to define what her vision of success looked like. Although every situation is different, the foundation of the conversation referenced in the preparation section shouldn't be. This type of preparation will help you prepare for any reaction. Just remember to stay calm and assess the situation. Dive deeper to find the root cause of the reactions you're receiving. When she noticed that I wasn't yelling back and I was asking meaningful questions, she calmed down and continued to open up enough for me to find the why. Once I accomplished that, I could earn her trust and her commitment. Her career path was put on hold, yet she still committed to improvement. Relating to these principles you're learning now, this is another example of how you can turn negatively perceived situations into positive ones.

Final Warning—A Secret Weapon for the Unwilling

Now, here is where we are going to visit the unwilling team members. Over the past ten years, I have only had one team member put on a final warning who was still a willing and improving team member. That was only because they made a huge mistake in allowing emotions to be involved in a client dispute and spoke inappropriately. Besides that, every single circumstance where this level of discipline was necessary was handling unwilling team members. By unwilling, I mean those team members who are not interested in improving themselves or the team. These are usually the team members who gossip about others on the team and spread negativity, the same we referred earlier to as the rumored cancers within teams.

However, just as the other disciplinary warnings, the final warning is still *not* a tool to slam your authority hammer and create a negative experience. As hard as it may be to accept sometimes, this conversation still needs to be just that—a conversation. Think of this stage as the last opportunity to help someone realize the passion they have within to become something great and help them connect the dots to their path to success. A manager will view this stage as a necessary stage to eliminate what they think is the problem. In most cases, it only minimizes the problems but never eliminates it. They're called cancer for a reason. A leader sees this stage as a final chance to encourage the best out of a team member, regardless if that is with your team or another. In the end, we want the best for every one of our team members, even if that path isn't with us.

Some individuals are not motivated by words or deadlines or even money. Some individuals are motivated by survival. By survival, I mean there are team members who push the limits until they realize it's the end of the line. Only then do they discover their spark to succeed in order to stay alive—in other words, keep their income. And through that discovery, these team members can become some of the best performers. They've been to the very bottom and discovered that it's not for them. For some, they need to see the very bottom, like the rags-to-riches stories you hear about. Again, that's why we need to see this more as a tool of hope than discipline. It is still a form of discipline, but to motivate, not discourage.

I created a tactic that helps unwilling team members find their spark, or in this case, kick-start their survival instincts. I call it the A/B ultimatum. I discovered this tactic by accident through a rough conversation I held with a team member while giving a final warning. The team member (we'll call him Josh) was arguing about how his position with the company was pointless and how the company didn't care about what happened on the team-member level. After going back and forth about adding value, I noticed that regardless of what was said and how it was said, Josh was stuck on not having to change since none of it made a difference. However, he certainly couldn't find it in himself to quit either. So instead of pushing forward with what seemed like an eternal argument, I gave him an ultimatum: improve or move on. It was a little more dramatic than that, but you can only add so much effect in a book. So we'll keep it simple. Notice I didn't say "move out" or "get out." Again, this is about helping, not threatening. You never want to earn your leadership through fear.

At that moment, it looked as though a switch just turned on—end of the line. Sure enough, he improved—not only improved but followed his action plan to a T and became one of my top Alpha performers. I knew I was on to something.

Learning from this experience, I created the A/B ultimatum with the intent of sparking the passion out of the unwilling. This is how it works. Complete the normal process of preparation and have the action plan prepared. Before the meeting, have the action plan facing down on the left side and a blank piece of paper on the right side sitting about arm's length apart. Must be in that exact order and you'll visualize why shortly. At the opportune moment, you'll make the presentation somewhat like this: "You have a choice, [team member]. Option A [under your left hand]: Sign and agree to follow the action plan that I created to help you become successful in your role and set you on the right path to reach your own goals with my full support to get there. [Do not turn over the action plan just yet.] Or option B [under right hand]: Admit that this position is not for you by completing and signing your notice of resignation, and you'll have my full support to do whatever it takes to get you into a role that best fits you, even if it isn't with us."

There is some scientific support behind the positioning. While I was in college, a survey was completed in retail stores that tested the direction in which customers walked toward upon entering a store. This data was used to form the layouts you see today. Typically, produce can be found to the right because of its fresh perception and higher margins. Ever wondered why they put the necessities like milk and diapers in the back? Not coincidence. Nonetheless, the connection was that the right direction appealed to the masses habitually instead of the left—makes sense. We're used to driving habits from the right lane instead of the left like in Europe. So if the choice you want to encourage is to the right of the team member, you'll have a higher rate of success the team member will choose the action plan. In addition, immediately going from the action plan to the resignation gives the team member the shock needed to spark their survival instinct and choose improvement. Although reading the presentation seems a little intimidating, notice how I described each choice. Under both options was my offer to assist. Again, in the end, we want what's best for our team members, even if it isn't with our team. Here is an example of the most opportune time to present the ultimatum.

REAL LIFE

I was recruited to take over a new team with approximately twelve team members under three departments. There were two Alpha performers, six Bravo performers, and four Charlie performers. Out of the bunch, there were two team members who had to be Alpha performers if I wanted that department to be the best. One of those team members was a Bravo performer who thought of himself as an Alpha performer. Let's call him Justin. Justin had some good experience in sales under his belt, and he had characteristics to be an Alpha performer.

What was missing, besides his goals, was his process, his behaviors. Each interaction with customers or clients was inconsistent with the next, hence his mixed results.

After my thirty-day observation period, which we will discuss in more detail under pillar V, it was time to put my process in place and develop each team member to adapt to it. Justin was one of the toughest to change because of his arrogance. To Justin, he was hitting his numbers (on and off) prior to my process, and one of his favorite things to say was "If it ain't broke, don't fix it." The problem was that Justin had a broken process but couldn't see it. As a matter of fact, on a few occasions, he insisted for me to trust him on how he takes care of customers. It's important to pay close attention to these types of personalities because the rebel bunch can pull your team south if you allow them to continue their broken behaviors. As you can imagine, eventually, their actions can and will encourage others to follow suit.

I already held an informal conversation with Justin in regard to neglecting the use of some of our assessment tools willingly; however, I reached my peak of tolerance when I witnessed another team member in a different department carry out the exact same actions. When questioned about why, he said, "Justin hasn't been doing it, so I thought we didn't have to anymore." That was the point I realized Justin was not holding to his commitment from our informal conversation. I then observed Justin from a distance and witnessed his continued actions of not following expectations. That was a transaction where he missed a lot of opportunities. We missed the goal that day by 4 percent. Justin didn't hit his goal.

His continued neglect for following the process brought him all the way to an upcoming final. The decision from my leadership wanted him gone. I knew he still had great potential to be one of our best. I prepared by forming his action plan, final documentation, and setting the stage to deliver my A/B ultimatum. I saw tremendous talent in Justin, and it drove me crazy to watch him waste it on mediocrity and stubbornness. He was with the company for over four years prior to my arrival, so perhaps he didn't have the experience of having a leader develop him. I had to help him see that he was capable of much more and that the team needed him to lead by example. I had to show Justin the pit in hopes that once he saw the bottom, he would fight honorably to the top. So I called in Justin the next day.

As Justin entered the room, the only thing visible between us were both of my pages facing down: the action plan and final to his right and the blank sheet to his left. After a quick greeting, I cut straight to the point as I prefer to do.

My presentation was like this: "The reason I was brought to you here was to help these departments become one of the best in the business, and in order to do so, I have to develop those team members in becoming the best in the business. It's important as a leader to have the ability to see the greatest potential within team members, in order to drive top performance, whether that means the team member does or does not belong in their role. When I observed everyone's interactions with clients and among yourselves, I saw a ton of potential. I saw the most in you. When I look at you, I see you as being capable of becoming number one in our district. I see other stores lining up to send their team members here to observe and to learn from you. I see you leading this store and area to top performance. However, you haven't shown that. No matter how much faith I put in your ability, you seem to prove me just as wrong. We made a commitment to each other to follow the previous action plan, and you have not fulfilled your commitment. More so, you have risked another team member's performance because they idolize you, and your decision to evade our process has rendered their capability to improve. Even more so, risk disciplinary action. I needed you to be the leader I knew you're capable of and all you had to do was trust my process in making you the best in this district. You're capable of far greater achievement than just hitting 100 percent of your goal 50 percent of the time. But it's you that needs to believe that, which leads me to ensure that I have the right belief in you. It's rare I'm wrong on this, but not impossible. Only you can tell me. Was I wrong? Are you not who I believe you can be?"

(With a mild pause, he responded, saying that he was that person and I wasn't wrong.)

"So today, you have a chance to prove it. You have two options. To your right [under my left hand] is option A. Should you choose option A, then you choose to trust my process, agree to, and follow the action plan that *will* help you succeed, lead your team by example, and I guarantee that I will do everything in my power to help you become the best that you can be in this industry. Or option B [indicated with my right hand]. Should you choose option B, you accept that this isn't the role for you. You are not capable of becoming the person I believe in, and you document in writing your notice of resignation with an agreeable date for your transition. Even with this option, I guarantee that I will do everything in my power to help you transition into any role you feel is right for you, regardless if it's with our company or not. In the end, I want what's best for all of us."

Of course, Justin had a couple of objections and comments in between, but I stayed on point. In the middle of offering option B, I saw it in his eyes. After I said "resignation," each word following appeared as a number counting down to when he hit rock bottom. His eyes faded into red. Tears moistened his eyes, but he held back the fall, struggling to avoid showing his vulnerability. He broke down at the end. He couldn't believe the conversation being held. He just realized he hit the bottom. As I mentioned before, his reaction is a great thing. I didn't see a weak man crying; I saw a passionate performer ready to prove to me that he was now willing to become the best. He still loved his job, the company, and the industry. After explaining why he was the way he was and apologizing for the way he reflected on the team, he promised me that he would not only change but become more than what I projected. He chose option A. Three months later, he proved me wrong. He was not only the one of the best in the district; he ranked thirteenth in the world.

I kept the conversation on point. Before and after the ultimatum, I created room for self-discovered questions, to gain their perception as to why he did what he did. If it weren't for those opportunities and allowing him to speak, I wouldn't have found out the whys. If I listened to my manager, we would have lost an amazing performer that brought tremendous performance and honor to our team. It turned out that he never had a leader to help him envision something better than what he had. He'd been living with his parents for years and was excited to know that someone else believed he was capable of much more. He just needed someone to help him unleash it. This is to the point I made about holding these meetings as conversations. I didn't see this as a point of punishment or as a scare tactic. This was a straightforward conversation to help uncover his barrier to becoming something far greater than he saw within himself. By doing so, he became a champion, exactly what I saw in him.

Now, depending on your style and the situation you have to address, the A/B ultimatum doesn't have to be an instrument only used during final warnings. This can also be used during formal warning if you witness a situation leading to that point. Again, it's not a scare tactic. It's a tactic to help the team member uncover who they really are and what they want to be, a moment for you to help a team member realize where their passion truly lies. I've had team members who have chosen option B. That's okay. I helped them realize that they weren't where they wanted to be. Even better, I've had team members come back to thank me for helping them discover that and assist in their transition into something they love. That's what this tactic is about: not fear, but self-discovery.

Typically, if a team member is put on a final warning, there is a higher chance that the team member will get discouraged or even scared. No one likes to work fearing that if they make one more mistake, they're fired, or the feeling of uncertainty about your leadership team wanting you on the team. Although they may choose to improve and, in most cases, do so, there is still a probability that the team member will leave the company. Remember the impact of a final on someone's record will impede their ability to grow within a certain time frame—most cases, even longer than a formal. With some companies, regardless of your performance, you committed career suicide having a final—just their policy. I don't agree with it, but now you lost a good performer that you spent time developing that you can't get back. Sparking their passion earlier will encourage and motivate top performance faster. Not only that, but their level of comprehension, respect, and loyalty will be much higher without that fear. The worst that could happen is that the team member will discover that they don't have a passion to continue on their role and move on to another. Best case, they will recognize a passion for their position and unleash it. In both cases, you help a team member progress in their career. So if you feel it is necessary, use this tactic during the formal conversation. Regardless of which option is chosen, honestly help them transition.

REMEMBER: As a preventive measure, if you identify a will issue early and you feel it's necessary, you can carry out the A/B ultimatum during the formal conversation. This will generate motivation sooner rather than later, saving time, which is your highest commodity, and minimize negative impacts on your team by addressing the issue sooner. However, if you didn't, it must always accompany a final warning. It's your last chance to earn their commitment to improve and minimize the loss from time and cost spent developing that team member.

Making an Impact

I've shown you the positive way not only to understand accountability, but also to act on implementing this new behavior. You can now effectively prepare, complete an impactful action plan, dedicate to a strong follow-through, perform accountability coaching, and complete a conversation on every level of developmental accountability. You are prepared to help team members adapt, grow, and thrive in their roles through accountability by encouraging the acceptance of mistakes and not to fear progression—and for those unwilling team members, how to ignite their passion to succeed regardless of which option they choose using the A/B ultimatum. I have used these tactics and behaviors in six of the biggest profitable and competitive driven industries and with over five major *Fortune* 500 companies. It worked in every single one because a team is a team. Although they operate different roles, they provide the same function: top performance. This is a powerful and effective resource to minimize turnover and increase production from existing team members facing performance-hindering obstacles. That's because it focuses on the passion of the team member. That focus *always* wins in one form or another.

These skills, upon practice, will also help you develop great social skills when handling confrontation. Especially when you're in retail, these practices will be considerably useful. Not to mention, think of the impact you'll make on new and existing team members. As a developing leader or a veteran leader, this is a skill set you can't afford to underdevelop. This is a powerful way to minimize turnover and a positive alternative to handling unwilling team members. Accountability is crucial in a team's development into top performance. Team members have to see the cause and effect of their behaviors with the team in order to make their passion a reality. This is a tool you'll need every day for their development. So make sure to start now.

REMEMBER: Although you can't teach will, you can definitely encourage it. Don't give up on him or her. Connect with them. Again, you never know how a team member can impact your life on or off the team. Help them develop wherever their passion takes them. I have even had old team members become huge clients and others present excellent opportunities to grow my career.

PILLAR IV

Alpha Sales 101

Sales and Strategy: The Elements of a
Top-Performing Interaction

BEHAVIORS PLUS ACTIVITIES equals results! The most important equation I've learned in retail, the very thing that helps you take your focus off the end result and put all your attention on how to get there. You've learned the MIL model and how to identify where your team members place within the model. You've also learned the importance of time and have a good concept on how to organize it through a priority list. Then you formed an understanding of the importance of accountability and how it's a tool for progress instead of fear. Now it's time to learn my favorite part about being in business, and that is sales and strategy. I'm sure you've read about or attend seminars regarding how to sell, what to sell, and the importance of sales in general. However, have you ever heard anyone incorporate the word *strategy*? If you have, you're lucky. I've been to dozens of seminars and read even more books, and I only heard it referenced a few times. If you haven't, you're about to get a crash course in understanding its importance.

Anyone *can* sell, just throwing that out there just in case you're doubting yourself. However, not everyone knows how or even takes the time to learn how to sell. For those who know how to sell or wish to learn, the difference between good, better, and best is strategy. Luckily, the more you practice, the stronger your strategy and your confidence become. Every company and every one great you know or have heard about involved having a great strategy in place. Regardless if it's a particular bundle, product, attachment, brand, service, or investment, the best already know exactly what they're going to sell you and how they're going to do it before you even walk through the door. They're already tactful, pen in hand, have an assessment ready to complete, and a target product or service waiting to share with *you*. The only thing that changes is the why. That's what they learn from your story during the interaction. Your story helps them tie the product or service into your life. Don't worry, though. This *is* a good thing, I promise. I mean, all the way up to the '80s, people were able to hustle you relatively easily by convincing you that you needed something you really didn't. Although we still hear about unfortunate stories like this, overall, people have gotten smarter, and technology has certainly made it easier to challenge questionable sales pitches. But the truth is, a majority of the salesmen and women you meet today have a sincere desire to help. Learning your story helps them determine what's right for you. It's all about strategy and having the confidence to remain consistent. If you're not strong in both, this is your time. A clear, consistent strategy will open up all possibilities, while confidence allows you to turn rejection into a closed sale. We'll discuss more in detail.

This pillar is going to help you form your perfect interaction into a strategic behavior that will yield success for you, your team, your customers and clients, and everyone's career you're a part of. As usual, if you already have a strategy that is successful for you and your team, you are more than welcome to use bits and pieces of my strategy to help you improve. Besides, in order to continue being successful, you have to be able to evolve as my strategy has over my career and will continue to do so. Some of the tactics I use have been around for hundreds and even thousands of years. That's business. If you're absent of foundation or need something new, this is all for you. Starting here will yield more success as long as you execute the plan. As I have told many of my team members, the meaning of anything written on paper is only defined through your actions.

Strategy can be something as simple as who you pick as partners within your team to the very language you use during your interactions. For example, have you noticed how I used the terms *customer* and *client*? Of course, in some industries, there will be specific verbiage to describe customers, like *guests* in hospitality or *friends* in social media, but they all describe either a customer or a client. Many see them as the same, but there is a very distinct difference. Merriam-Webster Dictionary defines a customer as "one that purchases a commodity or service." It also defines a client as "a person who engages the professional advice or service of another." I can see where some confusion can take place, but the difference lies in the word *engages*. No matter how it's referenced, no one engages anything without some establishment of trust. Thus, a client is someone you've built a relationship with, who seeks your advice and expertise to guide a decision.

In my trainings, another way I've described their difference is that a customer is someone who commits to a transaction for the short-term benefit because they believe you can only help them in the short run. In other words, they don't see the value of staying committed to you anytime they need assistance. These are people who only visited because your company was convenient at that time. Or it had the lowest price that day. All are examples of someone wanting something to satisfy the "now" crave.

A client is someone who commits to you for a transaction for the long-term benefit. These are loyalists and repeated business. These are individuals who enjoy seeking advice, learning about what's new, and consistently purchasing from *you* because they trust that in the long run, you'll provide more value. I remember a time where there weren't any loyalty programs like rewards. At that time, business CEOs in retail were still understanding the importance of converting customers into clients. After years of research, the results favored the acquisition of clients. How to do so was rewarding customers for constantly shopping at their stores. Thus, the reward programs were created—turning customers into clients, short-term shoppers into long-term shoppers, one transaction into hundreds, $5 purchase averages into $50, and so on. Both customers and clients are very important to the growth of a business as you can't have one without the other to thrive, all of which we will cover in this pillar to help you sharpen your sales skills so you can carry on to your team members.

See how just two words can make a big difference? As I referenced before, Professor Mehrabian's study showed that 55 percent of all communication between people is expressed through body language, 38 percent through their tone, and 7 percent through their words. Although that 7 percent is how you close the deal, it also means that whatever comes out of your mouth better be strategic. Otherwise, you'll lose the sale. We'll visit this in more detail. The point here is that this pillar is the most important and has the most impact throughout your entire life. Salesmanship doesn't just benefit an individual in business. It is also applied in all aspects of life. It is a scientific train of thought. It allows individuals to think on the spot and outside the box, which is exactly what fuels entrepreneurs to become successful businessmen and women.

From here, I will be teaching, sharing, and illustrating techniques, strategies, and behaviors that will improve your individual performance and, in turn, your team members' performance. I will share plenty of examples and illustrations to provide visual assistance to their applications, and I cover from the moment eye contact is made to when your customer or client leaves the building and beyond. I'll share how to set up the sale (proactivity, to prepare for success), the elements of an impactful assessment to organize your interaction, how to increase traffic through lead calling, and additional tips on how to succeed with small-business owners, who make up 89.6 percent of the employer firms in the United States, based on data collected and reported by the US Census Bureau in 2012. I want to help you develop a very strong sales strategy and to increase your confidence greatly in remaining consistent at execution and development.

REMEMBER: As we evolve, so must our strategies. You must constantly evolve your strategy in order to progress. So be sure to take this strategy and evolve where needed, as I did throughout my career.

Setting Up the Sale

You may have noticed how big I am on proactivity. It's a must for my teams. I've learned the hard way, regardless of how hard my parents attempted to teach me otherwise. Some of those experiences made me wish I listened, but in that experience, I truly understood the power of preparation. As I mentioned, I'm not a fan of surprises—the bad ones. Although they can't be completely avoided, I truly believe they can be minimized. The best way to do so is through being proactive. Whenever my team members went through a negative experience, I always asked them to remember what they said to see if what they could control could have made the difference. To minimize conversations going south, I always tell myself if it's controllable, then it's avoidable. In other words, focus on how to respond appropriately, proactively to avoid responding emotionally and making things worse, as we discussed in pillar III.

When I say "setting up the sale," I mean preparation for success. I train each of my team members to view every interaction as an already successful sale. This helps the team member build more confidence in themselves and helps eliminate any invisible barriers people tend to create for themselves like doubt or fear of rejection. Although there are many ways to set up a sale, I focus on three big contributors to increase your probability of closing just through preparation: utilize target products and services, read and reflect the appropriate body language, and be confident. I have tried many tactics, and these three have made the biggest impact on customers and clients, my teams, and my success in sales, each having a unique impact during every interaction.

Target Product(s) and Service(s)

Now, why do you think I recommend targeting products and/ or services? I'll give you a hint. I've worked for companies that held over thirty million SKUs (some departments with over 10,000 alone). That's a lot of products and services to remember, let alone sell. Keep it simple. Find your niche product and services offered by your company. For me, it was the products and services with the highest margins. For instance, in the electronic world, if I only made $10 off a TV, but $50 off an HDMI cable, I'd make sure to always reference HDMI cables and find a way to connect that product to my customer. An example question to set up would be "Do you have a Blu-ray player or gaming system?" If I were in hospitality, particularly restaurants, I would always offer an appetizer, dessert, and specialty beverages as they typically have higher margins.

Services are typically higher in margin in retail, or all the margin space for service-oriented industries in general. So if I had a list of services, I would look for the most impactful ones that I would be interested in or have enjoyed personally. In electronics, it was mounting and/or calibrating a TV for a perfect picture. In the automotive world, alignments, brake replacement, and oil changes have good margins. If you manage a spa, it could be a particular massage or an add-on like using stones or oils.

The value of each product and service lies within you and every single team member that tries to sell it. Only you can create its value, and the only way to do so is learning your product and service like this guide you're studying now. I was not afraid to tell a customer or client that I didn't know about a certain product or service if they specifically came for it, but I always told them that we could learn about it together from reading the back of the package or asking another trained associate or manager for information. Everyone appreciates honesty and courage to learn. However, if someone approached me with very little knowledge of what they needed, I already had products and services I knew they could be completely satisfied with. I just had to learn their story to determine which one was the best fit. So find those products and services that are most intriguing to you and learn them well. Knowledge of the others typically come in e-learning (electronic courses), through social engagement with other team members, or learning with your customers and clients. Specializing in those SKUs or categories can help you rake in great profits for the company and more income for you as you will consistently hit your goals, especially when you learn the power of the bundle.

The Power of the Bundle

Although we will cover this in more detail later in this section, it makes sense to at least reference it here. When you're targeting which particular products and/or services to specialize in, think about what complementary products and services you could pair them with to create a greater value for your customer or client and your company. What you'll learn later on when compiling your assessments is that we need to stop looking through the one-solution-fits-all lens. The world is evolving, and therefore, so are the people within it. Complications thirty years ago may have been created from one thing. This day and age, it is multiple issues causing one big complication. However, people are still being addressed with a one-solution-fits-all mentality.

If my ATM card doesn't work, the typical response is "Let me replace it for you," or "Let me reset it for you," an immediate one-solution-fits-all response. Because I said my ATM card is the problem, the team member believes it to be the problem. These days, you need to ask why. If you have the power-of-the-bundle mentality, you have a prepackaged solution that can solve multiple problems just waiting to find its use. As you ask why, you discover that the ATM card is being used at stores and was shut down for security purposes. In your conversation, you discovered that I needed a checking account coupled with a debit card and online or mobile access to monitor my spending. The problem wasn't the ATM card. It was multiple issues such as using the wrong card, not having the right product for its use (savings vs. checking), and convenient access that would help monitor its use. In the end, offering an immediate solution wouldn't have yielded any sales credit nor truly solved the client's issue. The bundled solution solved not only the client's current issue, but also potential issues in the future and resulted in three products sold.

Bundling targeted products and services doesn't limit you. It opens up your thought process, creating a desire to know more about why an issue has arisen so you can connect your bundle to solving the appropriate current and unperceived issues. You'll learn more about discovering and uncovering these opportunities later. For now, definitely find your complementary bundles. These bundles can also be accessories to a core product or specific sides to an entrée or one service to expand the use of another. Bundling not only solves multiple wants and needs, but also greatly impacts your sales goals, attachment rates, and bottom line. Take some time to write them down. This will prepare you for learning how to harness this strategy during your assessment.

Learn to Read and Express—Body and Mind

Do you walk the walk or talk the talk? If you want to be successful in this game, you need to do both. As I said, although that 7 percent is what closes the sale, it needs to be strategic. It also must have the least amount of focus. In other words, that 7 percent needs to come naturally. Have you ever heard someone talk oneself out of a sale or a date or an opportunity? It happens all the time. It's because they are too focused on that 7 percent. They throw out the other 93 percent and end up sending the wrong message. There is a technique that helps make you more effective.

Have you ever watched someone give a speech? In the first seven seconds, I can tell a lot about a person, especially on stage—things like what that individual focused on when they were practicing their speech. In many cases, it's remembering their lines. If they weren't practicing at all, that becomes immediately noticeable to even someone blind. When someone (and this might be you) practices for a presentation, they typically focus on one mode of communication more than the others. That's because the average person doesn't understand how to communicate effectively. Their innate behavior is expressed through body motion; however, unconsciously. That can be scary when your body is doing things you're unaware of while saying something completely different. Ultimately, the average person focuses on 7 percent of communication, and the rest is left up to their natural reaction, which results in mixed signals and a poor presentation. You can always tell who has effective communication skills because those who don't may talk for a long period of time, use a monotone through the whole presentation, forget certain portions of the presentation, use multiple fillers such as "uh" or "um," or may even stand in one spot with very little movement. Those who do are energized, moving up and down the stage, raising and lowering their tone during motivational moments, and really captivating the audience.

I've always played by the numbers. If I focused on effective body language and tone, I would have a 93 percent chance of captivating my audience. Of course, we're aiming at 100 percent, but if I mastered those sections first, I would have most of the hard work knocked out, like back in pillar II about tackling the harder, more impactful priorities first, leaving the easiest part last: closing the sale. Meaning I can use fewer words than the average speaker but make a greater impact and connection to the audience. With fillers, the average speaker adds tens to hundreds of extra words, further losing their audience. Therefore, when I practice for a presentation or a seminar, I'm practicing hand gestures, body movement, tone of voice, positioning, and eye contact while giving my speech. I make sure that at the precise moment I want a particular reaction from my audience, I reflect my body language and tone accordingly so when my words fill their ears, they're already motivated to respond. Acting as such really helps me remember my lines because I'm excited for the reaction. This is the same in sales or any other interaction.

A normal behavior I've practiced since college is that I tend to count the number of fillers in any given speech as if it was an OCD complex. For example, one of my assistant managers was giving critical feedback to their team member while I observed, to help develop her coaching skills. In ten minutes, she said, "You know what I'm saying" over twenty-five times—twenty-five in just ten minutes. Back in my college communication class, my friend said during his thirty-minute presentation "You feel me" over fifty times. The more interesting part is that I approached both right after to show them the tallies I collected throughout their discussion and both reacted in shock. As a matter of fact, neither of them even knew that was coming out of their mouths, especially that often. It was a natural instinct, a sign of nervousness, sure—more so a sign of lack of effective communication. If you look for fillers during speeches, you'll find this to be a huge fallacy across many professionals, especially in PR. I still hear decorated officers, executives, and even presidents have this issue. So it's important for you to expand your knowledge of effective communication for yourself. If you practice how to use your body and tone of voice during your presentation more than your words, not only will you help yourself remember your speech, but you would need fewer words to remember. Adjusting your tone during important, more captivating subjects and moving your body to illustrate what you want the audience to envision or become passionate around is an artistic skill, but by no means difficult. In fact, it's a heck of a lot more fun; it just takes practice.

Body language is only one side of the coin, however. You can learn how someone's body and tone are saying something about themselves and topics at hand, but they can't reveal what to say next to motivate a response or what to say to help someone understand a frustrating situation. If I gave you an hour to get your point across, do you think that would be difficult to do? I would hope not. That's plenty of time. Now, what if I said you only had one hundred words to express your point? Do you think that would be more difficult? Of course. Not impossible, though. You just have to be more strategic about what you say and how you say it. That's how it is with every interaction. That's where learning personality traits come in. It helps capitalize on body language. Understanding different personality traits helps you maneuver through and even avoid barriers with certain types of personalities whom you may have a hard time communicating with.

Sometimes, you come across people with whom you connect instantly. Other times, you meet those whom you can't stand to be within a mile radius of, the second they speak. Happens to us all. Have you ever wondered why you just don't click? You'd be surprised to find out that it's simply how your personalities are different. It's two unknowns not taking the time to make each other known. I hope that didn't confuse you. It'll make sense. It's like reading horoscopes. However, if you don't understand why people act so differently with one another, you can't learn how to adjust and communicate effectively to your customers, clients, or team members—even friends and family. You'll miss many opportunities simply because of a misunderstanding.

When I read someone's body language, I'm able to prepare for what personality trait I may encounter. This helps me form a good strategy on what to say and, in many ways, how to say it. Some personalities are rather dominant and straightforward. If I pick that personality up, I'd make sure not to beat around the bush and cut straight to the point about why someone may want what I'm offering. These are typically those who come straight in and tell you exactly what they want. If I took my time explaining features and benefits, these personalities may feel that you're wasting their time and not listening. They tend to think you're just trying to push products they don't need. As a dominant personality myself, I can relate, but would want to adjust accordingly because I don't want them to misinterpret my message.

Then you will have personalities that are very organized and love to go through every product or service to compare the benefits and detriments themselves, which means they are detail oriented. If you cut straight to the point with these personalities, they'll feel rushed or even pressured to buy. Not understanding personality traits can lead to these types of miscommunication. If I read that personality, I could adjust what to say, such as word-for-word details straight from the packaging, or details of my own experiences using a particular product or service.

Are you starting to understand the importance of learning personality traits as well as body language? There are many books you can certainly read that will go into further depth on how to read every angle, including more advanced techniques like micro-expressions and how to read personality traits instantly. By no means am I considering myself an expert, but I have a firm foundation as a continuing student in this field. If you haven't taken the time to learn more about how to read and effectively understand body language or personality traits, I recommend starting with a couple of options I've started with. For understanding the fundamentals of reading body language, I recommend picking up *Body Language for Dummies*, written by Elizabeth Kuhnke. She is a very smart and captivating author who has studied the art of effective communication for over twenty-five years. It is a very easy read, and she provides very lively and illustrated examples that will really help you envision how to read, adjust, and reflect desired behaviors. For personality traits, I'd recommend none other than the D-personality queen herself, Angel Tucker, and her book *Stop Squatting with Your Spurs On*. Pick it up to learn more about the personality trait classes, like Dominant, Inspirational, Supportive, and Cautious. Her energy and great spirits really reflect in this great read with hilarious but true examples of how to relate, compare, and adjust to different personalities you meet every day. More so, learn how to be the ultimate communicator by becoming one of the few who can effectively communicate with all types of people. There are many others I would invite you to explore, but here is certainly a great place to start helping you become a more effective communicator than you have been before. It opens a whole other world right in front of you.

Confidence

It's like what Will Smith said as Alex Hitchens to his client in the 2005 hit movie *Hitch*:

"So, tonight, when you're wondering what to say or how you look or whether or not if she liked you, just remember: She is already out with you. That means she said yes when she could have said no. That means she made a *plan* when she could've just blown you off. So that means it is no longer your job to try and make her like you. It is your job not to *mess it up*."

A very comical movie with a lot of good themes. The scene following had all three of his clients respond with "Huh?" simultaneously in complete shock, which is the typical response when I repeated a similar line. I tell my team members that each interaction needs to be seen as if their customer or client already said yes to hear their recommendation because they chose to come into their location to speak to them when they could have gone someplace else. They planned on learning more about what you have to offer. So the only way you'll lose the sale is if *you* mess it up, like what I referenced earlier about talking yourself out of a sale. As long as they are consistent with their behaviors and confident about why they came to them for help, they can't mess it up.

They controlled the interaction. It's much easier to win when you're in control, don't you think?

REAL LIFE

The thing about confidence, especially when you're trying to create it within your team, is that the simplest thing is all it takes. If you're thinking too hard, you're trying too hard. I had a team member who had the hardest time believing in himself to be a top performer. In a discussion we had, I told him that he could sell just me. Maybe even better. However, he would never be able to if he didn't believe he could if he wasn't confident in himself. His reply was that I was the supervisor. People respected me more and would listen to me as a result. After a few seconds, I had an idea and responded, "You're right!" I took off my name tag, which also displayed the title, and I put it on his shirt. After a couple of shared laughs, I convinced him I was for real. I said, "Now, you're the supervisor. Lead by example and help these customers find a solution."

With a chuckle, he said, "Piece of cake."

You should have seen his face. He held a broad chin. Straight shoulders. He even had a strut that to this day, he won't admit. He was proud and felt confident as the supervisor. He could sell anything. Would you believe that this guy sold over 115 percent of his daily goal? At the end of his shift, he turned the name tag back in with a huge grin. So I asked, "What's the grin for?"

He replied, "I told you! It's easy as the supervisor. People saw who I was, and I didn't have an issue. When there was, they trusted my solution. It's all in the title."

Smiling back, I said, "Maybe. Or something else. Want the role tomorrow?"

With the cocky head tilt displayed, he shouted back heading out the door, "Definitely!"

The next day, he came in to retrieve my name tag, but unfortunately, I forgot it at home. He looked me right in the eye with a grin and said, "This is just your way of avoiding being wrong."

Laughing at his comment, I replied, "Not at all. How about this? You're still the supervisor. If anyone asks who you are, you just tell them you're the supervisor."

Confidently, he agreed and went on the floor to start his second shift as a supervisor.

At the end of his shift, he turned in his goal sheet. With the biggest smile I have ever seen, I noticed he reached over 140 percent of his goal, the highest he's ever had in a single day outside of holidays. Smiling back, I told him I was proud of him. Our conversation went like this:

Me: So what did you prove?

Tony: I was right about being a supervisor.

Me: Is that right? So how many times did someone ask what your position was?

Tony: Well, no one did.

Me: How many times did someone ask for a supervisor?

Tony: Just once, but just for a warehouse issue. Why?

Me: Oh, nothing. You don't find that strange that you did so well, and yet no one asked for a title?

With a smile on my face, I led him on with self-discovery questions.

If it's one thing my team certainly learns about me, it's that I do everything for a reason. At the end of my question, I started seeing his face slowly shift as if the cogs in his head finally got on track. Then, his head lowered as his eyes wondered to his goal sheet on the desk. Right next to it was my name tag. It clicked. I never left it at home. It never left my desk. As a matter of fact, the time I told him it was home, it was right in front of him in the same spot. The point is, he didn't see it because he didn't look for it. More specifically, he didn't *need* to look for it. He already gave himself confidence the second I told him he was a supervisor without it. No one asked for a supervisor because he was the confident one out there discovering issues and hunting down solutions. When people see that, they automatically assume *you* are the authority. Supervisors and managers are asked for because the team member did not display confidence in themselves, therefore reflecting insecurity, which makes someone find a person in a position to give them a confident answer because it's assumed that managers have earned their position because they confidently know the answer.

Tony discovered that he was the barrier the entire time. The second he saw that name tag, he realized that he was capable of doing what he did the day before because the tag represented a confidence he already had in himself. Indeed, Tony became an Alpha performer.

REMEMBER: Confidence can be found in the simplest ways.

People make things harder than they need to be when they really just need a leader to help them look. It took just a title change to help Tony discover his confidence. From there, if someone asked, he said he was the supervisor. He was confident to go even above and beyond. In many other industries, I've used the same technique. I've had team members in finance call themselves relationship managers versus being called bankers. That simple change gave them the confidence that they *were* the best experts and could solve any issue given. Sometimes, that simple change from associate to supervisor is all that is needed. All you have to do is look.

You're always going to hear about the importance of self-motivation, confidence, and courage in sales because you need just that in order to show your customer that you know what you're talking about. If you walked up to someone searching for advice on something and all you received were stutters, a "maybe," or "not sure," I bet you wouldn't feel too confident about their advice. Most likely, you'll forget everything that was said immediately after—nothing disrespectful, just nature. You just didn't trust how the information was transmitted to you. That's exactly how everyone else interprets communication. They interpret how the information is transmitted, and confidence is the bridge. If it is a clear and precise message said with confidence and good eye contact, you can have someone believe the world is flat. This example is only to elaborate my point of how confidence makes an impact on your audience. Do not go out and try to convince someone the world is flat for practice (ha).

Nothing can stop confidence except insecurity. I learned that a long time ago. My marketing professor said to me when I was concerned about how to finish a big project that I would always get what I fear. It reminded me of a saying I've always heard that you always find what you're looking for. She meant that if I feared that I *would* fail the project, then I *would* fail the project. I had to be confident that I would ace it. If you don't build the confidence within yourself and trust that you have all the capability to accomplish your goal, then all your studies in sales, body language, personality traits, and even my guide will be forfeit. I loved a saying from Mel Gibson playing William Wallace in *Braveheart* when he said, "Men don't follow titles. They follow courage." You have the title of a supervisor or manager, or you will soon. If you truly believe that you have the capability to lead your team to great success as I know you do simply by picking up my guide, then you will achieve exactly what you and your team deserve: greatness.

Another great part about confidence is that it's contagious. When others see how confident you are about reaching goals and growing their business, they'll want to be a part of that. If not, it's like being stuck at a party where everyone is having a blast, but you're just sitting on the couch, watching. No one wants to feel that. They want to be a part of something better, something bigger. And the reason you picked this guide up is because you want to create that. You know what? You can! You know how I know? You had the courage to pick my guide up and improve your skills. You certainly have the confidence to lead your team to success. By the end of this guide, you'll have enough to share with your entire company and still live your life to its fullest with nothing to fear.

Your Greatest Tool—Your Assessment

First Impression Is the Only Impression

By now, I'm sure you have it ingrained that first impressions are everything. After centuries of sales conversations, some things have changed. As a matter of fact, it used to be where if you didn't make a good first impression, you might get a second chance because people preferred to go to one location and build a relationship—not as much these days. People prefer to go where they are treated the best, regardless of the distance. Not only that, but with technology, if someone ever had a bad experience, the whole world would learn about it before a survey was even submitted. I had a customer who drove over forty minutes to come into my location because a friend of his told him we would take great care of him. So in this day and age, the first impression is now the *only* impression you'll be able to make. Ever been told to get things right the first time? My team will tell you they've heard it from me a thousand times. It's not just the point of doing your job right, but more of making a great first impression. If you don't nail it on the first impression, somebody will, and you'll never see that customer again. All this being said, you have to nail your first impression the first time.

Through many different companies, I saw an assortment of systems and strategies that have been implemented across multiple locations, yet for some strange reason, I had different experiences at each one. I know they're all receiving the same information. I've been a part of big companies that ultimately experienced the same challenges and changes. I know we all experience this with fast food. I can't tell you how many restaurants I have memorized as the prime location to go to when I'm craving something because I know that when I order it, they'll be polite, order my food right, and deliver it fresh. And in order to get there, I'd have to pass up two or three of the exact same restaurants to get there. It made me chuckle just writing about it now—funny to discuss, but terrible to experience. Chick-Fil-A is one of the few companies that provide what I call a predictable experience.

A predictable experience is just that, an experience someone anticipates to have. At Chick-Fil-A, it's rare for me to go through the drive-through, order my food, and pay at the window without a cheerful greeting, repeating my order for accuracy, delivering fresh food with a smile, and of course hearing the famous "My pleasure" every time I said thank you. It's a predictable experience that makes every trip a pleasant moment *before* I even get there. I feel good about just making the choice to go because I anticipate they will treat me just as well as, well, always. Chick-Fil-A is a prime leader in creating that predictable experience. I created a system and this guide to help my team and you create a predictable experience and how to avoid those unpredictable experiences. As you move up the chain of command, if you're not doing so already, you can train your managers to utilize my system so all your teams, stores, branches, or chains can provide the same experience. Clients and customers alike don't have to guess which location is better or pass others up to experience something great. You never know when a competitor provides an unpredictable experience. My team knows very well how to capitalize on those moments because they're confident they provide the best.

What's the secret? A part of that takes place before the customer or client walks through the door—preparation. That's right. It's back. This doesn't mean exercising before your doors open, although that can help. This means having your home prioritized and your hand full. Now, *home* means home base, what I call your station or work area like a desk, cubicle, department, etc. Believe it or not, your psyche will become the environment it's in. That also means your home, office, etc. If you show up to work and the office is a complete mess, you're already starting your day with stress, which will display through your body language and tone. That means you're not prepared to make a great first impression. As we discussed in pillar II, productive time management, you want your home to remain clean as if it is constantly in view of someone important, like you want to impress them. So have your resources ready for your interaction and make sure it's always presentable. Easier to start your morning in a better mood when you complete this task before you leave at the end of the day.

Next, I said "your hand full"—singular. In sales, you should always have what you need within reach. This includes having your notepad or assessment and a pen in your hand, ready to take notes during your interaction. Why? Because you never know where your conversation will lead you. If you're pulled away from the office or asked to assist in another department, it doesn't look good to say, "Sure thing. I'll be right back and then I'll help." Be prepared. Why do you think your other hand is empty? To shake their hand. It's very important to initiate the handshake and introduction. If not, it's like walking into someone's party not knowing anyone. If the host doesn't introduce himself or herself, then it could make you feel unwelcome or uncomfortable at the very least. You want to avoid that. Make them feel welcome in your business.

Preparation is one secret. The other is your introduction. Now if you're not used to having a specific introduction memorized, then you're losing business. As funny as it sounds, it's very important to have a strong introduction memorized. Remember, it's about a predictable experience. To be predictable, you must remain consistent. To be consistent is to be prepared. Some organizations caught on to this, like Chick-Fil-A. Others are still struggling. Hopefully, your company taught you a thing or two. If not, this is what I have taught my teams for years that I've slowly collected over my experience as a leader, and it is very effective.

For every person who walks through our doors, I ask every team member to SHINE TWICE, a very simple method to remember how to properly introduce yourself the same way, every time. The acronym SHINE stands for smile bright, firm handshake, introduce yourself, ask for their name, and keep eye contact. Or smile, handshake, introduce, name, eye contact—a behavior I've learned from other leaders. The TWICE acronym stands for thank, welcome back, initiate follow-up, closing, and exit—a behavior I've created to complement the interaction as I noticed team members didn't provide a predictable experience at the close as they did during the introduction. They were inconsistent. It also has a sub-meaning to shine at the beginning and the end of each transaction. When you say your goodbyes, I believe you should share the same courtesy as when you said your hello. The only difference is that as a farewell, you will reintroduce yourself and use their name instead of asking, followed by the rest of the behaviors that assure future business. As a little bonus, I asked team members to make it a goal to use the customer's name at least three times during each interaction. Why do you think that is important? Of course, as I referenced previously, repeating something out loud three times increases your chances to memorize something, but more importantly, you are making the interaction personal, therefore building a relationship with trust. After your conversation, your customer will feel confident that you know their name and will provide the best help every time, thus turning a customer into a client. Starting to get it? Pretty cool, right? I hope you agree.

So following this basic, consistent introduction at the beginning and end of every conversation will immediately set you apart from the competition. Between your preparation with a clean home, a full hand, and SHINE TWICE, you have covered 20 percent of a great first impression. The other 80 percent is where I believe all the fun is at: the assessment, your greatest tool in sales. A single tool capable of uncovering great stories, identifying problems to solve, developing trust, building relationships, and making a memorable experience while greatly impacting your sales goals. Just talking about it gets me psyched about how amazing this tool really is. The unfortunate truth is that it gets very little recognition and even less respect. As discussed before, it's because of how the tool is communicated. If the person teaching you how to use the assessment is the same person who never used it during their career, how impactful does that turn out? I can always tell when an inexperienced teacher taught a team how to use an assessment. You can find it written in the team's excitement and passion around it. If it's missing, there you go. Your company needs some serious help. Once you understand what it's capable of and how to use it, everyone gets excited. It's your turn to build its excitement.

REMEMBER: A predictable experience is an experience someone anticipates to have. Keeping it consistent is the key to referral growth.

Constructing Your Assessment

Not all industries will or can allow putting an assessment in your hand. I can't say having your waiter holding an assessment in one hand while taking orders in the other will be easy. However, an assessment always improves sales. You see it every day, and you probably don't realize it. A doctor or nurse has an assessment they hand to you to fill out to determine common issues based on your medical history, even a digital one they may fill out in the exam room on a computer or tablet. A mechanic or technician will have one in hand while inspecting your car to reference all checkpoints have been checked. All are examples of assessments.

Having your assessment in hand will result in higher production and efficiency than not having one by far. Think of it as a tool to stay consistent. Thus, creating the predictable experience we talked about. However, there are some businesses (and this may be yours) that present holding one as an obstacle because you need all hands free, like the server example. If you can't have your team members hold an assessment, then let them at least have one to review prior to meeting a customer or client. I will leave it in your capable hands to determine if it can be in their hands or not, but you always want an assessment in place.

I will help you with one of two things: If you don't have an assessment in place, this section will help you create one from top to bottom with great real-life examples to help illustrate how it should look. If you already have one, this section will help you simplify your current assessment to make it more efficient and effective for your team. Of course, the illustrations are also for you. The other part is for you to act. That part is all you. The good news is, either way, you'll learn something very impactful. So get your highlighter ready or, at the very least, fold the corners of these pages because these are references that you will want to return to during your practice.

In your assessment, you want to have three sections. No surprise, right? Keep it simple. If you need more, then do what you must to help yourself and your team keep organized and structured. However, I caution having more than four sections. More than four can get overbearing, overwhelming, and in most cases, more stressful for all members. That includes you. Keep it simple, and you keep it easier to master.

The three sections should complete the following objectives: discover their story, uncover their situation, and define their goals. That's it. What do you see when you uncover these three objectives? The full picture. What made my teams and me successful is that we were able to uncover more than just the immediate issue. We were able to solve three problems over the competition solving only one at a time. That's because we asked the right questions to uncover greater opportunity for us and our customers. This is called selling deep, or what I prefer to call relationship selling, being able to sell multiple products and services to one customer that becomes a client. Each industry has a different term to call it, but all mean the same thing. The questions within these three sections will help you see everything you need to help solve past, present, and future issues so you can deepen your relationship with customers and convert them to clients. At the end of the day, regardless of your job title, business is in place to solve problems. Just be that team that knows how to solve more and solve faster than the competition.

REMEMBER: Whatever you do, do *not* sell during any of these sections. It is one of the easiest habits to pick up and one of the hardest habits to break. Eighty percent of the time, it will cause you to derail the customer experience. The point of these three sections is to learn and connect with your customer, to build rapport so your customer can learn to trust you. Your time to sell will come after, but for now, focus all on the customer at hand, listen to their story, and collect all the information you need in order to make a strong recommendation for solving their needs and wants.

Section 1: Discover—Discovering Their Story

Keep in mind that this comes right after your SHINE TWICE introduction. So you or your team member should be using the customer's or client's name during the interaction. Remember to reference their name at least three times during your interaction. Exactly how this section sounds, you need to discover why they are there and learn about who they are. This is the section focused on building trust through relationship development. Like a first date, you ask questions to learn about the other and try to find ways to relate your story to theirs. If you find common ground, you can open up an avenue to build a relationship. Therefore, in this section you want to ask open-ended questions as well as guided close-ended questions to discover information about themselves, where they are from, if they have other families nearby, the names of those family members, where they work, and so forth. For example, if I came up to you at an electronic store, I would ask you questions such as "How many people in your home watch TV and when? What are their ages? How far do you sit from your TV? How many windows do you have in that room? What is the layout of that room?"

Now it may sound like I'm planning a heist because these aren't the usual questions you may hear from an electronics associate, but I'm actually creating a full picture of your entertainment experience. The answers to these six questions will allow me to know exactly what type of television you need, which surround sound system will be suitable, the cables required for the best picture and audio from programs you watch, what type of installation will be necessary, the best place to position your system for optimum results, the universal remote needed to simplify that experience, and provided cable services. Just using six questions, I am able to create all of that. But that doesn't mean that's what the customer needs. That comes later. This is just an example of how impactful it is in discovering a customer's story.

When you are forming your questions or reviewing what assessment you have, think of this section as the connection stage of building a relationship. This section is used to build a bond between yourself and the customer. Our objective is to discover their story, and to do so, we have to ask questions about them, their family, and anything else that is relevant to the products and services you offer.

REMEMBER: These questions must be relevant to what you offer. If a customer or client doesn't understand the relevance to what you're asking, they'll happily call you out. In addition, be careful not to ask too many questions. It's easy to get pulled off target and suddenly an hour-long conversation turned into "I forgot why you're here," and then a $10 sale or nothing at all because of the loss in time.

Your questions have to be strategic, and you must be able to keep the conversation on track. Here are a couple more examples to help illustrate what type of questions to use. I will use examples from multiple industries to further illustrate its usage and hopefully be more relatable for you. After each example, I'll explain why those questions were impactful for both sides of the interaction.

Example 1: Financial

Where do you live?
How long have you lived there?
Are we closer to work or home?
Do you own or rent your home?
Where do you work?
What do you do?
How long have you worked there?
Do you have family or friends living with you?
If so, what are their names?
If kids, how old?
If married, how long?
What does your spouse do?

These are just a few example questions that I had my teams in the financial industries ask in order to learn about our customers' story. These questions help open up the conversation that allows the team member to connect. "Oh, your kids go to ABC school? So, does mine. Their names are Joe and Jane." "You live off ABC Street? That's about fifteen minutes from us. I appreciate you coming by to see us." This is the best time for the team member to connect and relate to the customer. After all, they *are* supposed to build a relationship.

Asking these questions opens that dialog and builds a foundation. In exchange, an experienced team member also knows that the answer to these questions will help him or her form possible services to offer in addition to other needs. These questions serve a joint purpose. They are strategic questions. If we added in there, "What is your favorite animal?" that may open up dialog for a continued conversation, but would serve no purpose for the team member because Bank A doesn't offer any pet products. Although you want to build rapport with them, your time and your customers' time is too valuable just to chat. Those questions must serve a dual purpose benefiting both parties: the win-win.

Example 2: Restaurant

What made you choose us today?
Are we celebrating anything today?
What is normally your favorite place to eat?
Why is that your favorite place?
What is your favorite food?
Where are you from?
Have you been here before?
Have you heard/seen our specials?

These are some examples that have really helped open up dialog with my servers and guests. It also helped them prepare recommendations. A lot of sales in hospitality are missed simply because there is little dialog outside of allowing the guest to make all the decisions. I have had guests admit that they came in for steak, but changed their mind to chicken because the menu didn't create a good picture. If the server asked a few questions and created an opportunity to recommend, that guest could have enjoyed our steak and we might have become a new favorite restaurant. Asking these questions helps build rapport between the server and its guests and allows the server to make great recommendations. I've heard many critics laugh at when I have my servers build rapport, but I always had the last laugh on the scorecards. I had an assessment that my servers would memorize before starting each shift so each guest, regardless of which server they were with, will have a predictable experience. In addition, asking questions like these opened up additional sales opportunities and increased our guest experience. As I said, a win-win.

These are just a few examples of questions I have used on my assessments in these industries. Some of my questions changed even at different companies within the same industry. As I mentioned, you want them to be strategic to what *you* need to achieve your objective and goal. This should help guide you toward which questions to create or tweak questions you may need for an impactful discovery section. As mentioned previously, we want to build rapport within the short time given, learn about our customers' story, and develop trust to move forward into our more personal section, which dives into more intimate information such as behaviors, ideals, experiences, etc. (personal information that is usually provided to those trusted with such information).

Although I know people who would simply ask personal questions out of jest, it isn't socially comfortable to walk up to a stranger and ask for their annual income. Even more so, someone to actually reply truthfully. That is information earned through trust. You have to earn that trust, and each section helps accomplish just that. It's exactly like building a personal relationship. As a matter of fact, that's what you're doing. You need trust to share personal information and even more really to consider saying yes to someone else's advice. Before you are successful moving on to the next section, you have to earn a certain level of trust. Before your advice or recommendation is really considered, you have to prove that the personal information that was given actually has a use. In other words, create a purpose with the information you've gathered, rather than just collecting information for fun. You do that just by sharing stories about helping others in similar situations, or mentioning a few options you will later discuss that will really help. Sharing stories and examples on how you've helped others in similar situations is one of the strongest ways to build that level of trust and strengthen your recommendation, especially if your customers are very personable.

Ultimately, their yes or no lies within the level of trust you've established. Either you have enough of it or you don't. It doesn't always mean that you did a good or bad job. I've seen magnificent interactions end with a no. I have even experienced it personally. That's because somewhere in the conversation, you overlooked a detail that threw off your solution. Sometimes, you may just think of the wrong solution. It happens.

You and your team have to have integrity and honesty. If a client is significantly in debt with terrible credit scores, applying for a credit card to buy Christmas presents will not be the best solution. If a guest with a family of five asked for a room, offering a room with a single queen-size bed will not be the best solution. As obvious as these examples sound, they are all truthful events that I've witnessed. Some were pretty comical, especially when the customer or client caught the mismatch. It happens a lot because members fail to interact with their customers or clients properly, hence the necessity of an assessment. Consistency leads to predictability. For your customers and clients, that's the best thing to offer: predictability.

Since you have a good idea on how to discover your customers' or clients' story and how to gain enough of their trust, let's start asking about their personal situation. I call this uncovering the unforeseen because you are now looking for specific, personal information that will help you form your recommendation. You are uncovering this information that normally would not be shared. Get it now? If you're hoping to get a full visual, don't worry. I've illustrated a full assessment toward the end of this section.

To Transition or Not to Transition?

Has anyone ever done something like this without a moment's pause? "Hey, the kids look great! What's your secret? You're getting evicted?

Why would you buy a Honda?" This person just threw completely different conversations at you, and you were probably still gearing toward finishing the first one about the family. These personalities are fun to talk to, but if you're in a business environment, this can be torture, especially if that person is you or your member jumping around like that. What's my point? You can't go from asking about your customers' kids to jumping straight into something more personal without a proper transition. You have to make sure the customer or client is *prepared* for the next level in the conversation. In a typical conversation, most of our replies lead on to different subjects respectfully. In business, you can change gears with a simple transition statement. Anytime you are ready to switch to a new section within your assessment, you have to apply a transition statement. This will help avoid confusion or, in some cases, distrust. Here are a few examples of transition statements:

"Mr. Smith. Thank you for sharing about your family with me. I enjoyed learning about Susan and Michael. Now, I'm just going to ask some questions to help me get a financial picture of your current situation so I can provide the best solutions for you and maybe Susan and Michael as well."

"Thank you for telling me about your previous experience, Ms. Jane. Now that I have learned about that, I would love to see how I can make your experience even more impactful by asking just a few questions about you personally. This is a great way to narrow down the most effective solutions."

Pretty simple, right? Hopefully, you've already been using this skill. If not, this is here to help. This is a very smooth and peaceful transition.

REMEMBER: Always use transition statements between each section. Without a transition statement, you risk the loss of a sale, loss of a customer or client, and loss in your brand image. It is never worth the risk *not* to use one.

Section 2: Uncover—Uncovering the Unforeseen

Once we've transitioned into our uncover section, what now? This is where the bulk of your strategic questions will lie because these questions need to support the products and services you have to offer. The answers to these questions will help you form a mental list of the best solutions you have available. Just remember not to offer yet. This is where most team members are challenged with patience. They tend to get really excited when they hear an issue that they know they have a solution for. Although they'll have a nice list of solutions to recommend, they won't officially know the best course until they've learned their customers' goals in the next section.

So, what do these personal questions look like? Here are a couple of examples I've used with previous teams to help:

Example 3: Retail Electronics—Computers

What type of security do you use on your computer?
Do you share printers on your network?
What router do you have and why?
During what times do you use your computer most?
What do you most frequently use your computer for?
When on the Web, what sites do you typically visit?
Do you game or plan to game on the computer?
How many people access the computer?
How many people access or have access to your network?
Do you check financial information or anything holding personal information?
What type of personal information do you keep on your computer?

Although some of these may seem simple, I'm sure you saw some thinking that's nobody's business. In this digital age, asking what a computer is used for, when you use it, and what information you store on it is like asking someone to unlock their phone to view it. You feel vulnerable with your privacy. In the computer world, these are intimate questions, but questions computer techs must ask in order to solve some of the most common issues people run into with their network or computer. What seems private to you is just another day at the office for them, which is why team members need to establish trust through discovery first, then transition to uncover. Customers don't know that these are common questions. These two steps help the customer understand why the conversation has become personal and increases the chances of a customer answering trustingly and truthfully yes.

Example 4: Automotive

How often do you travel?
What's the average mileage you drive per year?
How much are you willing to spend?
What seasons do you travel in the most?
How often do you change your oil?
When was the last time your vehicle was serviced?
Have you had any accidents in the past year?
How many people drive your vehicle?
When do you plan to purchase a new vehicle?

I'm sure you've heard these questions asked by a mechanic before. You may have even been dismissive. I've experienced it quite a few times and still witness others being dismissive. Without discovering their story, these questions could lead to incorrect information or none at all. Some people are embarrassed to answer because the answer may reflect their lack of knowledge in taking care of their vehicle (this happens a lot). Others may feel that travel information is irrelevant and puts their family at risk as if a mechanic will watch their home for the right moment to break in like the Wet Bandits from *Home Alone*.

Many people feel mechanics just try to rip you off and find a reason to replace more parts or add additional parts and labor. All scenarios can be examples of why you must discover a customer's story first. These questions are actually very impactful questions that help determine what tires to recommend, where to find a possible reason for your issue, understand how you use your vehicle, and how to make sure all are safe when driving it. Maybe you'll be more willing to answer next time (wink). Again, these objections, like many others in different industries, can be avoided if the trust is established early on. Team members just need the know-how.

You have discovered your customer's story and got a chance to know them on a personal level, which allowed you to successfully transition into uncover. During uncover, you and your team ask strategic but more personal open-ended questions to learn more about your customer's situation. These questions help uncover possible past, present, and future issues that you may be able to assist with. Again, the point of this assessment is to build relationships consistently with your customers to evolve them into clients and solve the issues they inquire about when you uncover. If you were thinking about products and services during discovery, then your brain will be turning here. If your questions are strategic, people will be pouring out information that will urge you to really jump ahead and start offering what you feel are the best options. That's a great feeling to have, trust me, but you can't make recommendations yet. Jumping in early can really risk losing the whole deal, but more importantly, their trust, as that behavior may reflect that you only care about the sale. Although you hear a ton of opportunities, remember that the conversation is to help identify what's important to your customer or client first. Think of it as the listening stage. Once you've collected all the information you need to make sound recommended options, you now have to learn what's important to them. It's time for you to discuss their goals.

Section 3: Define—Defining Their Goals

I hope for most of you, it makes sense why we have to define their goals. If you're confused as to why we define their goals, then I'm glad I have a chance to help you. Think of yourself here. Just like your performance goals at work, you have, or should have, personal goals as well. If you don't, I encourage you to put my guide down and write out three goals you would like to accomplish in the next year. Then in the next five years, come back. You'll toward the end of the guide.

Anyhow, before anyone in sales recommends a product or service, they really should know what the client wants and needs. The only way to know that is to ask. However, just like transitioning into uncover, to better set yourself up for a successful response, you want to transition here as well. Here are a few examples of how you can transition from uncover to define:

"Thank you for sharing that information. It helps me determine the best options to recommend. To really narrow down the best one(s) for you, I'd love to learn about your goals."

"Great. Thank you for that information. Now, before I can make the best recommendations, I would like to learn about your goals so I can help align the right solution with them."

"Thank you for sharing that. For me to really piece everything together, why don't you tell me about your goals? After all, it's my pleasure to help you reach them as best as I can."

As much as it will please our hearts to hear goals like ending world hunger or creating world peace, this isn't a beauty pageant. The goals we are looking for are those where *you* can assist in accomplishing them. For example, if you're in the financial world, you would want to ask, "What are your top three financial goals you wish to accomplish?" The answers should be related to finance such as paying off a car, becoming debt-free, or increasing monthly cash flow by $1,000. If you're in an industry that's hard to relate your product or service to goals, then use a different phrasing like "What are the three most important things about _____?" It sounds different but still provides the same meaning and result.

Say it again with me, "Keep it simple." We aren't airing our own weekend music countdown, so don't collect twenty. Keep their response limited to three. If you said, "What are your goals?" that could be *very* short or *very* long. I have found that three is just enough to help your customer stay in tune with their own progress while it helps prevent being overwhelmed. So in Define, you're simply asking, "What are your top three goals?" or "What are the top three most important things about . . ." That's it.

REAL LIFE

I had a client that I hadn't completed an assessment for. I'd known her for only eleven months. We had a great relationship, and we shared many stories about each other's families. Every now and then, she'd bring in her husband, who was a remarkable vet who served in the army during WWII. I've taken them out to lunches. They invited me out for coffee. We had a great relationship. One day, as I was implementing a new assessment, I noticed that I didn't have one completed on her. Let's call her Mary. So I called Mary and mentioned that I would love to follow up and see how her portfolio was progressing to set an appointment. Upon her arrival, I told her that I was introducing a new assessment that would help me capture very important details that I might otherwise miss in our very interactive conversations. I then asked for her permission to proceed. She gladly accepted.

Now, as I previously referenced, since I knew about 80 percent of the answers, we just chuckled as I validated my accuracy and wrote them down. However, the other 20 percent was pretty impactful (I didn't know that I didn't know). Discovery was a breeze, but uncover opened up additional opportunities I haven't noticed before. Of course, during those discussions, it opened up more dialogue that led to learning even more about her history and her family—most importantly, what was most important to her.

As the experienced salesman that I am, I developed an ability to reference solutions mentally for each problem that I recognize during an interaction, like a library with a computer searching for each solution as keywords and phrases are spoken. It's hard to really explain, but pretty cool. If you're experienced, you know exactly what I'm talking about. If not, this ability will come. You'll get there. Anyhow, with each answer Mary gave me that may have been an obstacle for her, I was storing up solutions. By the time she answered my last question, I already had close to eleven different solutions prepared for her. Eleven! But I had two choices. I could pitch each solution to Mary and see what could stick. Or I could learn about her goals and compare to how each solution, if any, could help accomplish them. Thus, I transitioned to define.

"Thank you, Mary. Just when I thought I knew everything about you. (Ha-ha). This information was very useful. Although I do have some solutions that could really assist you, I'd really like to know what your financial goals really are. What would you say are your top three?" Let me tell you, if there was ever a best moment to bond with my client, it was here. Her top goals were as follows:

1. Leave a legacy for her grandchildren
2. Make sure her husband was cared for after death
3. Help pay off her daughter's home

I knew that Mary had an unconditional love for her family, but I never knew she was striving for these particular goals. I helped her and her family with multiple financial issues and helped increase her wealth, and yet, I never was told this. It's because I never asked. The assessment allowed me to uncover this opportunity and connect my solutions to her goals. Now, out of those eleven solutions, I knew what she found most important and helped her understand which solutions were the best match for each goal. All other solutions I did reference, as you should when you find an opportunity, but we connected on her goals. I based my recommendations on how they would help her accomplish each goal. She was incredibly grateful and, to this day and forever, is a great friend.

Mind you, I could have said I don't need an assessment or I could have just filled one out with the information I already knew, but what would I have missed? Look at everything I discovered, uncovered, and defined between us. Never miss an opportunity to better a relationship. The assessment brought our relationship closer and allowed me to identify what was most important to her. Moreover, it allowed me to become a better leader, a better team member, a better friend. Learning their top three goals allows you and your team members to connect with the right solution. Although Mary didn't go with all my recommendations, she certainly chose the most impactful ones, those solutions that assisted her in accomplishing her goals. Also, more than a couple solutions sold. That's the gap many, many businesses have in their service. That's the gap you can easily fill just by defining their goals. Understand that this also helps increase your chances of a successful sale because you are able to link your solution to their story.

Some people don't take the time to think about setting goals, especially in specific aspects of their personal life. If they can't think of a goal or more than one goal, then don't be afraid to assist them. In fact, they love the attention. I ask for something they would want to accomplish within the next three months, then another within six to twelve months, then a third within the next two years—a win-win for now and later. If you look closely, I just created a good follow-up opportunity as well. A great salesman or woman knows that the key to longevity in success is not what you sell now, but what you can sell later. It's the consistent business. It's the evolution of a customer to a client. As I mentioned, this guide and these strategies allow you to take advantage of the time now and in the future. This helps you guarantee your business in the future, proactively. So they will appreciate your assistance, and both of you will accomplish your goals.

This completes the construction of your assessment. You have a strong idea not only on how to develop a strong assessment but also on how to build strong relationships. This technique has been around for ages. The only thing that evolves is how you use it, like I have evolved this tool for its many uses in multiple industries. This will help connect to all generations and, with plenty of practice, will help your team feel more connected to their mission with the company and their community.

"What do we do from here?" Glad you asked. Again, at the end of the day, our job in business is to help solve problems. I was told by an old manager and mentor of mine that if I'm not helping someone else in life, then I'm wasting it. I just taught you how to do just that on a silver platter. However, once everything you need is on your assessment, what's next? Well, typically the leader or team member would just jump straight into recommending. Why not, right? After all, you are all the best salespeople, right? You should believe so. For your team, however, they are just developing into your system. You have to help them become the best they can become. You can't do that by teaming up with them at the end of an interaction. That's reactive thinking. You're a proactive leader now. You want to help them have a plan prepared before jumping into a recommendation. Therefore, I present an amazing game-changing tactic referred to as a mid-session review.

Mid-Session Reviews

My second favorite part of the assessment is the mid-session review, or MSR. Many companies, especially *Fortune* 500 companies, like to have their own terms for it to fit their culture, and that's perfectly fine. It's branding, right? It's all the same though. If you're familiar with this, you're lucky, and I hope you're not neglecting it. This is a huge game changer. This is nothing new; however, it's interesting to see many *Fortune* 500 companies are just now adopting it or even more that aren't using this at all. Some are starting to understand its potential.

I've brought this behavior to life at multiple global companies and assisted in providing demonstrations on my effectiveness in mid-session reviews. About half of them came around to adopting it nationwide in some form or another. Trust me! I wouldn't waste all that time and passion on something that would leave your performance dead in the water.

So you may be asking yourself, "Self, what in the heck is a mid-session review?" The answer is very simple and doesn't involve special sauce. It's just as it's called, a mid-session review. More specifically, it's a two-minute review of your team member's assessment that is literally held in the middle of an interaction. After the interaction, as the manager or supervisor, you will discuss what the team member discovered, what are the best solutions to recommend, and you will be introduced to thank the customer or client personally for their consideration. To understand its potential, you have to understand the meaning and impact of it. Many of your team members, especially the veteran members, may push back or easily forget. So you must understand and practice this behavior personally so you can share the same passion. The meaning of a mid-session review is to develop your team in four unique ways:

1. Product/service awareness—learn about how products and services can be leveraged in multiple, and sometimes unique, ways to solve problems.
2. Solution-based salesmanship—strategic thinking
3. Leadership development
4. Creating a unique and predictive experience

Of course, there can be many others, but I'm keeping this simple as an example. Here is *why* we want to use this tactic. The following are the results of using this tactic:

1. Increase overall sales
2. Increase customer service scores
3. Increase average unit/SKU per transaction
4. Increase market share
5. Increase team member development
6. Develop role clarity
7. Decrease turnover
8. Increase loyalty
9. Increase brand awareness
10. . . .

Need I say more? I can go on, but I think you get the picture. The impact is self-explanatory, but we'll revisit the meaning. First, let's get a deeper understanding of what a mid-session truly looks like.

There are four objectives you want to fulfill during your mid-session: learn the customer or client's story, define the problem, identify a solution(s), and introduction. During your mid-session, your team member requires your full attention, so please do not attempt to multitask. Divided attention always minimizes results. Here is how a standard mid-session is conducted. Just like transitioning from one section of the assessment to the other, your team member will transition into the mid-session. Otherwise, you'll risk putting the client through a very awkward hold. That's not a good thing. Their transition can sound similar to these examples:

"Great. Now that I know what's important to you, I'll give you my recommendations. But before I do, I'd like to introduce you to my manager just in case I'm ever unavailable. If that is ever the case, he/she will be able to assist you. Sounds good?"

"Thanks, again, for sharing your goals. I have the perfect recommendation(s) for you, but first, my manager loves to meet our customers/clients to thank them personally for their business. His/her name is Mr./Mrs. _____. I'll get you introduced to them. You can also rely on their help if I'm unavailable. I'll be right back."

After their transition statement, they will bring their assessment (if used during interaction) and meet you where you choose. I always recommend a particular location to allow privacy, and it helps build a visual behavior of identifying when a team member is ready for a mid-session if you're not observing the interaction. At this time, the team member should hand you the assessment so you may quickly scan while the team member summarizes their interaction. This is learning their story. This is important for you to learn so you may have a stronger connection when you introduce yourself afterward—more to that later.

While they are summarizing their interaction, you're looking for a few things: the completion of the assessment, what the team member is sharing as if you're reading along, and creating your own recommendations to discuss later. This is an excellent practice because with the team member presenting what they've learned, you're helping them reinforce their interaction. That helps develop their communication skills and memory. If they said their customer had a daughter named Jane, then you should see that reflected in their assessment. If you see opportunities, such as missing information, you can help the team member identify some additional questions that may be helpful to ask.

TIP: Avoid coaching. This session is not for coaching, and a major fallacy is a two-minute session turning into six or eight minutes. Coaching comes after the interaction.

They should be briefly sharing their information from Discover to Define. Once you learn their goals, this is the perfect time to ask the team member what they recommend to the customer. Doing so is allowing the team member to take ownership of their decisions, and ownership creates pride, not to mention develops leadership. You want your team members to feel passionate about helping others. When they share their recommendations, allow them to finish. If you feel there is an opportunity to add another service or product, ask the team member for their thoughts on it. This is their client, and treating it like it's their responsibility will only make the team member more thoughtful about the recommendation and feel open to suggestions. In some cases, they may even ask for your recommendation. At that point, it's okay to provide it. This may also be a good opportunity for team members to revisit or learn about other possible products or solutions, even their uses for creative solutions. If there is a particular focus on a product or service, then ask your team member how that focus can assist their customer in reaching their goal.

These moments provide a support system for the team member. It gives them an opportunity to bounce ideas off an expert, which only increases their chances for success. I've had multiple team members even ask how I would recommend the solution. It's about working together. However, remember this customer is your team member's customer. You must let them have ownership. It's the best way to help them become passionate about what they do, especially millennials.

Although this may seem like a lot, this easily fits in a two-minute window, so don't be concerned. At first, it may take you a couple minutes longer, but as you practice, you'll progress. Everything will come naturally faster.

Anyhow, once you have discovered the best solutions together, it's time for your introduction (assuming you haven't formally introduced yourself already). This is the most impactful part of the mid-session for the customer or client because this is your moment to do two things: provide exceptional customer service and boast about your team members' ability to help accomplish their goals.

As a customer, have you ever had a manager introduce themselves willingly? I'm sure you have somewhere, particularly in restaurants or hotels. How about retail stores? How about on the corporate level? This is your opportunity to stand out, and when a manger interrupts their schedule to thank customers for their time and business, you make a big impact in their experience.

When you introduce yourself, it's important for you to SHINE TWICE. You want to thank them for their business, compliment their choice to see your team members, and assure them that they made a great decision meeting with your team member. Use their name to make it personable. Here is an example:

Team member: Here he/she is, Mr. Smith. This is my manager _____.

Manager: [SHINE TWICE] Hey, Mr. Smith. It's a pleasure to meet you. I just wanted to take the opportunity to thank you for seeing Cynthia here today. Cynthia shared with me what brought you in and some of your goals you wish to reach. She has some terrific recommendations for you that I know you're going to love. Also, going forward, she is going to be your personal account manager, so any questions you may have, she will be your go-to gal. However, if she is ever unavailable, I'll be happy to assist. Thank you for your trust. Cynthia will take great care of you from here.

If you can interact a little longer by connecting with their story, that is always a plus. It's really that simple. Saw what I did? Just in this thirty-second intro, I was able to thank the customer, reinforce the great decision he made coming in, reinforce Cynthia's trust in her upcoming recommendation, and assure him that Cynthia will take care of all his needs. It was all about Cynthia and our customer. You are supporting their interaction.

That's all! That is a full mid-session review. As I said before, it reads as though it's a lot, but trust me, it isn't. As you practice, this becomes a two-minute drill, and the two-minute time frame is away from the customer. Out of sight, if possible. This doesn't count face time. It's a very small and very simple addition to your interaction that makes a huge impact. To master my program, you have to complete a mid-session review successfully on every interaction when possible. It's about consistency in creating a predictable experience. When your team members execute these behaviors over and over, they'll master their interactions—therefore a dramatic increase in performance, not to mention the team members will see how much you can contribute to their growth. Therefore, loyalty substantially increases as well. Again, this is a support behavior for your team members and your customers.

REMEMBER: The biggest fallacy is turning a mid-session into a mid-coaching. Avoid coaching opportunities during their session. This is about encouraging development through self-discovery and guidance. Coaching comes afterward.

Section 4: Recommend

Just in case you were asking what my favorite part of the assessment was, the recommendation stage is my favorite. This is from presentation (or pitch) to closing the deal. This is where you see a lot of magic, and if you're an experienced salesman or woman, you know what I mean. This is where you're just within reach of your goal, where all the information you've collected is about to unfold multiple solutions. The best part is where you get to see the faces of your customers positively change when they hear how you're going to solve their dilemma and help them reach their goals. It's truly a very impactful moment. However, on the other side of the coin, it can also be where a customer notices they may have wasted their time or where someone can be demotivated from rejection. The recommendation stage is a very critical stage because the stage is really an all or-or-nothing scenario. Although someone could argue that "maybe" is a middle ground, I just relate it to sports. In basketball, the only way to score is to take a shot. There are many ways to make your shot, but it either goes in or not.

To a leader, much like a coach, it's a great opportunity to identify how effective a team member is during their transaction if you weren't present for the whole interaction. By just listening to the recommendation stage, you can determine quite a few things. You can determine if the team member was listening, if particular information was missing from the assessment, their product knowledge, ability to handle objections, self-motivation, salesmanship, and the list can go on. I'm sure you can think of a few others right now.

To a team member, much like a player, it's a great opportunity for them to identify how effective their practicing has been. Can they make the shot? In my experience flipping teams, I discovered that eight out of ten times, the reason for their failure to close a sale is because they failed to see their purpose. Many believe selling is their job, especially with millennials. If there isn't an endgame to helping others, they lose purpose, motivation, and confidence. They think their job is to sell. That means it's not their job to help customers as much as it's their job to make profits. There are many companies and many teams that still have this mentality. If that is your company or team, *stop it*. Be the change. Become the difference. If you have team members believing this, then correct it. As a leader in your industry, it is your responsibility to make the change. We are all here to make someone else's life better. The sooner you believe that, the more successful you'll be. That belief can be easily created with just a single word. We are not here to make suggestions. We are here to make recommendations. Did I lose you? No worries. I'll explain.

The word *suggest* means putting something (or someone) up for consideration. The word *recommend* means putting something (or someone) up suited for a specific purpose. If you look up those words, you'll find multiple meanings, but the majority falls right on the line of consideration and specific purpose. So when you visit your doctor, do they give you suggestions on how to get better? Or do they recommend a particular instruction? I don't know about you, but I wouldn't feel comfortable with a doctor who said, "I suggest you take some kind of antibiotic and a painkiller in order to feel better. Don't forget to read the bottle. Would you like to follow back up next week to see how things are going?" I wouldn't feel very comfortable with the confidence in my doctor's solution for me. I think we would much rather hear them say, "I recommend picking up prescription A from your pharmacy after this. Take both your antibiotic and painkiller twice a day with food, and we'll set up a follow-up appointment for next Thursday to see your progress." Huge difference, right? I'd do whatever he/she just recommended because it seemed like they were more confident in their solution. If people don't want their doctor "considering" solutions, then why should you be that way?

People visit the doctor because he/she is a specialist in that field. If they look, speak, and act confident, then I'm certainly going to follow their recommendation. I make it very clear to my teams that they *must* see themselves as the specialist in their field. If they are in finance, they are the doctors in finance. If they are in real estate, they are the doctors in real estate, so on and so forth. This doesn't mean for them to go out and order name tags with "Dr." printed before their name (someone would have done it). Their purpose (as a team member) is to be that professional that can guide customers with recommended solutions. Don't suggest. Recommend. That difference alone will build confidence in yourself and your team. If you put the customer (patient) first, the business will always follow as you've heard me repeat several times. Must be important, right? (wink)

Although a single word can make a huge impact, you still have to communicate your recommendation effectively to make sure the customer or client perceives that recommendation as you do—a valuable solution. Not only what you say, but also how you say it can add tremendous value. You want your customer or client to see the true value you can provide in solving their issue(s). Here are a few very successful strategies to use when making your recommendations. Keep in mind that there are hundreds of strategies on how to close a sale and thousands of resources available. If you wish to learn more about growing your ability to close a sale, I recommend you continue your education if you haven't already. I also recommend you find the names of a few top producers in your field or company and build a relationship. For now, I know these strategies will be very useful for you. Although I train my team to use a hybrid of strategies depending on the circumstances, these are a few that remain a consistent foundation for all my teams to utilize during presentations and closings: bundle, top-down, and bottom-up strategies. Because it is very important to have your strategy decided prior to your presentation, we'll discuss these strategies first. The strategy you choose should outline how your solutions will be presented.

TIP: Never let your customer or client see or hear the price for the first time at the register (close of sale)! Always share pricing during your presentation to maximize results. Sharing too soon, like before the recommendation stage, can cause you to devalue the recommendation because you haven't gained enough information to determine if it's the best fit (goals are the last thing to cover in your assessment, remember?) and the number will distract them before you can link their problem to the solution. Sharing too late, like at the checkout, can be a major surprise to consumers and create a negative experience.

Harnessing the Power of the Bundle

We touched on this earlier, if you can recall. The power of the bundle strategy is one that doesn't get harnessed as often as it should. Now, when I say bundle, I don't mean a package that is only available on Black Friday or holiday specials. I mean the power of creating a bundle out of complimentary SKUs like referenced earlier. It's almost rare that I walk into a business of any kind and I see a custom bundle priced and displayed. I always see branded, advertised bundles. The unfortunate part is that these sponsored bundles are typically low in margin. The purpose is to help drive traffic into your business so you can help identify more needs and build your attachment rate. If you haven't learned by now, the attachment rate is one of the most important metrics that should be tracked, yet I still see businesses in multiple industries that don't pay attention to it. All businesses should be tracking the attachment rate (or what other industries may call it, product penetration) if your company carries multiple products. Product penetration is just a fancy way of saying what and how many products are attached to a core, or focused, product or service. This measures the blood flow of your business. That's where you'll find out many secrets to increase profits and, ultimately, your performance. Anyway, what happens is that everyone focuses on selling a ton of these sponsored bundles, like on Black Friday. In many cases, if not all, companies lose money. It's up to you to help your team and your business understand the true nature of these sponsored bundles and create your own bundles to market right next to it.

The power of the bundle is harnessed through creativity, finding complementary products and/or services and bundling them into a packaged deal. Now, I'm not talking about finding two or three SKUs and taking 10 percent off, unless you feel it will make a big impact and your margins are large enough; then go ahead. I only apply discounts if I feel it will drive more traffic. Typically, I'd recommend starting with sticker prices of each item and adding them together. It's very interesting how the common person uses math. On average, they need everything simplified. Sure, everyone can count ten plus ten, but if someone offers the answer before they have to process it, it becomes more appealing.

REAL LIFE

When I was trying to figure out how we could increase our margins per transaction, I started experimenting with the idea of creating bundles out of regular-priced services, an idea I discovered walking down a popular college street loaded with small businesses. There were handwritten signs everywhere, offering their unique products or services. These businesses couldn't afford a lot of name brands. But when I saw a good price on the board for a meal, I went in and grabbed a menu. Surprisingly, I didn't see the special out front. However, I found each individual part under their respective sections of the menu.

Listening to everyone in the restaurant, I heard quite a few team members mention the special and some of the guests ordering it themselves. Looking at those items again, the price for each portion totaled the price outside for the combination. It was an appetizer, an entrée, and a dessert. I asked my waitress if it was popular, and she said, "Extremely," as they were complementing flavors. I then followed up and asked how often people ordered appetizers. She replied, "Honestly, only during sports events if you don't count our special." I was very impressed. The owner found a way to make the price of the appetizer look more appealing by offering it with selected entrées and desserts. It definitely got my gears turning. By the end of my delicious meal, I was convinced that this might be my solution because this special was terrific and I wouldn't have ordered the appetizer otherwise. I would have never known how delicious it all was.

Let's just say I had a couple of skeptics, including my store manager. However, confident that I was right, I asked to try it out. For one week, from Sunday to Saturday, I ran three services side by side on a display in front of the department, each individually priced. I also required all of my team members to show these displays during each interaction. To keep it simple, I only recorded the first twenty interactions I could witness and followed up with each team member about the results.

Out of those first twenty transactions, eight sold with at least one of the three offered services, and three of those had more than one service attached in that single transaction—not bad. To keep numbers simple, our service attachment rate for those selected services out of those twenty transactions was 40.0 percent, and out of that 40.0 percent, only 37.5 percent had more than one of those listed services. If you need a better understanding of the math, for the 40.0 percent, I simply divided twenty by eight and the 37.5 percent was simply dividing eight by three then I multiplied each by 100. A total of eleven services were sold. To some industries, that may be good. For others, it may not be. My manager loved it, of course. For me, it wasn't good enough because I knew we could do better.

The following week, from Sunday to Saturday, I held the same contest and required the same behaviors from my team members while recording the first twenty interactions I could witness. The only difference was that I offered the same services, but as a bundled service this time. I had one display with one price that showed a breakdown of each service and price on one sheet, but with a total amount in bold (we never want to confuse our business or mislead anyone, just help them work the math—KISS).

Out of the next twenty transactions observed, nine sold with at least one of the three services bundled, seven sold with bundles, and two of them were sold with only two of the three services. The attachment rate for those services out of the twenty transactions was 45.0 percent, just one transaction more than the previous test—not much to brag about. But let's look a little deeper. Out of nine transactions, two sold with one service, two sold with two of the three services within the bundle, and five sold with complete bundles (or three services). In the first test, we sold eleven services in twenty transactions. This week, we sold twenty-one services in twenty transactions. We actually average over one service per transaction, and we only sold services to one more person than the previous week. My store manager was excited with eleven services sold in the first twenty. If you were the store manager, how would you react when you found out that we almost doubled performance in one week? As predicted, he went head over heels in hysteria and ultimately applied this practice throughout every department almost overnight.

After the big success, I pulled my team in with my store manager to get their feedback about the different experiences they had with our customers when offering these services in both ways. The results were surprising. Not only was I right about the customers' perception of math, but it turns out that my team members thought it was much easier to talk about one package deal than separate services. One even said "less to say, but more to show." That just ties back into the 7 percent of communication that comes from words. Be strategic. We put more power back into body language. Their feedback said customers found it easier to interpret what they can and cannot afford. Those who didn't see value in one or two of the services in the bundle just deducted it. However, it increased the chances of closing additional services because customers found it difficult to see the added value of each individual cost. They saw 100 plus 100 plus 100, which appeared larger than just seeing 300. In addition, my team members felt it was easier talking about a bundled service than multiple services. That made me think back to my waitress that didn't even have to mention what appetizers or desserts she'd recommend. Just offer the special and ta-da, appetizer and dessert—much easier. This new strategy made the experience easier for both my team members and my customers. In addition, it made our business more profitable. This was truly a win-win.

For some of you, this may be a new concept, but this practice has been around for a long time. I only discovered what small retail businesses have been doing for centuries, with just walking down the street—another example about how we must continuously evolve our strategy. However, I hope you have a good grasp on how to harness the power of the bundle. This is a terrific strategy on how to increase profits, reach sales goals, increase customer experience, and help your team become more successful. Another way of working smarting rather than harder. Sit back and think of how you can bundle your products and services. You can do it with any SKU in any industry for anything. I recommend trying the same way I did for your own research. I think you'll be surprised.

The Top-Down Strategy

The top-down strategy is a great closing strategy to use when you're building value for higher-priced products and services not in a bundle or talking with price-conscious consumers. The name "top-down" means starting your recommendation with the most expensive product or service first. Then follow the same order when completing their transaction. I'm sure you've experienced times where a salesman or woman would add up values like this: "Okay. It's $300 for A, $135 for B, $495 for C, and $80 for D," then later repeat during your checkout, "It's $495 for A, $80 for B, $135 for C, and $300 for D for a total of . . ." Saw what happened there? If this was you, you'd probably think twice about your choices. This form of pricing can be overwhelming. Even if you heard the prices prior to being rung up on the register, you could generate an anxious situation at the end of your recommendation stage simply because of being out of order, disorganized. It looks even worse when other potential customers are watching these types of experience. We all know and have experienced in some way the expressive consumer. You know, the ones who have emotional responses and say everything on their minds. That is where the top-down strategy comes into play, to provide structure and organization and create a more positive experience to minimize the negative reactions.

When you share each individual price during your recommendation and at the close, consumers feel more comfortable hearing prices get lower as they're read back. It's like our instinctive reaction during negotiations. The buyers negotiate a lower price and feel more accomplished and at ease the lower it gets. When pricing is referenced from highest to lowest, it gives the same positive reinforcement received from negotiating, helping to minimize negative reactions: "Okay, great. It's $495 for A, $300 for B, $135 for C, and $80 for D." Once their subconscious catches on to your pattern during your recommendation, then your pricing at close becomes predictable and easier to absorb, therefore easier to recognize and accept the value of what you're selling. Their subconscious recognizes the price pattern and anticipates the total price slowing down as each item is read back. This type of predictability brings consumers at ease during the closing process. Amazing how powerful predictability can really be. Pretty cool, right?

As I mentioned, this strategy is used during your recommendation stage twice: during your presentation and at the close. It's very important that the items you've recommended are priced while you make your presentation to maximize your opportunity. If your customer is not prepared to hear these prices at close or able to predict when the pricing will stop adding up, you'll only increase the chances of losing the sale and a consumer. So this strategy should be utilized during your presentation and again when completing the sale. There should never be surprises when you're closing the sale.

The point of the strategy is to truly assist and ease consumer transitions to close. For example, during your recommendation stage, you'll recommend an abundance of products and services and you'll reference the price of each item individually. However, the majority won't add it up, leaving a big possibility of a dramatic surprise at the register if you start throwing prices in unpredictable order—the perfect time for the top-down strategy to ease their anxiety.

If your team is in auto sales and your team member discovers a need for a vehicle to seat a family of five, you'll want to start with the highest and best models to accommodate, such as vans and SUVs first. Once an option is chosen, then the same process for the attachment services. If your team is in the restaurant business and your server discovered that their guest loves steak, they would want to recommend the filet mignon signature steak first, then a runner-up like the T-bone, then the upsell substitutes and so forth. If your team is in the hotel business and your guest relations specialist discovered that the family plans to stay for vacation, then they would want to offer a suite first because of the space available, a better experience, and a higher comfort value for their long stay. Then follow up with a queen suite and so forth if declined.

The point here is the importance of using a very effective strategy when recommending higher-priced or mixed-price products and services. If you observe interactions during the recommendation stages, don't be surprised if you hear team members recommended lower-priced products and services only or first. People who fear confrontation and/ or rejection usually prefer to start with or recommend only lower-priced products and services, assuming the consumer is only after a cheaper price. This, of course, is proven wrong time and time again through the assessment. I can't count how many times I've heard team members recommend a four-door coupe to a family of five, or a Salisbury steak to a steak lover, or a twin-bed economy room to a family staying for vacation as their first option. That points to two things: either the team member didn't assess their needs or they didn't have a strategy in place to make the appropriate offer first, both easily addressed and coachable from this guide.

REMEMBER: The top-down strategy is most effective with higher-priced SKUs or if there is a mixture of prices involving

higher-priced items. It is also most effective with items not within bundles and with price-conscious consumers.

If your product or service doesn't necessarily come with a single price tag like in banking or using monthly membership services, then you would want to start with the solutions that have the highest risk of being rejected, or in layman's terms, the hardest-to-sell solutions first. For example, in banking, before recommending a checking or savings package, it is more effective to recommend the credit card application first as determined through the assessment. If your team recommends memberships, they would want to recommend the biggest package with the biggest advantages first, starting with the membership that best fits their needs, like the auto sales example, working your way down the membership options until a balance is accepted. This strategy is effective in any industry. Give it a try the next time you're engaged with a consumer in a similar scenario.

The Bottom-Up Strategy

So you may have asked yourself, "Self, what if I don't have a bundle or all the items recommended are all low-priced?" Although the top-down strategy can also be used for lower-priced solutions, you may want to build a different value behind your recommendation, like a bargain. I have many team members who utilized the flexibility of all three.

When you recommend products and services starting with the lowest-priced items first then work your way up the ladder, that is called the bottom-up strategy. It creates the same attributes as the top-down strategy, such as organization and predictability to minimize negative responses. However, it is most effective under one condition: All solutions recommended are low-priced or on sale. Therefore, it depends on what value you're trying to build with your consumer. The bottom-up strategy is not as effective as the top-down strategy when you involve high-priced solutions, but very effective to present a better deal. I'll explain further.

When I say high- or low-risk solutions, I am referencing the difficulty to sell those products and services. This could be due to price, or a new product that requires educating the public, etc. A high-risk solution increases your chance of losing the sale because of the previous factors mentioned. A low-risk solution decreases your chances of losing the sale. It's nature with consumers. So, how does the bottom-up strategy work? The bottom-up strategy works the exact same way as the top-down strategy, just in reverse. This strategy is used twice during your recommendation stage as well. You will use it to organize your presentation and then once more during the close. For example, you'll present your solutions like "Here is A for only $10, B for $20, C for $35, and D for only $70." Remaining consistent when you're closing, you will repeat in the same order like this: "Okay, we have A for $10, B for $20, C for $35, and D for $70. Making our total only . . ." When the numbers or the simplicity of the solutions are easier to interpret subconsciously, then they view the transaction as simple and easy, or in other words, affordable. Notice how I referenced the word *only*. Take a look at where I've referenced *only*. Do you see the pattern?

The power behind the bottom-up strategy is creating the value of the bargain, as I said before. Our subconscious associates lower prices with terms like bargains, deals, or sales—all found to be very positive associations with consumers that you want to use if the value you want to build behind your recommendation is the bargain, best deal, or sale. The word *only* is very powerful in this context because it implies that the price is indeed a bargain. In my example, I used *only* in three positions: Solution A, Solution D, and just before the total. I used *only* for solution A and Solution D because I'm associating that the $70 solution is just as much of a bargain as the $10 solution. Then I follow through with one more just before the final price to continue that positive reinforcement that the consumer is getting a great deal. After all, based on the team member's assessment and the recommendation you and your team member discussed during the mid-session, they are getting one, right? Using the bottom-up strategy helps consumers envision how great a deal it truly is, hence why this strategy isn't as effective with higher-priced, higher-risk solutions. On those solutions, consumers aren't looking for a bargain as much as the best solution to help accomplish their goals as determined from the assessment. The bottom-up strategy works with consumers who are either looking for a deal or trying to get the best solution at the lowest price they can reasonably afford. Now we're ready to learn a foundation in presentations.

BEST PRACTICE: During your mid-session reviews, while discussing your team members' solutions, ask them, which strategy do they plan to use: bundle, top-down, or bottom-up? Not only will this help reinforce their training, but it maximizes their chances of a close. This will also keep them focused on presenting consistently since you're adding accountability by asking, further developing each team member to become an Alpha performer.

NOTE: The person who sets the standard in determining a high price and low price is *you*. Each industry and market carries its own interpretation of high and low prices. The examples I gave were only to keep it simple in determining the differences between the strategies. Please use your industry and market standards to determine when the top-down and bottom-up strategies are best utilized.

REMEMBER: If you're recommending products and services and you don't share pricing until you ring up the consumer, it decreases your chances of success and may lead to a deceptive perception, which can tarnish your brand, your company's brand, team morale, and your production. Always aim to share pricing following during your presentation. If you forget to price during your presentation, utilizing one of these strategies can still make the close more successful than shooting out unpredictable pricing or one big total surprise amount.

The Presentation

Any time you're recommending solutions, you and your team should always provide a professional presentation. Just like I discussed about making goals tangible, you would want to make the solutions tangible for your consumers. It's easy to give a nice speech on why someone should choose one thing over the other, but it isn't so easy to get them to say yes. Why is that? Think back to how we communicate. If what we speak is only 7 percent expressed, how on earth will you be able to make a strong connection to your solutions? A presentation. A combination of ways that will excite your tone of voice and allow your body to express its passion to help solve their issue(s).

As I mentioned previously, the strategy you choose must reflect in your presentation. For example, if you choose to use the top-down strategy, then during your presentation, you want to demonstrate each solution in order from highest to lowest in risk or price. Makes sense, right? Organized. When you present the total, you follow the same order, no surprises. If you use the bottom-up strategy, then you present solutions in order from lowest in risk or price to highest. It's a simple, organized process that encourages the customers and clients alike that you're confident in what you're recommending.

Think back in school when you were instructed to do a presentation on a certain subject. Or try to remember a recent business, sales, or leadership meeting that you were in where you or someone else gave a presentation. Hopefully, it was a great one to learn from, but if not, no worries. The point is presentations are a necessity in sales and you've witnessed hundreds to thousands in your life and may not have noticed, definitely wouldn't remember the ones where people just talked. However, I bet you can recall at least one or two that were captivating. This is how you and your team need to present your recommendations, just like giving a speech, you must captivate your intended audience (in this case, your customer or client) to help motivate their passion and envision how your solution is the best option to reach their goal(s).

When presenting, you want to use all the resources you have. Not everyone will have access to a computer or tablet to provide a presentation. Not everyone may have that exact solution on display to see it in action. And that is okay. If you haven't learned it by now, then catch up. You can only do what you can with what you have. However, the more stimuli you can visually provide, the higher the success rate you'll create. So take advantage of all you can, when you can.

Here is a list of very impactful resources and tools I've listed in order from most impactful to least impactful, although the least impactful is still more impactful than your 7 percent speech. I will also provide brief descriptions why.

Demonstration/live example—There is nothing better than a hands-on experience with a product or service in action. Being able to witness the unique features live provides the best experience when deciding to purchase. Demonstrations can be the solution in active use, a display showing videos of its active features and even granting participation from the consumer to engage in the use of the product firsthand. This tactic can incorporate all the senses, providing the greatest chance of success, but the most important is the sense of touch.

Tours—For many, when deciding to make a purchase, experiencing is believing. Tours are the next best way to provide a captivating experience if you are selling an experience over an actual handheld product. For example, if you're a mechanic, a tour of the auto shop can really empower a buyer to feel comfortable about using your services as they see how your team works with vehicles. If you're a real estate agent, tours are your life. How does a buyer feel comfortable about buying a home? Through touring the property. Tours can also be witnessing other installations, where the service takes place, showrooms where products are exposed and active (if interactive, it's considered a demonstration) in their specific setting, or even introducing consumers to additional partners who will help showcase some of your recommendations.

Product displays—Just as it sounds, nothing is more tangible about the product than the product itself. Putting the product in the consumers' hands is the oldest trick in the book, and it still is just as effective.

The sense of touch is one of the most impactful senses connecting to a decision. So if you can, put the power of the product in their hands.

Games—This is how you take a sense of humor to another level. Games are very impactful because they require interaction and make the decision process more fun. If you make your presentation interactive with a game, it can truly show a consumer how much fun it would be to witness your solution achieve their goal. Not everyone likes the same game, but everyone likes a game of some sort. Make it fun, and you'll make a sale.

Sense of humor—Have you ever heard laughter is a faster way to someone's heart? It truly is. Have a sense of humor. This doesn't necessarily mean you have to tell jokes all the time, but when you have an opportunity to lighten the mood, definitely do so. Many salesmen and women focus so hard on getting everything perfect, they accidentally make the environment too serious. For some consumers, this can be a turnoff. After all, if they didn't need your help, they would've shopped online. Since they came to you, don't be afraid to entertain them with stories, jokes, or a quirky laugh or two.

Analytics—Graphs, charts, and math, oh my! Some consumers just like to get to the bottom line. You can spend an hour presenting, but for some, all you needed was the right graph. Math doesn't lie. Applying graphs, charts, or even writing out the math for a consumer in person can really help them put things into perspective. This is most effective when money is a priority. If you are selling a product or service that doesn't have any of these resources available, rely on a tour so the consumer can see the result of its use in real time.

Reflection—You're going to talk about a lot of things with your customers and clients, some of which they may forget. Another huge advantage of having an assessment is to assist in this situation where they may have forgotten what they told you. Reflection is where you use your assessment to point out how your solutions will help retain a goal based on exactly what they said. "Ms. Jane, you said here you were concerned about not meeting your deadline because you didn't have what you needed. Here is how this will help you achieve that deadline and more . . ."

Partnership—In order to be a team, you have to know when to utilize that team. A partnership is when you have another team member, or partner, assist with the sale of your solution. For example, if I was a salesman, although I am the forefront of selling a service, I'm not the installer. To better describe the value of a service, I would invite the installer to join my presentation and provide their experience to add incredible value. This can also help provide answers to questions you may not otherwise know. Even a coworker or team member who has more experience with a particular product can make a huge impact in your presentation. Other similar partnerships are lenders to real estate agents, mechanics to technicians, tax advisors to a business, etc.—a single product or service that links their expertise together to solve a common problem.

Role play—As funny as it sounds, role play isn't just for training. It's a very effective way to put clients into different perspectives. Not to mention, it can also make interaction fun. This is just putting your consumer into the role of another who may have experienced a similar situation and helping them self-discover that your solution is the key to their success—like telling a story, but through first-person, making you the narrator.

Formal Presentation—This is probably what you've had the most experience providing, thanks to schools and the standard training in communication with corporate businesses. This is simply putting your speech in a presentation software program, like PowerPoint as an example, and hosting a formal presentation on a screen or using other means of resources to put words into writing so the audience can read along. It's easy to lose an audience in a formal presentation because it's out used. If you must have a formal presentation, remain interactive. Be sure to keep your body moving so your audiences have to adjust their positions to follow. Adjust your tone to incorporate what's important or humorous, and when you can, gain participation from the audience for engagement. Again, it's all about experiences. Make sure your presentation is an experience. It works best coupled with other tactics above. There is definitely a ton of material out there to learn how to maximize this form of communication.

If you have others you've discovered that are impactful, as before, please feel free to add them in their respective order to train your team appropriately. These practices are very impactful at increasing your rate of success to close the sale. However, I will add this: Make sure all your team members are consistent in how they present. Just like in sports, inconsistency can cause disaster in the long run. The more practice they have at their presentation, the faster they become the expert in their field and build the confidence to show it—more importantly, the faster your team member can become an Alpha performer. Although the way they present will be unique, how they present should remain consistent. A predictable experience, remember?

BEST PRACTICE: Although you've put together the perfect package, consumers may not always select everything you've offered for multiple reasons. Don't be offended. However, make notes in your recommendation section of what they did and didn't accept. I make the list of recommendations and then put a checkmark next to those accepted. This way, I'll be able to refer to the rejected options in the future.

I've led teams where I had all team members provide the same exact presentation following some form of script, and I've led others where I've allowed each team member to provide their own personality (without a script) still using a particular presentation. Both are very successful as long as there is a predictable experience. The difference was industry specific. I recommend that if your industry is more customer-based like retail sales, then train your team to follow an exact presentation you

VERNON MASON III

feel is more impactful and hold all accountable to the same standards. However, don't be shy in letting them use their creativeness, like humor, to make the presentation *theirs*. In other industries where it's more client-oriented, I recommend having team members create their own unique presentation and keep them accountable to their own standards. Be sure to have them share their best practices to help the team as a whole grow. Regardless of what you decided is best, help them remain consistent.

REMEMBER: You can review their plan through the mid-session review and their consistency through observations. If you remain consistent in your follow-up, your team will remain consistent in their performance.

TIP: If you're thinking of utilizing a single presentation for all team members to use, but don't know where to start, don't be shy to ask your current top performers to help put something together. I've always said that everything you need for a team to succeed can be discovered by the team. Just ask. After all, you're in it to win it together.

REAL LIFE

Here are two examples illustrating when and how I've used presentation strategies. One of my favorite examples to use in retail is with one of my teams in the electronic industry because they did a great job providing all the necessary tools to create great presentations. In addition, those tools were consistently available, no matter which store or which department you worked in.

My teams had to provide specific presentations if they were presenting our top three most popular products. I used our reporting to determine our most popular products, which were televisions, computers, and surround sound systems at the time. Every time a customer came into the store to look for either of these products, my team members were accountable to provide the appropriate presentation during their recommendation stage. They had to give a tour of our showroom, demonstrate the calibration display, and allow customers to interact with the suggested accessories with a good, better, and best approach. If a customer was looking for a TV, my team member had to do a presentation with a projector, an LED, and a plasma TV, which were the three most dominant types at the time. We had each type set up in low-lit studios connected to our top sound systems. The presentation *had* to take place in the studios where an active surround sound system and connected Blu-Ray player were accessible for a better-quality experience. Afterward, the customer was taken to our calibration display, where they were able to compare a manufactured TV with a calibrated one, side by side (a service I would still recommend you to check out yourself), then a walk to our accessory section and physically providing the recommended accessories to the customer to interact with while discussing the features and benefits.

Anyhow, these were required presentations regardless of which TV, theater system, or DVD/Blu-ray player a customer looked for. If it was a computer, we would do the same presentation with monitors and speakers. Why? Because each product and service provided the best experiences for our customers in the store and could do so in their homes. Not to mention, in our studios, you couldn't see a single wire and all the TVs were mounted in different forms. Again, all demonstrating covertly what our services can provide. There were thousands of customers who didn't even know that type of experience was available, even affordable.

Notice what were connected in our studios: the top products and a view of our services. If the customer was shopping for a surround sound system or a computer, my team members would still bring their customers into the studios. That's because it provided a complete experience. Our customers were able to hear, feel, see, and even smell (we had a clean aroma with a lavender scent) what a great experience could be like in their home. We brought the solutions to life in our tour and demonstration. As you saw at the top of my list, demonstrations and tours are the most impactful because a solution is seen in action. The more customers that were able to experience my team members' solution directly, the higher the chance of success in the sale—in addition, making additional attachments. It became an experience they needed in their homes. Thus, we were able to provide. My teams here utilized demonstrations, tours, and product displays to achieve success.

Now, not all stores and industries can provide these experiences. My teams in finance certainly didn't have a showroom where you could see high-definition colors zoom across the screen with surround sound during an action-packed scene about someone getting a return on their investment. Honestly, the end result may not be as gratifying as the hero walking through fire after saving the world. However, as I mentioned, every company and industry is different. Finance is more client-based. Although they too have customers, they truly seek to turn customers into clients. Retail likes to set up repeat customer business but can't truly establish one-on-one long-term relationships because they operate in the mass market, surviving through quantity. Client-based industries work to establish their business through one-on-one relationships. And to do so, a unique presentation can be accommodating.

I had two team members named Howard and Jamie. Although on the surface it appeared they had similar personality traits, underneath, they were day and night, an I personality and a D personality. If you sat with both during their interactions, you'd notice that their interactions were very similar, but how they presented their recommendations were completely different. Howard relied heavily on humor and role play, while Jamie relied on analytics and reflection.

When Howard would collect information from his clients during the assessment, he would always make it engaging and comical, to keep the atmosphere calm and fun. That was just him. So when he would present his recommendations, he always had a comical story to accompany his recommendation for perspective and to lure the customer or client into engaging in conversation. If he received any objections, he would do a role play putting the customer into the shoes of another to emphasize perspective and why the solution would be a perfect fit. If he really struggled with an objection but knew this was the best solution for them to reach their goal, he would tug on a partner for additional value. Howard had a way of making the most frustrated person laugh, with a solution in hand by the end of their interaction.

When Jamie would collect information, she would stick straight to the script. Unless someone mentioned puppies and kittens, she didn't stray far from the path. I knew that if she was with a client for two hours, someone brought up dogs and cats—very humorous unless the lobby was full. Nonetheless, when making her presentation, she would involve analytics to prove what a perfect match her solution was to obtain their goal. To Jamie, a confrontation wasn't her comfort zone, and if she had any chance of avoiding it, she'd prefer to be proactive about it. If she displayed the facts first, it would reduce the chances of objections. If she still received an objection, she did incredibly well taking notes during her assessment and therefore reflected what the client told her. "Well, Mr. Smith, you said here [pointing to her notes] you were most concerned about making your car payments. If that is truly your top concern, this solution will take care of that by reducing your payment and saving you over $100 a month." Since she learned to be very particular about taking notes, she utilized this presentation tool often and was very effective with her style.

Two Alpha performers offered the same products and services, but in two completely different ways. Although these aren't more impactful than demonstrations, they did use the best of what they had available and were still successful. Like I said, use all that you have to make the best presentation. Over time, it will evolve and become one of your most powerful closing tools. All that will be left is for you and your team to close the sale.

TIP: Presentations are like puzzles. Move the pieces around until you find the perfect match. Although you allow your team members to have their own presentations, you can still require each team member to present a particular product or service if it's a part of their solution. For instance, if you heard a great practice that is yielding better results from another manager, you may want to incorporate that script into your team's presentation.

The Closing

TIP: Always ask for the business—literally. It doesn't always have to be in the form of a question, but you need to ask for the business. All team members performing less than Alpha-level performance are very inconsistent about asking for the business. Just this simple change can make a huge impact on their results.

I have seen some of the biggest and most well-planned presentations end making the biggest fallacy of all: they didn't ask for the business. Even many big stars I've heard giving seminars have made this mistake. I've asked many of my team members if they are in entertainment or sales because that's the difference. Without asking for their business, all you did was entertain them. In many cases, without asking, many consumers think about what you've discussed, then go to a competitor for the services you presented, just to buy theirs because they asked. You can have the biggest performance and make such an incredible presentation that will wow the audience with an unforgettable experience, but if you don't ask for the business, that's all you did, make an unforgettable experience. I can get that at the theater downtown. In sales, you have to ask for their business after your presentation. You should never end your presentation with "This is why it's best for you," or "This is why you'll reach your goal faster." Instead, you should be saying, "So when should we get this started?" or "Let's accomplish this goal right now!"

A powerful closing strategy that has contributed to much of my successes and I have trained all my teams to utilize is the assumptive strategy. Heard of it? If you have, I hope you're using it. It's an incredible strategy that has been successful for ages to help maximize your closing rate. If not, don't worry. Here is a brief explanation on how it works. In sales, you have a ton of things rattling in your head about what to say, think, do, and respond. However, the biggest thought and concern is typically rejection. One of the biggest contributors to having that fear of rejection is anticipating their answer to be no. So the biggest secret to reduce the fear of rejection, in turn boosting your confidence to close, is to *assume* they'll say yes. That's it!

You may be asking yourself, "Self, I thought if I assume something, I'd only make a you-know-what out of you and me?" Not in all cases this remains true, even if it is fun to say. In the world of proactivity, it's the exact opposite. It's literally the science of assumptions if you think about it. I'll create that new scientific subject right here. Let's call it assumology. I don't think that will stick enough to earn its shot for college credits, but you get the point.

Sounds crazy? Think back to my example about being the doctor in your industry. When you're with your doctor, do they ask what you want to do, or provide direction on what to do? That is the principle of the assumptive strategy. The doctor doesn't worry about you saying no because they *assume* you want to get healthy quickly. That's why you're there after all, right? What they advise, you will do just that and follow it. Now think about what you're doing. Aren't you doing the same thing? You're doing a thorough analysis of their history and making a strong evaluation that leads to the best solution you have to offer to help them reach their goal. For a patient, it's health. For your consumers, it's whatever you have available to provide: wealth, a home, a car, a career, volunteer work, advice, security, etc.

Going forward, since you and your team members are the doctors in your industry, assume that your consumers will say yes because you know you have the best solution available to help them accomplish their goal. Period. After the first couple of times practicing, you'll notice an immediate, positive change in your confidence, therefore a positive change in your closing rate. That's because the confidence is observed through your body language and tone. Therefore, your customers and clients alike will trust you more when you make your recommendation. If you're confident it will work and you're the professional, your consumers will too. With that mentality coupled with my presentation guide previously, your odds of success go through the roof. The only thing standing in the way is, and will always be, your ability to act.

Therefore, make yourself a promise for you and your team right here out loud. "My team and I only offer the best solutions to help our consumers reach their goals. Therefore, we will be confident that our consumers will always say yes, and we will never forget to ask for their business." There you go. At the end of the day, asking for their business is just plain courteous and, honestly, expected. I've spoken to many consumers who were actually disappointed that their business wasn't asked for. Many responses were similar to the consumer believing the salesman or woman didn't really want their business. If they're expecting it, you shouldn't feel uncomfortable doing it. This fallacy is typically made because of a lack of training. That's where you come in. Train your team to provide what they asked for.

So I ask you, "Are you in the entertainment business? Or are you in sales?" Always ask for the close. Like my example earlier, assumptive closes may sound like these examples:

"So, since we both agree this is the best solution for you, let's go ahead and get this rung up so you can get started."

"Now that we know exactly what to do and how to do it, let's get it done."

"I don't know about you, but the anticipation is killing me. I'm ready to get you started on achieving your goal(s). Let's get everything ready to go."

The Complete Assessment: Putting It All Together

Here is an example of a full assessment using what was previously referenced:

Customer/Client Assessment (Questions from examples)

Customer/Client Name:	Date:
Appt: ☐ Walk-In: ☐	Reason for visit:

Discover	Uncover
Where do you live?	What type of security do you use on your computer?
How long have you lived here?	What router do you have and why?
Where do you work?	During what times do you use your computer most?
Do you live with family or friends?	How many people access the computer?
Define	**Recommend**
What are the top 3 goals? Why?	(This is a note box. Team members are making notes here while uncovering issues throughout their interaction. This is where they would put down recommended products or services during their interaction to help remember and reference after all goals are defined)
1)	
2)	Best Practice: Have team members put a check next to the products/services that were accepted. This can help with follow up sales for the products/services that did not sale that
3)	day.

Great job! You've learned the basics in constructing your own assessment. By now, you have a firm idea on what questions to ask in the discovery and uncovering sections. You also have a great understanding behind the importance of completing a mid-session review. That is a *huge* piece. Then during the Recommend stage, you've learned some techniques on how to provide great presentations and using impactful strategies like bundles, top-down, and bottom-up to make a more valuable connection with your consumers and their solutions. Don't forget, a reminder of the importance behind asking for the sale, utilizing the assumptive strategy to gain confidence in yourself and for your consumers choosing your solution(s).

You're now ready to lead by example and train your team to make incredible experiences for your customers and clients. However, this success only lasts for the moment. The true power behind this is creating these moments consistently with a solid follow-up, or should I say, follow-through strategy. The term *follow-up* is a thing of the past. These days, follow up means to check in, say hi, make sure all is well, then move on. That's not how to build a business. What your team needs is a strong follow-through strategy. Not all industries in sales will require following through after an interaction or any phone calls to generate business, but this is still important for you to learn. I once had my supervisor at a restaurant chain call the neighbors to offer specials to increase awareness, and it worked beautifully. So you never know when this may come in handy. This could be the very thing that sets you apart from the competition.

Do you have to complete an assessment every time? The answer is of course not—and yes. Lost you? I'll explain. You certainly want to do this with every customer and client you haven't already completed one for. Once you have one in place, then the next time, all that's necessary is just updating any changes. After all, situations do change, sometimes daily. You never know what has changed since your last interaction unless you ask. Back to our discussion about a strong first and only impression, using the assessment allows all team members to provide a predictable experience and a strong first impression. All interactions after that won't have to be the same because you've established trust, a relationship. This tool serves as a great reminder when you have multiple customers and clients visiting every day. So be sure to keep them in alphabetical order to reference later. When that customer or client returns, refer back to your assessment, hold a general conversation, and update anything that may be necessary to update. This includes referencing your list of recommendations that may have not been selected before, but could still apply.

I can't tell you how many compliments I've received from my clients I've had for years when I return to complete my assessment after I created one. They all understood and complied with answering my questions. About 75 percent of it, I was able to fill myself, but a necessary behavior to have with everyone. All your customers will witness it as a first experience, which is much more impactful. When my customers understood what I was doing and why prior to engaging, I've never had one say no. As a matter of fact, many customers who said they only had five minutes to spare ended up spending thirty minutes to an hour with me because they understood the importance and really enjoyed the experience of building a relationship with my team and me. This is the magic you're creating.

The Era of the Follow-Through

Following up is service oriented. Unless you intend to call someone just to chat about their experience, the age of the follow-up has changed. Actually, it evolved. We're in the age of the follow-through. Follow-through speaks of the actions taken after an interaction to close additional business—in other words, actually fulfilling behaviors that yield consistent business. This is the key to turning customers into clients. This is a salesman or woman's loyalty program. But instead of buying their loyalty with some form of monetary value, you provide them with knowledge, expert advice, and of course, *you*.

It is a common practice still used by top producers to call consumers at intervals such as a week after the sale, a month after the sale, six months after, and one year after. For some that want to track anniversaries, they would just simply add one call on the anniversary date after that. If you follow through, this is still a very impactful and necessary behavior. However, don't fall into the same fallacy that underperformers do: not asking for additional business, in other words, referrals. Although it is a nice gesture and just plain courteous to follow up to see how your consumer is doing with the recent sale, you must follow through to achieve additional sales, either from the same consumer or a referral to someone they know. After all, your team is in sales, right? Besides, catching a customer in a short time frame from an unforgettable experience encourages more participation. The longer you wait before the first contact, the greater the chances that they'll forget you exist. Don't be offended. It's nothing personal. It's just nature. I can't tell you how many times I've seen real estate or insurance professionals discover a friend or someone they know choose to go with another agent. It's because at the time they were deciding what to do, there wasn't any reinforcement from the agent to help aid their memory of you. You have to have a strong follow-through.

If you or your team don't have a follow-through system in place, please start with the sequence of calls I've described previously. As always, you may alter as you see fit. It will need to be customized to your specific industry, although don't stop at just adding calls to your priority list. Just calling to check in is a follow-up. A follow-through has to be strategic. Be sure to have a script and your assessment prepared. The script is for you to stay focused on your objective and remain consistent with each call. The assessment assists in leading your conversation. Your assessment will have important information under the Discovery section that you should use. As a recap, it should contain information such as family, friends, where they live, etc.—very important information that you'd want to revisit to reestablish a strong connection, or reconnection, to your consumer. Not only does it make their experience more personable, but it also reinforces their trust in you and your advice. As we talked about in previous pillars, we're building relationships here. That has always been the secret to great success in sales. Always have these two prepared for your follow-through calls.

The assessment will also assist your memory on what you sold to your consumer. As you and your team bring in more business, this will become extremely helpful. Do you remember my tip about keeping track of what sold and what didn't? This is where that information can come in handy. During your call, you'll have an opportunity to discuss the missed opportunities, if any. In addition, if there was a solution that you didn't think about until after your interaction, this is the perfect time to bring it up. Perhaps your customer left the conversation saying, "I'll think about it," or "I don't know." Again, it's the best time to follow through on that conversation.

I mentioned two ways to earn business here; following through on missed opportunities is one of them. As I said, if you just called to follow up on whether they are satisfied with their products or services, then business wouldn't move forward, and you and your team will waste a lot of time. Always reference missed opportunities. The second and most impactful way to increase business through your recent sales is asking for referrals. There is over a 90 percent chance that your competition is not doing this. That means just applying this behavior to ask for referrals will already provide a competitive advantage in your market. Be the difference by training your team(s) with these behaviors, and you'll make the difference between underperformance and top performance.

Over the Phone

Since we already touched on what follow-through calls should look like, this would be a great transition into one of the most impactful ways to increase your business: call times. Regardless of what business you're a part of or what industry you're in, you'll only be fooling yourself and selling your production short if you believe that call times cannot grow your business. If any part of your job requires managing sales of any sort, call times can and will grow your business. Of course, this activity is also one of the most feared, mainly because of inexperience. Inexperience leads to anxiety, which is a form of fear about rejection or confrontation. Call times are one of those activities that, once you practice enough times, will become second nature and your confidence rises along with your sales. If you've participated and still have a hard time making those calls, then that just means you haven't had enough practice. Time to pick up that phone! If you wish your team to follow the very principles you're teaching, then you have to be fluent and lead by example during call times.

Now, you didn't think I was going to let you figure it out on your own, did you? Throughout my years of sales, training, and team development, I've been able to create core behaviors to truly maximize your opportunities over the phone. So don't worry. This guide is a great starting point for you to fight your fears and become successful over the phone. The first thing to understand is that unless you are a part of a phone sales department, your objective is not to sell over the phone. Your objective is to set an appointment to sell face to face. If you are leading a phone sales team, then your objective is obviously to sell, but these behaviors will still support your business.

Each call time should only need to last one hour and ten minutes. I've discovered during multiple experiments that production and willingness begin to drop significantly after an hour and ten minutes. The first ten minutes are used for preparation, so the following hour is strictly left for smiling and dialing. During call times, I expect all team members to have the following prepared: their scripts, a predetermined amount of scrubbed leads, and their goals to reach by the end of their call time. In the next few sections, I'll guide you through how to be successful using scripts, learning the difference between scrubbed and non-scrubbed leads, the power behind smile and dial, and the best times to make your calls. So let's get started.

Scripting: Friend or Foe

You should know by now that scripts are our friend. If not, then either you don't have experience using them, or you have had a bad experience due to improper training. Regardless, there is a reason why all the most profitable, top sales and investment companies utilize scripts in both sales and customer service. They're extremely effective and consistent. It is the most powerful tool any salesman or woman can have for over-the-phone interactions, and yet it is still highly underrated and underused overall, across the business platform. Whenever I train a team on scripting, I always start with the why, then I put it in the form of a benefits-versus-detriments chart. I typically draw a table on the board, with two columns. On the left side, on the title row, I will write "Benefits." On the right, I will write "Detriments." Then I would allow the team members to write out benefits and detriments to compare under their respective categories. The discussion comes afterward. I am all about self-discovery, if you haven't noticed. So of course, I would recommend this exact same approach if scripting is something new to your team or team member. Since this book is the portal I use to share this example, I will just provide the chart. Just as I have said multiple times, your team's understanding of the why is very important. Otherwise, this part of the training becomes a writing class, and I know those two words didn't just make *you* jump out of your seat with excitement. Let's take a look at a brief list of the benefits versus detriments of using scripts for call times.

Benefits	Detriments
• Efficient	•
• Consistent	
• Predictable	
• Accurate	
• Flexible	
• Adaptable	
• Goal oriented	
• Focus driven	
• Increased production	

Notice that I left the detriments column empty. I left it for you to illustrate my point further. I personally believe there are zero detriments. However, that is only my perspective. Just as I trained my team members, I would like you to come up with some of your own to compare. If you can come up with detriments that completely counteract all the benefits *and* would negatively impact your production, then scripting is not for you and your business. However, I believe you will come up with your results in one of three ways.

You won't think of any. It will take too long to come up with more than a couple (meaning not enough).

Or you will make some up that can easily be adjusted or corrected by altering your script. Either way, you will come to the realization that you will have nothing to lose, but much to gain. If this is the case, then why not do it?

Or if you have already begun, why not perfect it? If you did come up with more detriments than benefits, then I believe you're trying to avoid this practice (wink). Embrace this tool. It's a huge part of your growth and your success.

If you take another look at the list of benefits, what would you think is the most impactful one? It's not a trick question. There is a reason efficiency leads the list. That's right; efficiency is the most impactful benefit. Believe it or not, increased production is last. Now, it doesn't mean increased production isn't important. That's what keeps the doors open and the business thriving after all, right? However, you can't be a result-oriented person to become a consistent Alpha performer. You have to focus on behaviors. If your behaviors are consistent along with the appropriate strategies, your results will be just as consistent. It's also less stressful in the long run. So efficiency is the most important benefit. During call times, time is of the essence, as we'll discuss a little later. This tool is how your time is maximized to its full productive capability.

Unless it was necessary through a job description or special event, I always had my team members avoid sales over the phone. The reason relates back to body language. Over the phone only leaves room for tone and words. That cuts out over 60 percent of what needs to be communicated, which makes sales very difficult. Not to mention, time is the biggest factor. Your team will only have a set period to hit their appointment goal, and those experienced know that it only takes one person to get off topic and talk for over an hour. So my team members' primary objective was to get their consumers through the door to learn their story. Again, the goal is to set appointments during call times.

There are two scripts that I have my team members create: one for all voicemails and one for appointment setting. Of course, depending on your industry and job requirements, you can have three, four, or even more different scripts for all to use. Just be careful about having too much for team members. Turning all your conversations into scripts can come off robotic. It's inevitable. As humans, we were not wired to read off our conversations, so keep it minimal. Not to mention, some team members will find this practice more difficult than others. I create two scripts to keep it simple. My motto, right?

Scripting Voicemails

There are a few rules to follow when having your team compose their voicemail script. As a matter of fact, this is a script that I keep each team member consistent by following a single script. This should be a very simple, straight-to-the-point message with your name, your company, and your contact information, spoken with sincerity and enthusiasm. However, before we see what that sounds like, let's review what it should *not* sound like.

Rule #1: Unless it *is* an emergency, *don't* make it sound like one.

"Mr. Smith. This is Jeff with XYZ. Please give me a call as soon as you can at 123-456-7890. Again, it's 123-456-7890. It's very important that I speak with you. Thank you."

As a consumer yourself, I'm sure you understand the frustration behind receiving a voicemail asking you to call back as soon as possible just to rush to a pitch about a sale. Like the boy who cries wolf, when an actual emergency call is necessary, you may get ignored. Not to mention, leaving these voicemails can also impact future team members trying to reach out. Always think about the team.

Rule #2: Don't leave a message without leaving your contact info.

"Mrs. Smith. This is Melissa, assistant manager with XYZ. You can call me when you are ready to set an appointment. Thank you."

I don't know about you, but thank goodness for caller IDs on cell phones. It is a big pet peeve of mine when a voicemail is left and a number is either not provided or it is only referenced once. It always requires me to either call the number that dialed (which isn't always the number they want you to call back) or listen to the voicemail all over again to write the number down accurately. In my opinion, this is why voicemail apps now allow you to transcribe your voicemails. However, not even those are 100 percent. In fact, what they transcribe is quite comical (mostly way off from what was actually said). Always leave your contact information, and a best practice would be to repeat your information more than once as a courtesy and to increase the chances of your consumer to call back the right number or in a reasonable time. Think of it this way: you're helping them buy time to find a pen or remember your number. Trust me, they will definitely appreciate it.

Rule #3: Keep your message within five simple sentences.

"Mr. Smith. Jessie here. I just wanted to thank you for all the time spent with me Thursday. I also wanted to check in and see how your services are working out for you. I remembered that you wanted to discuss installation further, so that is why I'm calling you today. You can reach me anytime between nine and five tomorrow and nine and two Wednesday at 123-456-7890. Again, that's 123-456-7890. If I'm unavailable, I apologize. Just leave a message and I'll return your call as soon as I am able. Thank you, again, fo— (*beep*)."

Have you ever hung up in the middle of a voicemail because you either didn't know if it will ever end or didn't have time to hear the whole message? Don't be that person leaving those messages. Keep it short and sweet. If you keep your message within five sentences, you'll have a greater chance of a call back. Too much detail can detract from the importance of returning your call. Beating around the bush can also create the same effect. Keeping it short and sweet will make a greater impact and increase your callbacks.

Regardless of the reason you're calling (checking in, asking for referrals, recommending a product or service, etc.), your objective is to set the appointment. Therefore, at all times, avoid leaving the reason for your call in your voicemail script unless it's an emergency. Although you feel that what you have to say is very important, remember that your customer or client has a thousand things going on at the time they hear your message. They will not provide 100 percent of their attention. If your voicemail is misinterpreted, difficult to remember, or very detailed, your message may not carry the same importance as your message if they answered. That is why you want your team to keep it short and sweet, following the three rules. The only exception to this rule is if you share a close relationship with a client.

"Hey, Mrs. Smith. This is [your name and title] with [company name]. When you have a moment, you may reach me at 123-456-7890. Again, that is 123-456-7890. Thank you and I look forward to hearing from you."

Simple *and* effective!

Scripting Conversations

As difficult as it sounds, it truly isn't. It's about aligning the conversation with your objective. Set the appointment. As we mentioned before, the point behind creating a script is to save time and increase productivity. Repetition, repetition. Of course, each conversation will have different responses; about 90 percent of each conversation will follow your script. To help with how to keep your consumer on track to setting an appointment, the following is a four-point foundation for what your script should contain:

Introduction—Unless you established a comfortable relationship, share your name, title, and company.

Breaker—Like the icebreaker, this is just how you set the tone to your call. Always start the conversation with asking how the consumer is doing. It does help to ask if it is a good time to speak with them. This is a courtesy move that can possibly set up a good callback time where you will have the consumer's undivided attention. The more they focus on you, the greater your chances of success. If this is a follow-through call, always reference the family, such as "How is Susan?" and "Are the kids home yet?" If you are making calls to consumers you have recently sold to, you will want to follow up on their experience with the sold products or services after the icebreaker.

Objective—State the reason for your call. If your objective is to set an appointment, be upfront and say that is why you are calling.

Conclusion—Always thank your consumers for their time over the phone whether they did or did not set an appointment with you. Like the thought of burning bridges, you never know when they *will* say yes. Therefore, always treat them as if they'll always say yes. This is also where you will repeat the time scheduled if the appointment was set for confirmation.

That's it. Not difficult, is it? Those four points will help guide you and your team through each script, regardless of why you're calling. In this perspective, setting appointments. Here are a few tips to help your odds of success. Following are a couple of examples of personal scripts my teams and I utilized from different positions to provide perspective and a foundation on what these scripts look like.

TIP: Always have your team use their natural voice. Believe it or not, the natural reaction to speaking with strangers over the phone is to lighten your voice. Why is that? It's because when we like someone or meet new people, we naturally change our voices to make it seem pleasant to the other. Over the phone with a stranger, we naturally change our voices in hopes they will like us. Unfortunately, that natural reaction is trying too hard, and you make yourself unknowingly uncomfortable. Many consumers take notice and often misinterpret it as deceit. Keep your ear out for their tone during call times. Their natural voice is the best choice!

BEST PRACTICE: Use the assumptive strategy here as well. Just as you are confident that the product or service recommended is the best solution, make sure your team is also confident that setting an appointment is just as important. Besides, how else are they going to hear about those recommended solutions? When stating your objective, state it as if you know the answer is a yes. In the following example, you'll notice that we did not ask if they would like to set the appointment. It's assumed that answer will be yes and, therefore, going straight to asking when.

Assumptive strategy—"I was calling to see when is a good time for you to come in and speak with me about your account. I have Tuesday available between ten and noon. Would a time between then work for you?"

TIP: Stick to the script. It's all about consistency. It's easy to get pulled away from your script, but the second you do, you'll lose much necessary time to achieve your call time goal. Focusing on your script will help your team guide the conversation and maximize efficiency per conversation. It also serves as a means to help bring the conversation back on track. As mentioned before, the point of the script is to maximize the time you have to achieve the goal you need in appointments.

Here are a couple of real scripts used with previous teams:

"Good morning, Mr. Smith. This is Jamie, your account manager at ABC Bank. How are you doing today? Great. Is this a good time to catch you? Okay, well, I certainly respect your time. What is the best time I can reach you? You got it. I'll call back _____ at _____. Thank you for your time and I hope you have a great day. Goodbye."

Or

"Good morning, Mr. Smith. This is Jamie, your relationship manager at ABC Bank. How are you doing today? Great. Is this a good time to catch you? Perfect! Thank you for taking my call. I noticed that we haven't had the opportunity to meet yet and as your relationship manager, I strongly recommend that we connect to review your financial relationship. It's important to hold regular reviews throughout the year about your financial position because our business and industry evolve just as your needs do, not to mention assisting you in staying ahead of fraud and identity theft. I was seeing if you will be available Tuesday or Wednesday to meet? Okay, great. [If no, follow up with 'Okay, what would be a better day for us to meet?'] Do you prefer morning or afternoon? [Fill the 10:00 a.m. or 2:00 p.m. slots first if available.] That's perfect, Mr. Smith. I look forward to meeting with you on _____ at _____. If you don't mind, I'll call the day before to confirm to make sure that is still a good time for you. Have a great day!"

"Good afternoon, Mrs. Smith. This is John, your assistant manager at ABC Store. How are you this afternoon? That's great to hear. I hope I'm catching you at a good time. Okay. When would it be a more convenient time for you? Sure thing. Looking forward to catching up with you _____ at _____. Have a great day."

Or

"Good afternoon, Mrs. Smith. This is John, your assistant manager at ABC Store. How are you this afternoon? That's great to hear. I hope I'm catching you at a good time. Good. Thank you for your time. In our line of business, our products and services constantly evolve just as your needs and wants do. I wanted to personally invite you here so I can learn more about you and get a better opportunity to learn more about your priorities. I currently have Tuesday and Wednesday available. Which would work best for you? That's great. [If no, follow up with 'Okay, what would be a better day for us to meet?'] Are you more of a morning person? Or an afternoon kind of person? Nice. Then let's get you in on _____ at _____. I'll be personally meeting you along with one of my best sales associates, Ryan. Looking forward to meeting you. For your convenience, I'll call to remind you of our appointment the day before. Does that sound good? Great. Thank you again, Mrs. Smith. Have a wonderful day."

These are just examples of previous scripts that were used with two of my team members, both Alpha performers in their respective roles. Both moved on to leadership positions. You can see their differences, but take a closer look. Can you see how they're alike? They both had the four-point foundation: introduction, breaker, objective, and conclusion. The TIPS were also followed to make a strong script. These are just examples, but as always, you and your team have the freedom to make them yours. I encourage it. Just make sure you cover the four points and follow the three rules, and you'll have a strong foundation to build off. As you and your team are able to practice, you can alter what works and what doesn't work in order to perfect your craft. That's how you maximize your opportunity over the phone. However, to truly maximize your time, preparation is extremely important. The first step to preparing for a successful call time is scrubbing your leads.

Scrubbed vs. Non-scrubbed Leads

As a training guide, it's important to emphasize the basics for all levels of experience. So before I go any further, what does a scrubbed lead really mean? Some say getting phone numbers prepared; others say validating contact information, etc. Although they are both sort of correct, it's really the full picture that makes the impact. Scrubbing is like profiling or researching a lead. If you were given a list of names and numbers, then you would simply have a lead list. Non-scrubbed leads are just that, a list. The problem with a list is that there is no clue to what is needed or wanted, or even if the information is up to date. If you jump into a call time with a list like this, you'll have scattered results. In addition, it will take up a lot of time. I would never allow my team members to call what I called yellow-page lists unless all other options were exhausted (which they never had to). If you're in a big *Fortune* 500 company, I'm sure your company pays for lead generators somewhere. If not, you or your team can certainly make your own.

Back to a scrubbed lead, which is simply researching a list of leads to make sure they best fit the reason for your call and you have the most current contact information, if possible. For example, if I had a list of customers or clients that had anywhere from one hundred dollars to one million dollars in household income and were placed in alphabetical order, but the reason I was calling was to set appointments for a product that is priced over $100,000, would it make sense to call in alphabetical order? Of course not. Out of the first one hundred people, maybe only ten have the assets available to make the purchase. That means I would literally spend 90 percent of my time with those who wouldn't even qualify for my product. You or your team would ultimately set up yourselves and your consumers for failure. Bad experiences equal lost opportunity costs, bad branding, and loss of market share. Instead, during scheduled downtime, your team member will take that list and review each person's relationship to qualify them as the right candidate and, if possible, review their most recent contact information to make sure you don't hit a brick wall. Incorrect contact information is another leading factor in lost time during call hours. This doesn't mean you toss out leads that aren't qualified. Keep every lead as they may be qualified for other opportunities as your business progresses or focuses change.

While preparing to research your lead list, you want to either make a separate list using a notepad, use a spreadsheet, simply print out of the list so you can edit with a pencil. You're simply going to make a sub-list of qualified leads. Every time you verify a consumer's contact number or email and their qualification, you will add them to your list or place a mark to identify whom to call. Always aim for at least twenty-five qualified consumers. We'll get into more details as to why in the next section. After your twenty-five are compiled, you and your team members are ready to reach your appointment goal in your next call time. This activity typically takes an hour to complete. The more you and your team practice, the faster this activity will be completed. My Alpha performers would either have it completed in a thirty-minute time frame if scheduled or compile the list during their downtimes between customers and clients. This behavior develops quickly, so get started.

If you are with a company that does not generate leads for you, don't worry. Thousands of companies don't because of the cost, but that doesn't mean you can't create a list without the costs. Companies pay for leads because they typically come partially or fully scrubbed for your specific product or service offered. That's expensive because some poor person is pouring out their time researching each person in the market. However, you can find leads everywhere. You can look online, the Yellow Pages, your local city sites, DPOR, etc. They are everywhere with the help of the Web. Although you may be limited on certain information because of a lack of certain systems to help, you can still cross-reference names down to zip codes. There are also many resources out there that provide more options to obtain those kinds of lists. The important practice here is *getting* one, and do what you can with what's available to scrub each lead and maximize your call times.

Smile and Dial

Have you ever heard the phrase "smile and dial" before? Ever wondered what is meant by it? I've heard some funny responses to those questions throughout the years. Some have said it means "Shut up and call," "Do your job," "Stay positive and pick up the phone." However, there is a strategy behind it. Surprise, surprise. Studying body language, you'll find out that the best way to brighten your mood is to force a smile. Sounds funny? It's true. If you're ever in a bad mood or just a blah kind of mood, try to force yourself to smile for a certain period. When you smile, you tighten all the muscles in your face, which pulls back the negative expression and literally lifts them up, turning negative into positive expressions. In turn, it sets off positive triggers in your brain, and your mood will essentially begin to feel better. Pretty cool science, right? That was the short way to explain it. Over the phone, people can tell from your tone of voice if you're smiling or not, if you're in a positive mood or a negative one. Smiling during calls is a technique to help lift your motivation and to brighten your tone during calls so you will sound more positive over the call, in turn, reinforcing a positive response from the recipient.

The other half of the magical phrase (dial) is the numbers. They don't lie. It's simple math, really. The more you call, the more you get on the phone. The more you get on the phone, the more appointments you can set. Period. However, if you're really strategic as I am and you are becoming, you can help your team achieve more with less. Work smart and not hard, right? Using scrubbed leads will increase your appointment setting effectively and dramatically. We got that. Now, we need as many scrubbed leads as possible. If you know that next week's focus for your company is a particular service or as a business owner, you want to focus on a particular sale, then you have the power to prepare a scrubbed list proactively for your call times that week. Use that knowledge and line them up. The list you've created is a list of money. If you don't see that, you certainly will soon.

The magic number that has made my team members successful during call times in all industries is 25. So the simple equation is that you should at least start with twenty-five scrubbed leads per hour of call time. The results will vary, based on how effective your scrubbing is, the time in which you call, and why you're calling. Don't be alarmed if you discover that your team members zoom through those twenty-five in forty minutes. Or they only accomplish fifteen calls in the hour. It's about the results. If they at least hit their appointment goal, they're on a roll. If they're shy of their goal, adjust their next call time accordingly to make it realistically achievable. Smart, right?

REMEMBER: It's a numbers game. The objective is to get as many people on the phone as possible. The more scrubbed leads you have, the more you'll be capable of growing your business. I managed a team with a top company that held its lead in the industry simply because we had more business in the pipeline than any other. Never underestimate the power of a scrubbed lead, like our competition. Rack them up!

When my team members prepare to go into their call times, I always have them recite their dial goal, contact goal, and appointment goal to me. Is it a coincidence that I have them set three goals like this? Of course not. It's a strategy. The dial goal is to keep them focused on dialing. The contact goal keeps them focused on procuring scrubbed leads. The appointment goal is the ultimate result to measure their success. Makes sense? Although they have three goals, as leaders of the business, we naturally care most about the result goal of appointments.

However, remember behaviors plus activities equals results. Always encourage them to hit dial and contact goals, not just results. The results will come every time! So set three goals to keep them focused on the behaviors and activities as well as the results.

Recommended Times for Contacts

Finally, when should you call? First off, any call time is better than no call time. You need to get the practice, reinforce the behavior, and even setting one appointment is better than none. However, are there better times to call than others? Definitely. What are they? It depends on your business, or the target market you are trying to reach. Although this is by no means standard, these times that I'll reference below have been very similar across multiple industries I've led in. This is only sharing my research, but this is one heck of a place to start. If these times don't work for you, then trade off each day by an hour as I did. I literally started once at 8.a.m. Monday, 9 a.m. Tuesday, 10 a.m. Wednesday, and so forth until I found the best times that maximized contacts. I even went further to see which was the best way to contact them (home vs. work vs. cell vs. email) to have the greatest impact.

Unless permitted, I don't have my team members call work numbers. Keep in mind that this is the general public. You can't predict who are strongly reactive or nonresponsive. In addition, be familiar with the laws in your state. Some states have restrictions before and after certain times in their respective zones. Others either have none or completely forbid marketing calls. I call these curfews, or call curfews. Please be very familiar with your call curfews before scheduling your call times. This chart below can increase your chances of success during weekdays. Make your scripts, scrub your leads, nail the practice, hit your goals, and grow your business. Here is a chart to start with:

Residential Consumers	Best Response Times	Business Consumers	Best Time Periods
Home	12:00 p.m.–1:00 p.m. 6:00 p.m.–8:00 p.m.	Home	8:00 p.m.–9:00 p.m.
Cell	8:00–9:00 a.m. 11:30 a.m.–1:00 p.m. 6:00 p.m.–8:00 p.m.	Cell	6:00 a.m.–9:00 a.m. 11:00 a.m.–12:00 p.m. 6:00 p.m.–7:30 p.m.

REMEMBER: Always be aware of the Do Not Call Registry and always be aware of local laws around particular times of the day. Some states don't allow cold calls after or before particular times.

Partnerships

I saved partnerships for last because it's a big factor in growing your business. Partnerships are a crucial part of your business. Just as you want to diversify any investment portfolio or experience, you want to diversify how you acquire business. Just as they say don't put all your eggs in one basket, you want to be sure you have sales coming into your business through multiple streams for security and acceleration. I can't tell you how many times quotas, goals, and awards were achieved because of a referral from a partner. The same goes vice versa as the business I referred to my partners has saved their businesses. Just that, it's a partnership. A strong relationship between two or more business goal-oriented individuals who seek to assist in each other's growth. There are two kinds of partnerships to help grow your business: complementary and supplementary.

Complementary partnerships are partnerships between two or more individuals that sell complementary products. For example, if I led a team of real estate agents, then partners they would have could include title companies, attorneys, contractors, lenders, etc. They have products that complement their clients' needs that help reach their goal: selling a home. In return, they have clients they need to fulfill their goals because they need a loan, a closing agent, possible contractors for repairs or renovations, and so forth. They can also refer clients to the agents. If I led a team in the traveling or vacation business, then partners could include hotel managers, convenience store managers, timeshare salespeople, etc. They all can provide complementary products to their clients while on vacation *and* these partners can refer business back. In turn, my team can recommend their partner services during their purchased vacations with discounts, coupons, and specials for motivation.

However, partnerships don't just stop at trading or sharing business between each other. You also need to make sure you keep a strong competitive advantage, which is your process. That is the power of having supplementary partnerships. Supplementary partnerships are formed to enhance your process. For example, if I led a team of bankers, my team would have a go-to partner or two behind system operations, particular loan officers or underwriters, department managers, etc. These are partners that can help a banker push approval on a loan product, help solve an unknown issue with accounts in a faster time frame, get approvals or answers required to solve an unknown issue. They enhance the team member's solution by supporting the process, not adding products. If I led a team in a retail store, my team could have partners from corporate, district staff members, warehouse managers, etc. These partners could help track down missing products, provide key directions in solving issues, or provide overrides that may be necessary to take care of a rare situation to satisfy a customer issue—all supporting roles to accommodate the process and take care of the consumer.

TIP: Work outside the box. I had partnerships with managers from competing stores and partnerships with managers from competing companies. For example, while I led teams at some of the biggest, most profitable banks, I had partnerships with managers from nonprofit banks like credit unions because they had particular products we did not provide. However, I knew it would work to take care of my client. Guess what? They had similar situations.

We referred each other business, and we were *competitors*. That's the magic of growing your business through partnerships.

It's all about the relationships, not just on the consumer side, but also within your organization. Partnerships expand your tree of business. That makes it a necessity to have both complementary and supplementary to grow your business. Building this kind of trust within your company and outside your company is what develops confidence in your abilities and how you provide your solutions to your consumers. As we discussed before, confidence is a key ingredient to become an Alpha performer. With a powerful team supporting you and your team, you'll become unstoppable. In addition, as I mentioned earlier, both partnerships refer business right back to you. Win-win.

REAL LIFE

Here is an example of a partnership you don't want to have or a partner you don't want to be. I had the honor to work with an incredible and well diverse team that adapted quickly, competed valiantly, and knew how to have fun every day they started their shift. A strong mix of Alpha and Bravo performers who made our team one of the best in Region. We had team members who were among the top fifteen, with one ranked as high as fourth in the region. This team dominated in every metric but one. This was no surprise as there was history to that particular challenge, but present nonetheless.

One day, the regional manager of this challenged department (we'll call him Ronnie) visited to hold a meeting with my manager, myself, and his team member. The day Ronnie showed up was a surprise to me as I wasn't aware of his arrival and neither was his team member (we'll call her Kobee). We met in my office with the two of us on each side as if Kobee and I were in a lawsuit and being represented by our managers acting as attorneys.

Ronnie began to ask questions to uncover how we were a top-performing team, but in his particular metric, were one of the lowest. I told him one word: *trust.* To sum up the history, Kobee and my leading team members did not share a good relationship because of decisions Kobee made that made my team members uncomfortable with her partnership. Questions about ethics, behavior with minorities, and her desire to close business. Regardless of misunderstandings or misrepresentations, my team downright didn't trust her with their clients or to close the business. If she was the only person left to offer the solution, they would have to sit in the appointment to make sure the conversation was fulfilled. There were previous occasions when clients walked out within minutes because Kobee disqualified them when they *were* qualified for the products she offered. Once, I recall my team member chasing her client down in the parking lot to turn them around, go back into the room, and assist the close because Kobee didn't look over the client's profile to see that they did qualify. I myself had also experienced this unfortunate scenario too many times. In addition, my team members, one in particular, had tried countless times to build a relationship with Kobee, but she avoided such meetings. Relationships could not be established.

Ronnie, Kobee, and I discussed back and forth from how the situation started to how we could resolve it. Ronnie insisted that our team members lacked the confidence and ability to bring the business to his team member. After showing him a matrix of our successes and that my team dominated every category across the board except his, I kindly replied, "It's the failed partnership. If your team member builds a relationship with my team members, they will have a solid foundation of trust to refer business, therefore a solid and healthy partnership, which will vastly bring more business. The issues lie with the lack of relationship between the parties, not either of their abilities to close the sale. My team members, including myself, don't trust Kobee to take care of our clients." That was when I heard one of the most ridiculous comments I've ever heard in business: "You don't need to build a relationship to have a partnership." To me, that sounded like a desperate attempt to cover the obvious issue at hand. By this point, Kobee walked out of the room because Kobee believed it was my team members' fault.

My manager remained by my side, like a mediator, shaking his head because he didn't understand the statement Ronnie made as well. I asked Ronnie what was his secret in growing a business with partners he couldn't trust. The only response that was given was that we should just do business together. Give Kobee business and end the day. At the end of our discussion, we all agreed to reset, shook hands, and said, "Let's make some money" as D-personality leaders would do. However, I would never forget that unfortunate comment, mainly because Ronnie's team could be accomplishing so much more if he really encouraged building such trust between partners.

Months later, I found out Ronnie was demoted, Kobee lost a lot of business, and my team members were promoted into management positions. I was told Ronnie's lack of understanding of the power behind relationships was a contributing factor. A strong partnership needs a trustworthy relationship. If you're just learning this, embrace it and start building your partnerships by building relationships. Don't be like Ronnie or Kobee.

Partnerships are a necessity for your business to thrive beyond its required reach and a secret step in achieving top performance. Be sure to get involved with your partners' lives. Try to hold regular meetings to discuss each other's goals and target markets, and do not forget to ask how you can help impact their business. The fastest way to build a strong relationship is through communication. It's difficult for someone to help someone else who doesn't communicate how. Think about that. Do you know your partner's goal right now? Do you have a plan on how to help them hit their goal? You should. The door always goes both ways, but take the first step. Improving their business will come back to improve yours. Behaviors plus activities equals results. It won't hurt to learn about them over lunch.

Lead from the Front

Although we've concluded the sales section of pillar IV, there is still one more very strong point that has to be made. A strong ingredient that, if missing, can throw out everything. However, if noticed, it will amplify your team's performance and passion faster: leading from the front. I'm sure we can all agree that the strongest leaders lead from the front. If you're unfamiliar with this saying, it means "lead by example." I'm sure from your own experience, you know that it's difficult to follow the advice of someone who doesn't follow their own, right? The same will go for your team if you are not committed to the same behaviors you will hold them accountable to. The simplest way I've explained it to my management teams is that you should act how you want your team members to reflect. If you want them to reflect the behaviors of an Alpha performer, then you need to reflect those exact behaviors. Now, does it mean that you have to be the top salesman or woman on the team? Absolutely not. As a matter of fact, I discourage it on the leadership level. You get into leadership by being a top performer. Now you need to develop top performers. At this level, when you're leading from the front in sales, you have to have a purpose for development, not to boost your ego or feel number one, but to demonstrate the Alpha behaviors in real time to show your team members how to become Alpha performers themselves. At this level, it's about the team. Be strategic as your time is priceless, as we covered in pillar II.

Although reflecting behaviors is a huge piece of it, it doesn't just stop there. You can also lead from the front by being the first to embrace change, the first to accept a challenge, the first to encourage others that a goal is possible, the first to motivate others to believe in themselves, and sometimes, the first to prove other team members wrong (in an encouraging way). Here are some fun examples of how I have led from the front to illustrate further how you can too.

REAL LIFE

Once, when I was a branch manager, I had a teller working the drive-through. She had the biggest challenge speaking to clients and recommending a visit with a banker to uncover opportunities. She was intimidated using a camera as opposed to face-to-face interactions in the branch. She said that it was too difficult and didn't believe it was possible for her to hit her goal. As a branch manager with zero experience in the teller role, I stepped up and asked, "If I can make two appointments, would that encourage you to beat me? Because I think you're better than me, and yet I know I can set two appointments through the drive-through." Challenge accepted. I took the next eight clients and got two appointments set. Motivated to beat me, she ended up becoming the strongest drive-through teller we ever had. I knew she could do it. I just helped her see it in herself.

I took over as a supervisor of a team that had challenges reaching their service goals. So much of a challenge, there were team members on the same team that doubted their team's ability. One most of all stood out continuing to be negative, referencing how unrealistic goals were and how difficult it was to sell particular services. I knew I wouldn't be able to establish trust through words, so I decided to put actions to the test. I asked him to choose one service and I bet that just I and one other team member would be able to sell a week's goal in one day. With a hard laugh of doubt, the team member (let's call him Jerry) chose what seemed to be one of the most difficult services to sell, based on their history. When I asked for a volunteer to join me, one named Jon stood up to join. After a few minutes of sharing my sales strategy with the volunteer, we went out with only eight hours to work with. Six hours later, we sold ten services (five each) with a weekly goal of six. There were five members working that day. Shocked, Jerry asked how we did that. My simple reply was "Teamwork." Encouraged to learn, he became a top three Alpha performer.

When I was a technician at an auto shop, my shop manager, shop supervisor, and the veteran mechanics were having a difficult time trying to increase business. They had recently launched a campaign to encourage minor vehicle repairs and services to help increase long-term business. However, the campaign was coming up short. It seemed that customers didn't really come back a second time. Respectfully, as I was overhearing their conversation, I interrupted to let them know that I believed it was because our service line was taking too long, completely nervous as they stared me down. They eventually asked questions to help determine why I thought that was a challenge. I explained that I happened to notice that standard services like oil changes usually took about twenty minutes at that time. We were just like everyone else, but one company promised fifteen minutes. I suggested we could promise a faster time. Amused, the shop supervisor said if I could do a change under six minutes (with no idea where that time came from), then they might consider it. I was a little taken back from the time frame given, but I accepted. A car rolled in, and off to the races. I completed it under four minutes. Although they decided that four minutes was too much at risk, they agreed to guarantee eight minutes or less if I trained the other technicians on how. We had our most successful year.

I had a team of managers that shared their successes and challenges during a monthly meeting. One particular manager would always share a challenge that all their clients already had everything they needed and that they couldn't expand any more business. Taken back, our district manager pushed back with some objection as to why but was countered with similar excuses. One week, the manager called out sick, and the district manager reached out to ask if I could cover their store. During my visit, I noticed that the team members were inconsistent with their interactions. When asked why, they all replied differently, but all very similar to their manager's excuses in the meeting, all related to the point that all the clients were satisfied with their services. So I began to use my system. The first three clients I completed an assessment with ended up purchasing new products and services. Two of the clients were long-term clients; that surprised the other team members. When I asked the team members if they wished to know how it was possible, they jumped straight on the opportunity to learn. That week, I helped them become consistent with a system and complete their assessments with every client. That was their most productive week in over four months. The last time was during their busiest season. All they needed was direction and a consistent process. The manager came back to a team that outperformed them. Luckily, with the manager impressed, they asked to learn too.

These are just some examples of how I led from the front as a team member all the way up the ladder. Regardless of your position, when you have an opportunity to improve yourself, your team, your peers, or your business, then be the first to make the difference. As you saw in these scenarios, people tend to follow those who are confident in making the change. Becoming the first doesn't mean you *have* to be successful. It means you don't have to be afraid to fail. At the end of the day, people don't follow titles. They follow courage, remember?

In pillar I, you were able to learn how to read the performance levels of team members in order to analyze your training structure using my Mason influential leadership model. You learned how to bend time to your advantage and maximize your priorities in pillar II. Then in pillar III, you truly understood how to harness the positive powers of accountability. Now you have an arsenal of tools, resources, and strategies to strengthen your teams' ability to build relationships through assessments, develop partnerships, discover the best solutions available, and close the sale over the phone and in person. The only thing left is how to train them. In pillar V, it's time for you to learn just how—time to develop an Alpha-performing team.

PILLAR V

Building A Culture
(Flipping Your Team)

If you don't take action, you won't make a difference.

TEAM DEVELOPMENT HAS always been a crucial part of constructing a team, sure, but we're not just constructing a team. We're building a top-performing team. In order to do so, we don't just need to develop a team; we have to build a culture. My favorite definition of culture was collected from a dictionary web search some time ago that said culture was "the arts and other manifestations of human intellectual achievement regarded collectively." Now, *that* is a powerful definition because that is exactly what you have to create. Like America's Manifest Destiny in the nineteenth century, you are collectively utilizing the achieving behaviors of all your team members to grow your business beyond its limits, to reach a reality those before you haven't seen yet, or for quite some time.

Think of the companies that didn't just develop a strong business but created cultures that many other companies have adopted. How many times have you heard an associate somewhere say, "My pleasure," and you immediately thought of Chick-Fil-A? For me, it's every time. I know I can confidently credit that now-popular response to Chick-Fil-A's culture, for bringing such courtesy to multiple industries as a whole. How many times have you asked someone where they would like to meet (or they asked you) and the response was Starbucks? Starbucks redefined the modern look and experience on cafés and created an environment that individuals would go to use their facility like a library with professional and courteous services available to serve your favorite Grande. What do you use to search the web? There is at least a 65 percent chance you use Google. Google is still one of the highest rated companies to work for with one of their top respected categories ranked being the most fun place to work. If you haven't seen the movie *Internship*, with Vince Vaughn and Owen Wilson, you should. They do a great job depicting the life of an intern or employee on the creatively diverse grounds of this tech giant. Google found out that in order to generate the best ideas in the tech industry, they have to allow their members to relax and be themselves. They have sleep pods, free food/beverages, and slides for faster transportation from the second floor, for crying out loud. That's a culture!

Now does this mean you need to install a slide in the lobby to create happiness? Or provide free Wi-Fi to generate traffic? Not at all. However, you have all the knowledge and power to create your own culture of achievement. Whether it's at seminars or face to face, leaders have always asked me for one or two good practices to help make their team top performers, and it is always a tough answer to give. That's because the unrealized truth is that building a top-performing team is like building an engine. There are a lot of moving parts. However, if you fine-tune each part and get them aligned to work together, they will take you anywhere. What do Chick-Fil-A, Starbucks, Google, and many other successful companies have in common? They all had and currently have great leaders like you that were able to build their engine to outrun the competition, using the greatest power source: culture. This section is going to help you develop just that. This section will help you with the principal foundations of building a culture. If you follow the guidance of this pillar and use your imagination on implementation, you will create a very successful culture and, with that, a top-performing team.

Branding

Team Differentiator

In China, during the late Han Dynasty around the year 185 AD, there was a pirate warrior named Gan Ning, who took a group of local crooks to become one of the most infamously feared pirates wearing bells on their belts to warn their enemies in a battle that their doom was approaching. This tactic was used in many of their ambushes to strike fear in their enemy regardless of the army size. When Gan Ning was offered to become a general, eventually serving under the Wu army, he continued to wear his bells to continue his legacy with spread rumors of his ferocity in battle. During a battle, men were known to flee the battlefield at the sound of his bells. In addition, those bells boosted the morale of his soldiers. Although he was a formidable warrior, the bells he wore made him a terror to his enemies and a battle cry to rally the courage of his allies. Even in the second and third centuries, people understood the power of branding. Gan Ning understood the power of differentiating himself from others. This distinct tactic clearly isn't new, but it's amazingly still effective and impactful today.

Now don't go out and buy bells to wear around your belt in an attempt to scare the competition and rally your team, but definitely learn from the concept. When you take over a new team, everyone's perspective has absolutely nothing differentiating your leadership from that team's previous leadership, nothing from the previous managers. You want to reset your team's reputation, and rightfully so because they didn't have your leadership before. It's crucial to set your leadership apart as soon as possible. If you don't, either you'll fail at creating a powerful culture or you'll make your attempt twice as hard to accomplish. What you'll need to get started is a rallying point.

A rally point is your center of inspiration. It provides encouragement to reach your goals, reinforcing your purpose to be what you are, a beacon of hope that when times get rough, your team can rally around for motivation and drive. Every great leader ever developed in human history had and currently still uses a rallying point of sorts. Rally points are the pinnacle of passionate performance and can be represented as a mascot, a phrase, a chant, a person, a song, a memory, or a combination thereof, anything that can influence courage and passion. Gan Ning of Wu gave the sound of his bells. The samurai warlords called the Daimyo used to call out "Ei! Ei!" (pronounced like "A"), and the samurai would respond "Oh!" loudly for all to know who was charging forth. Today, "Oorah!" is still the preferred battle cry of our Marine Corps. And in American culture with sports, we cannot forget our favorite team's mascot. Every school in the United States has a mascot to identify with and rally around. Even "The Star-Spangled Banner" is a rallying point for all United States citizens to unify under just before watching their beloved sport. When the song plays, all stand, place their right hand over their hearts and admire the flag just before they unleash a huge roar of pride afterward. Many even sing along, like me, every time. It's because it creates a purpose, a why for what we do, courage to be what we are—a team. These are all examples of rally points. These are all examples of how you can unite a team. During these moments, all differences are cast aside, united under a common ground. I personally use a combination of these techniques to unite a "broken" team successfully. So should you.

REAL LIFE

There was a team I took over in the banking industry. I spent the first thirty days observing the team and the performance reports as you've learned in my Mason influential leadership model discussed in pillar I. We'll cover more about this thirty-day tactic later in this pillar. After my observations, I determined that I had an overall Bravo-performing team with a few Charlie performers and one Alpha performer. What was also unfortunate was that I had an *invisible* Bravo-performing team. By invisible, I mean call after call that I participated in, from district calls (approximately 10 to 12 branches) to regional calls (approximately 320 branches), I noticed the tone that managers were using when talking to or about certain branches and their performance. You can always tell who the disappointing ones were, who the average Joes were, and which ones were solid favorites. A clearer description: you could tell which ones were the top performers, mid performers (they neither do the extraordinary or the worst), and bottom performers. The mid performers get zero attention on calls or at events, hence invisible. Although I was new, when my branch was called upon to discuss, there wasn't any enthusiasm. This told me that the team I inherited didn't accomplish enough to earn enthusiasm. We had an Alpha performer, sure, but the team as a whole was too average. I knew I had to brand the team in a way that would get the attention of the top performers and management, by saying we were going to be a force to be reckoned with on the leaderboards.

I had to look within the team. I watched their body language and their social skills with each other to discover any anomalies in their interactions. Specifically, I was seeing how well they worked together. From my observations, I could tell that a couple of team members had much resentment from past transgression, one or two with little motivation to care, and a few that had a desire to progress. If I told the team to stand in a room together, they would probably huddle into three or four subgroups. It's hard to prove to executives that you're going to be a force of top performance if no one trusts each other enough to stand close to one another. I had to find a way to make the team believe in themselves and excite upper management about our potential. I needed multiple rally points for this situation, each serving an individual purpose to a common unified goal: become one of the best.

First, we needed to eliminate our common name that our mediocre history was attached to. However, you can't just change the name of a branch. Therefore, we needed a mascot. A mascot is a very effective way to change the image of a team for those who don't see them day to day, like upper management. They would only see it through email and hear through word of mouth about my team, so I needed something that would sound like greatness, something that when they saw the name, it would stand out and give a positive impression of my team, generating passion. We needed an image that towered above the mediocrity that this unfortunate team developed. Thus, we became known as the

Titans. Some team members bought into it. Others thought something else would have been more fitting. Some even believed it to be a joke and thought it wasn't going to last. Regardless, overnight, we became the Titans.

Second, to become a Titan, you had to believe in yourself to be one. Obviously, the whole team wasn't on board, but that's because it's human nature not to believe everything you see or hear. In most cases, you must be shown how to believe. One of the most effective ways to get different personalities to unite is through a commonality. Unfortunately, we didn't have that, so I had to create one.

Years prior, I was watching my favorite football team, the New Orleans Saints, getting pumped in their pregame huddle when it hit me. If you haven't seen their pregame huddle yet, you are missing out on one of the most motivating, adrenaline-pumping, passion-packing chants you have ever experienced. As a matter of fact, take a second to briefly put down this book and search for one of many of their pregame huddle videos from 2011, then return. I think it will be impactful. Regardless of their differences, when they chanted in unison, following quarterback legend Drew Brees, their words had power because they believed in themselves. They believed in their leader. Regardless of the game's outcome, they played with their hearts because they believed in each other. That's what your team needs, something that will bring them together to remind them of who they are prior to starting each day, like the Saints at the start of each game. During our sales huddles, this is what we chanted.

Me: What do we have?
Team: Faith!
Me: In who?
Team: Us!
Me: And who are we?
Team/Me: Titans!

Over time, the team not only embraced this new culture; they became it by taking turns starting the chant. Thus, the branch was reborn into the Titans, the sole purpose of encouragement to outperform and to outlast our competition.

Together, we created a brand. More importantly, the team had fun. Once the team experienced how much fun you can have working together and winning together, they easily bought into the culture, making it much easier for them to accept the training and conditioning they were about to experience. It starts with you.

Every team is as different as the leaders who lead them. Depending on your leadership values, vision, and personality, you may use only a mascot. Or if mascots aren't your thing, then perhaps it's a principle like our rally cry during our huddle. Regardless of what it is that fits your leadership style, having a rallying point is a crucial part of your branding. It's a crucial part of inspiring your team when the possible is possible and the possible seems impossible. That is how you call your team to action. Create the best rally point(s) suitable for your team. Each team you lead will react differently, so change accordingly. However, never let a team led you away from this important step. You must lead your team into accepting it. Embed your rally point into your language. Every chance you have, reference it. The more they hear it, the more you'll reinforce the very culture you're trying to build. Over time, they'll buy into the culture you chose to create. And the culture I'm teaching you to create here is a winning one. Later in this pillar, we'll cover when to implement and how to make your rally point become a culture.

Tactfulness

In a perfect world, we can have a general guide for tactfulness that can fit into any industry, but all managers within every company and industry are different. Some may have specific greetings and others may have very flexible dress codes. Even though there are many differences, here are some basic, professional policies to implement that you can use, regardless of where you work. As a matter of fact, I'm willing to bet that if you're working for a strong branded company, these may already exist in your dress code policies one way or another. If not, it will only help your brand to add them. Here are some of my must-haves under my leadership in regards to personal presentation as examples. These are not listed in any particular order.

1. At all times, any facial hair permitted must be trimmed and groomed (clean and neat).
2. Regardless of what is required to be worn, it must be clean and stain/wrinkle-free (within reason for wrinkles, but certainly "pulled out of a hamper after three days of sitting crunched in it" wouldn't fly).
3. Good hygiene is an absolute must. Body odor of any sort due to lack thereof is unacceptable.
4. Hair must be dressed and/or groomed (guys and gals) in a presentable fashion.

As crazy as it sounds, without these small additions, I have had serious challenges with team members willing to address it independently. Having these listed for accountability proactively keeps them motivated, professional, and more productive—most of all, prepared to make their strongest first impression when they SHINE TWICE. This is an area where details are often missed, which will speak volumes about your team and your brand image, not to forget your company's brand image as well. In addition, as previously discussed, in many cases you only get one shot at earning someone's business.

Each company has their own dress policy, yes, but you have to look beyond the obvious. Whatever you do, don't deviate from your policy. So be sure to stick to your required conduct, but don't be afraid to add to it to reflect the image you're building with your team, as long as your leadership approves. For example, if your policy states that all men must wear a buttoned collared dress shirt with a tie, feel free to add that they must wear a jacket to complement a complete suit. If women are to wear either skirts or slacks, you can say slacks only—again, whichever complements the image you're trying to brand.

Tactfulness, of course, is not just about how you dress. Tactfulness, by simple definition, is when someone carries out a combination of actions that is appropriate and pleasing to others. So not just your attire, but also what you say, the tone in your voice, your body language, eye contact, salutation, etc., all impact your first impression. The importance of the dress code is because it's the attire is typically the first visual to attract someone into an interaction. However, your behavior has to match that exact perception. So be sure that your team is trained to speak clearly, listen sharply, keep good eye contact while listening, have great posture, and always firmly shake hands with a smile. These interactions reach multiple senses like touch, smell (hygiene), sight, and sound, which means customers and clients alike will naturally use these experiences to identify and remember you. Make it a positive memory on every level of the senses.

REAL LIFE

I once had a customer come in to ask about a product we had available. After a great first impression, our customer became our new regular client. Since our new client was pleased with their experiences, I asked how they heard about our services and location. Excitingly, she replied that she was recommended by a competitor. Curious about that competitor, I asked for more details, and it turned out that our client was frustrated to hear that her preferred company was merging with another organization that she wasn't pleased about. While complaining to a team member there, that team member said that he had a great experience with us once and that we would be the best fit for her.

I reached out to this competitor team member, and it turned out that he came into our location months prior to her visit because he was shopping around for rates and prices. He was so pleased with the service he received from start to finish during his initial visit that his experience left a lasting impression. He complimented how we greeted him immediately through the door, stood and walked around our desks with a firm handshake and a smile while introducing ourselves. During his interaction, my team member remained professional and asked genuine questions to learn about his needs. Although he chose another competitor in the end because of lower prices, we provided the best experience. When his client needed someone she could trust, he remembered his experience with us and trusted that we would be able to provide the same trust and service that he did with her.

Because of this great first impression my team provided, our *competitor* recommended a very strong client to us. Our *competitor* trusted us and so did our new client. Now that's a first impression. That is the tactfulness you want your team to be consistently on. That is the brand image you want to reflect.

The behavior I've trained my teams to reflect consistently to maintain the brand image we needed was the introduction. It evolved with every industry I applied it to until it became what I believed to be the perfect first impression. It has all the elements that not only people expect in a greeting, but additional elements that almost seem rare to find these days. In all introductions, my teams are required to SHINE TWICE, as referenced previously, but it doesn't stop there.

Process

A lot of people wouldn't think of having a process in place as a sign of branding, but they would be completely wrong. How is that? Well, if you walked into a Coca-Cola manufacturer and then walked into a Pepsi manufacturer the next day, do you believe that you would see the exact same process? Of course, there are some behaviors that appear alike, but each culture and their process is completely different. Why? Because of their brand preferences. Disregard those copycat products and businesses only there to take a piece of a market share. I'm talking about all the brand names you know and love. A process is not only a behavior. It's a brand, ultimately part of a culture. Not just what is made, but how it's made can create a completely proprietary culture.

I'm a huge advocate of leaders who grow businesses and business teams alike. One of my favorites is Marcus Lemonis, whom you can find on shows like *The Profit*. This business-savvy CEO who spends his own cash to invest in failing businesses points out a huge weakness in almost every episode. Nine out of ten times, a business is failing because of their process. He is *absolutely* right. The same applies for failing teams. Nine out of ten times, the team is failing because of the process, either a failed process or the absence thereof. With every team you gain throughout your experience, if they're not an Alpha-performing team, then they're lacking the process, therefore missing the leadership to help provide that process. They're missing you.

What you've been learning up to this point is how to prepare to implement this process by focusing on specific skills you'll need such as leadership, utilizing morale, identifying levels of performance to make the appropriate decisions using the Mason influential leadership model, organizing your time to take full advantage of every minute, making accountability work for you, and salesmanship. Now you're learning how to build that brand you want to create. First, you have to understand that the team you are expecting to flip into top performance lacks a process. When implementing any process with a business or with a team, you must be patient, but remain vigilant. You have to observe and learn how the team performs by providing time to adapt, but you can't allow problems to occur in the process, like falling behind on their given tasks; otherwise, team members begin to fall behind in performance. Imagine a Monday full of appointments, and because you didn't inspect your tires, you didn't notice a tire relatively flat. You get a blowout. How would that impact your schedule? That's how one team member can derail your process. So you have to have a process that cannot only help with the daily flow of business but help identify those opportunities as well. The training section later in this pillar will lay out a fantastic, well-balanced process to implement for every team you lead, from identifying opportunities to how you can maintain their top performance. As a bonus, I will also teach you how to identify when it's time to move on to a new team to flip and how best to negotiate a higher salary.

Environment

Natural Competitiveness

At this point, hopefully you've thought about what to make your rally point. Now, you need to create a competitive environment. I mean, what's the point of having a rallying point if you don't have opportunities to use it? What sounds more competitively attractive, "Go Heights County" or "Go Wolverines"? This should naturally be a no-brainer, but to get a team to buy into the competitive spirit, you can't just let the language end with you. Every opportunity you have, say your rally point out loud. Remember the Titans example (no pun intended). Every sales meeting we had, I had the team call out our chant during our huddle. Every time we discussed our sales compared to the district, I always referred to us as the Titans, reinforcing exactly what I wanted them to adopt. Over time, your team will begin to refer to themselves as whatever mascot you chose. Over time, they will begin to memorize the slogans or chants or rally cries that you've created. This is the process of building a culture. Over time, team spirit will motivate them.

Another means to help them adapt to your system is to develop a competitive culture by utilizing contests. These old tricks always work, but you must be creative. Some team members have a hard time believing that they're capable of accomplishing top performance, especially on their own. These contests can help generate just the spark they need to bring out their best, and they'll have fun doing it.

After I have trained a team on how to execute certain behaviors and techniques, I launch a very special contest. It's special because this contest is really a test of knowledge, teamwork, competitive spirit, endurance, confidence, and ultimately, their capability. This contest helps open up the avenue of their capabilities and how they effectively utilize what I've taught them. Think of it like a scrimmage. Every other contest thereafter is the Friday night game. Now, only you need to know it's a test. While they'll have fun adapting, you'll be observing, motivating, coaching, and developing the team into their top performance.

The test that I've used multiple times with multiple teams is what I call the Chip-Off Challenge. You're more than welcome to use this idea entirely or develop your own. We'll discuss details of the best times and best practices to introduce these games under the training section of this pillar. The point here is that you'll need to get their competitive spirit out by having them compete against themselves. If they can't compete against themselves, they won't compete against another team, district, or competitor. This is their training ground in disguise.

Although it may sound like a golf game, it's far from it. "Chip" refers to poker chips, which are used to motivate team members and tally scores at the end of the day. Here's how it works (note that you can modify this contest to work however you wish):

1. Put together a list of how the team members can earn their chips. You must have clear communication on how they can achieve their goal, which is winning. For example, for every specific sale they make (depending on your focus) or task they complete, they receive up to three chips.

2. The chips are distributed and collected daily. In addition, each team member must have their chips where they can be exposed to the other team members. At the end of the day, they must turn the chips in to you to add to their total score. This not only helps you track progress, but it keeps them honest and motivates a more naturally competitive environment. Just for extra motivation, I always give the chips out loud for all to hear.

3. When the chips are collected, update a created leaderboard to keep an overall score for the team. Be sure the board is only visible to your team. I simply bought a poster board, asked them to take a fun profile picture, and draw their own names on blade-shaped plates to act as a ticker for the rankings. This allows the team members to stay involved, use creative skills, make the contest more tangible, and have fun.

4. The prize should be displayed out in the open. Whatever you decide, keep it displayed in a high position as if it's on a pedestal. Having to look up gives an impression that the prize is worth far

more than the monetary value. For some, it represents pride. For others, it represents a trophy. Every time they look up, they're reminded of the goal and are encouraged to keep climbing for it. This higher positioning is a symbol of moving up or progressing in their performance. It's human nature to revere higher positions as superior. Everyone wants to move up.

5. Lastly, you want to send out weekly updates or cover the updates in weekly meetings. Think of it like sports highlights. Most people watch the highlights than the actual games because of time constraints, so statistically, you'll receive more attention on the progress of the competition if you only broadcast the updates once a week. Let the team members track it themselves on a daily basis. They must have some ownership in the contest in order to develop their buy-in. If someone doesn't, that only displays an area of opportunity for your coaching.

I strategically chose to use the chips because I needed to make the contest tangible for the team. Also, poker chips make it a little more fun. To make something real and encouraging, you have to appeal to the senses with positive reinforcement. If a team member achieved a task or goal or sale, I wouldn't just hand them a chip, I'd call out their success and flip the chip toward them, like a quarter, right into their hands. The bigger the impact, the more chips I'd flip toward them. Since touch is the most powerful sense, you'll need a creative way to help them physically interact in the contest like my chip-flip maneuver. In addition to touch, they'll also experience visual and auditory responses because the chips are exposed in the air and on their desks. You *have* to make the game tangible so the team can truly believe and deliver. So instead of using a notebook with a tally board, I used poker chips. If Dave had one chip but witnessed Sue receiving three chips, Dave would experience the pressure of losing while Sue would experience the excitement of taking the lead with the chips falling into her hand—by the way, two experiences that are very necessary in order to achieve greatness in building competitiveness.

What typically happens from here is if Sue had three chips and Dave had one, Dave would be more motivated to work harder toward beating Sue. Once Sue realizes that Dave is on a mission to beat her, she'll be encouraged to keep her lead, thus creating a naturally competitive drive that all could witness and enjoy. If there were only a board with tallies on it, it would be hung in the back somewhere that no one could see throughout the day. Out of sight, out of mind, right? Therefore, no reinforcement leads to no development. This game is physically interactive. In other words, it's a real experience. Remember what I keep saying? Winners keep score. The next thing you know, you've opened up the natural competitive spirit of the entire team, and they'll have a blast doing it.

Now, you might be asking yourself, "Self, what should the prize be?" Great question. I always play the game in ways that appeal to the teams' motivation. I come up with different prizes that I feel would appeal to them and then let them choose. You'd be surprised at what motivates them. Whatever you do, don't get greedy and pick the prize yourself. Otherwise, you risk losing their motivation to win. You also don't have to go crazy (like a free cruise), and you always want to verify what can be used with your company policy. Some are lenient and some are really strict. Whatever it is, keep it simple and keep it fun. I've had teams that were motivated by gas cards, coupons, trophies, certificates, gift cards, gift sets, or even lunch with the boss. One of my favorite examples was a team I led in banking years ago. It wouldn't have mattered if I offered $50 cash; they wouldn't have been as motivated as the alternative they offered. They became motivated to fight over who was going to throw a pie in my face! An actual cream pie. As I said, you'd be surprised at what motivates them. That was one of the most competitive tests I've ever held. The team had crazy fun keeping track of their progress and competing against each other to win the honor to pie their boss at the quarterly meeting. When word spread about what motivated their performance, my boss and a few other outside partners decided to attend the meeting to witness it firsthand. The top three were within four chips, and first place won by one. I got pied for the first time in my entire life, just like the movies. It was so motivating, uplifting, and fun for the team that my boss challenged my team to become his top performer by the end of the year. If successful, he would allow the top performer of the year to pie him. Before the end of the year, we became not only his top-performing team, but one of the top-performing teams in the company. Guess who got pied? As I said, keep it simple, and keep it fun. It's contagious.

Team Participation (How to Develop Team Interaction)

You would think that getting a team or a team member to participate would be one of the biggest challenges that leaders and event planners face, based on how much planning goes into creating interactive speeches and activities. Well, you'd be right. Anytime you attempt to encourage free will, you'll always have a challenge. Everyone is completely different from the next on perception, which, in turn, makes it difficult for you to predict their reactions. However, there is an easier and effective way to increase the participation of your team. The secret is allowing that team or team member to develop naturally over time. "How?" Glad you asked. By creating a series of activities that encourages and even requires interaction.

Team members may not interact or participate because of a lack of trust. Trust that other team members won't react negatively. It could be a fear of offending others, starting a confrontation, or just giving the wrong answer and being judged. Over time, the series of events will eventually encourage all team members to become naturally comfortable with each other, which will develop more trust among themselves, therefore more participation. Why is their participation and interaction important? The more trust built within the team, the more their performance can achieve.

Now, how often is "often" for having these events? What type of events or activities can help increase participation? To develop and maintain participation properly, you want to create a mixture of predictable and unpredictable activities and events. I established monthly and quarterly meetings with every team, something predictable so they'll be prepared to participate and know how to participate when participation is required. An example is randomly asking a team member to give us a great customer service story or about their goal progress. Every team member is aware that they may be selected, so they'll have a story prepared just in case. In addition, during our quarterly meetings, I would also introduce an unpredictable activity that would make the team members interact under a different setting. They are the best. This mixture will allow requiring the team to interact diversely. More importantly, it develops trust, giving all team members a chance to find the best time and moment to participate. Some participate through organization, like planned events. Others participate through spontaneity, like playing an unexpected team-based game. We'll cover in more detail how to organize these events and activities to maximize the outcome in the training section of this pillar.

Interaction is key for any team, team member, and even a leader to develop your skills. It's very simple, if you think about it. The more people interact, the more those individuals develop. So your objective in planning these events and activities is to keep their interaction active. Standing up at the meeting and reading off paper to a team for thirty minutes is a great way to disconnect their interest. Through personal experience, you ought to know how that feels.

REAL LIFE

I developed teams that anticipated participating in four things when they attended our quarterly meetings: team contributions, individual contributions, awards, and a team activity. If they were writing this, I'm sure they would include a fifth, lunch, since I always fed my teams. Ha. Anyway, they knew that in every quarterly meeting, they would have to be prepared to discuss our team and individual quarterly performance, followed by having a little award ceremony to celebrate those successes while having lunch. Not too long after, we'd have the team activity. I strategically placed the awards second to last and the game last in order to keep their interest and to keep them engaged.

The first twenty minutes is basically data crunching on our strengths and weaknesses, taking votes and opinions on how to continue our success and improve our opportunities. Once we start the awards, the team gets fired up, ready to see who has earned which award, some anxiously awaiting the sound of their name just to feel the team roar in cheers for their accomplishments. By the end of our awards, the team is energized, very interactive, and motivated to have fun, the perfect time to introduce our team-building activity.

Up to that point, the team only knew to expect a team activity, but not what it was or the rules of it. This is very important. They knew they would have to interact in some random way, but didn't know enough to prepare. This is a great strategy so team members avoid what I call interactive shock (when someone is called into participation without expectation), which causes team members to get embarrassed or shut down, like paralysis. There will be moments where this can't be avoided, but you can certainly minimize those moments by setting up the expectation that there is participation in something every quarter. It's necessary to make team members comfortable with being uncomfortable. This is one of the strongest ways to help them overcome neophobia throughout their careers. You're helping them develop with these unpredictable interactive activities.

One of the activities I used with a team had a set of numbers up to six written on individual sheets of paper and then taped throughout the lobby in strategic locations. Throughout the lobby, there were also three red x's marked on sheets of paper that indicated a penalty if stepped on. Team members were divided into teams of two, with one as the navigator and the other as the pilot. The objective was to reach all the points in numerical order within record time to win. The pilot was blindfolded and had to navigate through the lobby, fully trusting the navigator, who must remain at the starting line in their respective 3' by 3' boxes they could not step out of. The pilot must travel through and touch all the points with the assistance of the navigator. It is the navigator's responsibility to effectively communicate and guide the pilot from one station to the next while remaining stationary in their specific box. If they lose, the navigator takes full responsibility. The pilot, blindfolded, is responsible for listening and acting on what the navigator communicates in due time and for using initiative when necessary, if communication is not clear. Even if the pilot appears at fault for the loss, the navigator still takes full responsibility. This is a leadership development technique.

There were four teams strategically chosen. One team, as my control variable, were two team members who were pretty close. The other teams weren't used to working with one another closely. After I explained the details between each roll, I then provided ten seconds for them to decide who was going to be in each roll. If they didn't make the time frame, I chose for them. Only one team didn't make the time frame. Once we established clarity on their roles, the activity began, and boy, did it turn out to be quite the event.

All four teams were excited to go head to head. After the award ceremony, how could they not be pumped up? In the end, two teams didn't make it past four, and the other two finished to six. The fours were eliminated. Among them was my control group. Ironically, they had the hardest time accomplishing their task and only made it to three stations. The final two completed within four seconds of each other—a successful activity. The team members took a lot away from what they learned and had a blast watching each other, particularly the pilots, navigate through the lobby. The prize awarded and another successful meeting at a close. The outcome, new friendships were developed and previous disagreements forgiven. Now that is the biggest success. Trust was developed.

So if you were participating in this activity, who would you chose? Would you be the pilot, having fun being the pioneer and leaping into the unknown with only the trust of your partner's verbal guidance? Or the navigator, who has complete responsibility of the outcome and is responsible for leading someone else's fortune? Both have their advantages and disadvantages, but what these positions really represent is being a great leader and a great follower. People say leading is easy. No, it isn't. People say following is easy. No, it isn't. Strong leaders and strong followers both require effective skills that take practice to develop. Majority of your pioneers are strong followers who had strong leaders that provided them the development and opportunity to explore for the greater good. Ultimately, this activity taught team members communication skills, healthy competition, listening skills, on-the-spot decision-making, trust, team development, teamwork, leadership, and the list goes on. These are the activities you want to incorporate spontaneously during your planned events.

Notice in my example that I didn't say "games." That's because there's a distinct difference. These are not games because there is more than just one objective. Games only have one, and that's to win. Activities aim to learn and develop. They can build trust, teamwork, communication, decision-making, or any other skill you wish to focus on developing. You are creating these activities to develop the team through participation. Avoid the word *game* when describing these activities. This will help the team understand its developmental purpose. Don't let this be a secret, though. Team members love development and, most of all, having fun doing it.

Community Involvement

This is a crucial part of developing a top-performing team, especially when millennials are on your team. Many top-performing teams that I have trained, led, and interviewed were very active within their communities. Those that weren't couldn't compete for long. That's because of my simple rule. Take care of your community, and the community will take care of you. There are a lot of positive impacts that go beyond your business just from assisting your communities— absolutely zero negative impacts, in my opinion, unless you perceive them as such. Participating in community events and activities is a *must* in helping team members open up to effective communication and develop many other character skills like teamwork, relationship building, leadership, and more, depending on the event. I have six major reasons why it's very important to participate in your surrounding communities that relate back to my simple rule:

1. The community gives you their time, their valuable feedback, and their business. The least you can do is give the same back.

2. It increases exposure of your business and your brand, therefore putting you at top of mind to bring more business back to you when the desire for your product or service arises.

3. For all generations from baby boomers to millennials, participating in community service develops a sense of purpose and pride. As your community develops, so do you. This will ultimately give your team members a more passionate reason for why they should have more pride in higher performance.

4. It builds strong long-term relationships. Some of the biggest business opportunities and deals have been made through strangers working together on a community project. Many successful entrepreneurs are also philanthropists who seek to give back to their communities constantly.

5. Business diversity. No one learns more about themselves and their business until they've worked for free. Once someone eliminates the root cause of why many Americans have to work, like making money, team members find something else more gratifying and passionate within themselves, like the impact of helping others—an amazing feeling, more gratifying than a dollar can ever afford.

6. It's your responsibility!

Did that last one catch you off guard? For many, I'm sure it did. Yes. That's right. It's your responsibility. If you really think about it, I'm positive that you can determine why. It's *your* community. And as any community, or let's call this a team for perspective, you have to work together effectively in order to grow and progress your business. Just as you're building a team of top performers, what you do in a community is build it to become a top producer. The more your community performs, the more you and the community get in return—a simple investment strategy. As being a part of a team holds you responsible for performing, so should the community. It is everyone's civic duty to care for their community and help it progress, help it develop, help it grow. Only through that growth can one's own goals and dreams be reached.

REMEMBER: Take care of your community, and the community will take care of you!

Birthdays and Anniversaries

We've discussed quite a few ways to build trust among your team, and I definitely wanted to dedicate at least a section to one of the easiest ways to show appreciation and to build long-term loyalty. Many times, this little recognition is overlooked, which is a misfortune. If this is already a behavior, then you're doing great! Always recognize birthdays and anniversaries. When you think of ways you could go the extra mile with developing teams, this is one small overlooked idea that could create a huge impact, which is why this behavior deserves recognition itself.

Every year, I always celebrate my team member's birthday by bringing in a birthday cake of their preference, something enough to honor them for spending another birthday with my team when the day is all about them. Pretty selfless, right? I think so. I know a ton of people who take their day off for themselves (as well deserved). However, my team members wanted to spend it with the team a majority of the time and, therefore, recognized that we appreciate them. There is always a cake available for the team to celebrate in the break room. I'm even known to come in during my vacation time just to bring that team member their cake on their birthday. On anniversaries, I always give a shout-out through our morning meetings and email to thank the team member for their contribution and continuing to help us succeed. After all, they could have spent their time elsewhere. Why not take the time one day a year for each to celebrate these milestones? The impact is priceless so stand out.

To this day, I still have team members who've referenced how great their experience was just because they remembered that I celebrated their birthday or anniversary and how I honored them with something as simple as cake and recognition. Many of those team members followed me to other companies and teams. Again, if something so small can make such a great impact, why not take advantage of it? Celebrate your team members' milestones like birthdays and anniversaries with your own expression of appreciation. With technology these days, there really isn't a reason why you shouldn't. Just that start will generate tremendous loyalty. With those small changes added to your strategy, you're ready to start implementation.

Implementation

Phase 1: Analysis and Strategy Development

Day 1–33

Up to this point, we've talked about what behaviors to create and build to reflect the culture you want. Now I'll teach you how to implement it. The implementation process is very crucial. Any sway from the timeline will only risk delaying the fast results you're aiming for. However, don't believe that you won't run into challenges that may derail you. You will. Notice I didn't say anything about quitting. As long as it's in your control, stay on your timeline. If something pulls you back or derails you for any reason, just get back on it and push forward. To overcome the challenges of the unwilling and your competition, you have to work fast and effectively. Any time you fall behind, just keep in mind that they'll adapt more slowly, which will drastically reduce the chances of encouraging their acceptance and development. Of course, your unique personality and skill set is what sets you apart from other leaders and managers in your industry, but it's the timeline and the behaviors that follow that will thrust your performance and career. You will develop your team through three phases totaling approximately one hundred days of implementation. You might be asking yourself, "Self, why one hundred days?" Believe it or not, like the president of the United States just inaugurated into office, the prediction and perception of your performance are judged on your first 100 days in your role. Sure, your bosses and executives will tell you that it takes six to twelve months for anyone to adapt to their role and become successful. However, the unfortunate truth is that they're judging your capabilities much sooner.

Think about it this way. If you have just bought a sports car, would you be patient enough to wait six months to a year for it to perform the way you expected? How about three months? It's tough to wait one day, but that's reality. You're their new sports car. With acquisition costs for a new employee reaching up to three times their salary, you're the company's newest driver, and they're expecting you to drive to their expected performance. The average breaking point for a company to break even on its investment on you is around six months. Imagine if you were that driver who could drive home their return on investment sooner. That means more promotions and more money for you. This process will help you drive results faster and make an impact on your business from day 1. In your first one hundred days, you'll become an Alpha-performing leader.

The first phase has a thirty-three-day observation and research period. The second phase has an implementation period between the thirty-fourth and the seventieth day. Phase 3, or the last thirty days, is the scrimmage. This final phase marks the beginning of your team's evolution into becoming a top-performing team by throwing everything taught into action. Please keep in mind of the size of your team and off days/holidays, etc. Larger teams may need longer, of course. Smaller teams may evolve faster.

There are only four quarters in a year. Any process that takes two or more to complete is not competitive enough in today's market, certainly not enough to reach your goals faster. If this is your process currently, you can still adapt to my model. This process is adaptable to any industry and can be implemented any time. Even if you've managed a team for years, you can still implement this new process and help your team evolve into an Alpha-performing team. Although your title, company, or industry will change throughout your career, this process shouldn't (unless adding to it), making you more efficient and effective at building top-performing teams and becoming a successful top-performing team leader yourself.

SWOT Analysis

Before we begin this part of the phase, it's crucial that you understand what a SWOT analysis is—more importantly, my modern interpretation of it as well. Unfortunately, SWOT, in this case, has nothing to do with law enforcement (not to be confused with SWAT). SWOT stands for Strengths, Weaknesses, Opportunities, and Threats, which refers to your business both internally and externally. It is a powerful developmental and assessment tool that's been used since the '60s (when the name became popular in business) and beyond. I've provided a couple of illustrated examples under Resources. Strengths and Weaknesses refer to your internal factors that you identify within your team to develop their behaviors further—ergo, their performance. Opportunities and Threats refer to external factors that can impact the performance of your team, such as variables that can be taken advantage of to excel or that could cause challenges and delay performance. During your first phase, this is a tool you'll be completing, your team's SWOT analysis. However, I'm going to teach you a trick taking this tool a step further.

Typically, this tool is only developed through one perception: the leader's. Your new process will require you to see through both sides of the lens. From the leader's perspective, and the team members' perspective. This diverse perspective will allow you to develop an all-inclusive strategy that truly incorporates the team and all of its strengths and weaknesses. Bottom line is, you strengthen and grow the team together. Some of the struggles with many top executives have today and have been for years is that many have been disconnected from the middle to lower leaders for far too long and lost that perspective, hence where you see a new strategy or campaign launched from top executives that crumbles upon execution. In other words, it's an inconsistent process across multiple stores. In almost every case, that failure is blamed on the middle and lower leaders. The real truth is that the executives failed to communicate. They failed to gain perspective. They failed to see how their strategies and campaigns would impact the teams throughout the company. They failed to create a proper SWOT analysis and implement an appropriate strategy. This is something that you can't afford to do, in order to drive consistent performance and your career in this competitive market. My SWOT analysis incorporates both perspectives to minimize deficiencies. However, to believe truly in this tool, you have to understand the structure. Here is what a standard SWOT analysis quadrant looks like:

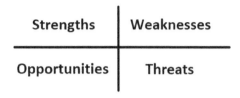

This is how you want to interpret your SWOT analysis with my model:

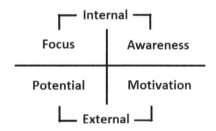

We'll continue to call it a SWOT analysis because we're not reinventing the wheel here and let's face it, FAPM doesn't sound as cool. Nonetheless, I just want you to interpret each respective category as I've shown to understand how each one will benefit you and your team. Can you see why each quadrant translates as such? You must master your internal factors before maximizing external factors. By focusing on your strengths, you'll remain aware of your weaknesses, become motivated by the competition, and discover creative ways to maximize your potential. Don't fall into the notion that focusing more on your weakness will make you stronger. However, I'm not saying ignore your weakness. As a strong note, you should always be aware of your weaknesses, but never focus more on your weaknesses than your strengths. This is where your mind may disagree and believe otherwise. Just stay with me here.

American culture has taught itself to believe that you're only as strong as your weakest link, so many people will tell you to focus on your weaknesses. I prefer not to have a weak link. There is a huge problem in sales about focusing on weaknesses and not your strengths. That's what many people were taught. However, you neglect your strengths. Developing weaknesses are important, but not at the expense of neglecting your strengths. In regards to a team, that holds entirely true. Keep in mind that you're running a team, not just yourself. Develop your weaknesses, of course, but keep the majority emphasis on keeping your strengths at their peak.

Here is an example. If a running back had a difficult time evading a tackle or running through a defender but had incredible ball-handling skills and speed, you would think the best thing to do is to make that running back practice evading or ramming into defenders. However, in focusing solely on developing the weakness of the running back, he now becomes a powerhouse to run against, hard to stop and hard to tackle. However, with all of his thoughts on his opponent's next move to decide to spin or ram a defender, he disregards hand and ball placement. Now if touched, the ball is fumbled easily—remind you of any players?

Focusing on his strength, the other option is to develop a play where a teammate can secure the run for him so he can use his strength to push past a defender, where he can't be caught or fumble. Focus on strengthening his strength and relying on borrowing the strength of protection from his offensive-line teammates to protect his weakness. Instead of focusing solely on his weakness, he trusts his teammates' strength to protect him as they trust his strength to run with the ball (which is their weakness). The team works united completely aware of each other's weaknesses, but using their strengths collectively and complementarily to maximize their potential together.

Here is a historical example just to illustrate how far back this tactic goes. In 430 BC, the king of Sparta, Leonidas, who led the infamous Spartans and his allies against the Persian army of over one million soldiers in the Battle of Thermopylae, mastered this tactic. Each

Spartan knew that one major weakness was their exposed left hip in their formation once their shields were raised for defense against a frontal assault. They could have focused on their weakness and created a bigger shield, but the shield would have been heavier, which would weaken their arms in combat. It would have also been harder to maneuver when fighting multiple enemies, making them slower to defend, and not to forget that it would have reduced their line of sight, which would have made it more difficult to view their opponents' movement. Their strength was remaining light, swift, and strong, united in combat. Instead, aware of their weakness, they took the strength of each Spartan and created the infamous spear wall, where each Spartan's exposed hip was covered by their brother in arms to their left. Together, their wall couldn't be broken in a frontal assault, even against a million men.

Again, don't ignore your weaknesses, hence why the meaning is awareness. Remaining aware also implies development, but not as a top priority. If one of your weaknesses is computer skills, then instead of holding one computer course a day, hold a weekly training session instead, followed by practice. When the Spartans broke their wall formation to engage in battle, they still had their weak side exposed, but they were trained to maneuver constantly to make their weak side a difficult moving target. Continue to develop your weakness, but your Alpha priority is to continue developing your team's strength, completely aware of the weaknesses.

As I mentioned earlier, by focusing on your strengths and remaining aware of your weaknesses, you'll maximize your team's potential. That is exactly what your opportunities represent: your potential. And your threats do not serve as a fear tactic, but a motivator. If your competition is achieving more, you should be motivated to do even better. If your competition developed a better product or service, you should be motivated to outperform them. That's the beauty of competition. To summarize how to interpret your analysis, focus on your strengths, be aware of your weaknesses, maximize your potential, and let your threats motivate you. Now that you can better interpret the SWOT analysis, let's move forward.

Observation Period

The first ten days are spent observing from your perspective, as the leader. During this period, you will carry out your normal daily functions, incorporating your new time management skills, utilizing the Mason influential leadership model, and introducing the team's new brand, all while making your observations of how they conduct business. The following days are observations from your team member's perspective, meaning standing on the front lines as one of them. This is your opportunity to understand existing operating systems, processes, goals (if any), and daily expectations of your team members. During this period, you'll be able to witness great interactions since you'll be more covert being in their shoes. Accountability will be at its all-time low during this phase. It doesn't mean we don't hold team members accountable when applicable. We'll go into greater detail shortly. Think of the good cop/bad cop routine. During this observation period, we're playing the good-cop routine. Although there will be situations where we have to change roles, those will be on a case-by-case basis. The objective during this phase is to establish trust, brand awareness, and generate a thorough SWOT analysis for phase 2.

There are four main reasons why it's crucial to play this role during phase 1:

1. Builds trust faster. This is the initial period where you are building or reestablishing trust. Coming in with an iron fist or having an on and off switch for good and bad can disengage team members early on, especially if you inherited a new team. Think back to the importance of a first impression. A strong first impression is more attractive and faster to trust.
2. Accurate observations. You'll always obtain the most detailed observations when team members don't feel constant pressure worrying about saying the right thing. This condition will allow team members to be themselves during your observations, thus a more accurate picture of their engagement.

3. Faster team member acceptance. Having a view from their perspective with no biased opinions will increase team member engagement. How many times were you told to do something you knew wouldn't work? This is about gaining perspective. By doing so, you'll gain their trust and respect faster.

4. Team member preparation. Believe it or not, you're covertly preparing your team members for phase 2. When building a culture, you have to provide a strong balance of engagement and accountability. This first phase introduces engagement. The next phase will introduce accountability, secretly building a well-balanced beam that your team will trust to stand on.

Imagine how much easier it would be for a team to learn and grow from a leader they trust compared to one they don't. Now, imagine how motivated a team member would be if they were developed by someone they trusted. Coming into a new team with an iron fist and immediately assuming you know what's best for each team member without knowing their strengths and weaknesses always results in some of the most unpredictable outcomes. Many times, a new manager comes in, and the old team moves out. That's because the manager prefers to skip steps, which unfortunately puts great people out of a job. You're different. You have the ability and capability of flipping underperforming teams into top-performing teams with this process. This is the fastest way to do it. Build a strong trust upfront. For phase 2, you'll have a path of least resistance.

Day 1–10—Leader's Point of View

Majority of your competition is going to take the first few days to learn, just from the wrong perspectives. The typical manager will spend the first three days just absorbing so much information, calling it learning, until their brain develops paralysis. The outcome? Three wasted days because less than 10 percent was even obtained. The unfortunate part is that upper management allows it. For other managers, even more days are lost, especially without guidance, which in today's unfortunate truth is over 80 percent likely. Each day during your first one hundred days is crucial, just like the president of the United States.

For the first ten days, you should spend about 20 percent of your time searching reports, but only those crucial to reading your team's performance and behavior metrics, both individually and overall. Be sure to include a comparison to other teams in your district and/or region. The other 80 percent needs to be face time with your team members. Feel free to increase your face time to a 90/10 plan with 90 percent being time spent on the front line once you feel more comfortable with the reports. That is ultimately our goal to reach. For some industries or if you're already familiar with your company's process, you may use the 90/10 plan sooner. However, never spend less than 70 percent of your time on the front line. A 70/30 rule should only be incorporated if your position is more demanding on reporting.

This is a great opportunity to introduce your personality and charisma. In addition, it sets the pace for the team to determine if they can trust you as their leader. It's crucial to have an active presence during your first thirty days engaged with your team members. If you spend more than 30 percent of your time in an office before team members learn who you are, they'll began to misread your leadership capabilities and begin to distrust you. It's not a road you can't return from, but it makes your goal twice as hard to achieve.

REAL LIFE

I had a team member, John, who was promoted to an assistant manager position because he was the top performer—a great salesman and certainly had great potential. A few months later, he was struggling with a new product release. When he held sales meetings and taught team members how to present the product, before the end of the day, execution was ultimately absent. Their production, especially in that product category, was terrible. His, however, was phenomenal, as expected. So when I visited his store one day, I walked into his office to meet him, and he asked me for some input on this challenge. I told him, "Sure. Wait right here." I left the office, walked up to each employee I could find, and asked where their manager was. These team members were on the register to the other side of the store. Their response was either "I don't know" or "He may be in the office." Three out of four had almost identical answers. The fourth said lunch (that made me laugh a little). After further questions, it turned out that the team members were under the impression John was in the office because he was "always" there (their words). Since he didn't have a strong presence, team members had disbelief in his capabilities to lead and support, therefore disconnect from communication, execution, and accountability. Without leadership on the floor during this early stage, confidence in a leader to assist the line diminishes into defaulted, unhealthy behaviors—unhealthy for their own careers and for the organization. This immediately created barriers from the start, making his ascension up the ladder even more difficult to pursue.

When I reported back the results I gathered, John was shocked. In his mind, he was on the floor all the time. Turns out when he was on the floor, he was directly selling to customers, which (without the guidance) he assumed was face time with his team members. Once I gave John some direction on how to combat that perception with a higher involvement on the sales floor, he was able to turn his team around within sixty days and became second in the district within that category. Team members want to see an active leader, and they are begging for it right at the start. You just have to believe it. They want and need to see heavy engagement through the gate. Even if they don't admit it or bluntly say it, they *want* it, so as their leader, provide it starting on day 1.

Be sure to have your mental pencil sharpened and notepad ready. Although you'll be taking time to introduce yourself and learn about your team members, you'll also be observing. The best practice for you is to remember the rules in pillar II: productive time management. Prepare the next day the day before. Discover the busiest times for your team and schedule accordingly. Typically, the morning is slower, so you'd want to schedule time to find your reports in the morning.

Doing so will allow you to focus on your team for the rest of the day (during those busy periods).

At this stage, the only Alpha priorities should relate to executing your one-hundred-day strategy. Unless given a different priority by management, stick to this routine. If your busiest time is in the morning, again, schedule accordingly. When observing, stay active, bouncing from one interaction to the next, immediately documenting afterward. Try to avoid taking notes during interactions in *this* stage. However, if you need to, then something is better than nothing. If asked what you're doing and why by a team member, definitely let them know that you're taking notes in order to help develop the team later as you learn their processes. For the most part, they'll love it. Being familiar with personality traits really helps at this stage.

The key here is to maximize your listening skills, which is why the pen should come afterward. Your first thirty days is all about listening and observing. If you're new to a company, you won't be observing specifically the details of their process, as you're still learning those yourself. Instead, what each of their processes looks like (if any), look for similarities and differences. If you're new to the team but not the company, then you're observing their specific behaviors to make sure they reflect what's expected, still looking for similarities and differences between each team member. Either way, compare those behaviors to the elements of a perfect interaction that we covered earlier when observing team members' interaction with a customer/client.

Observe their body language, how they introduce themselves (rather if they know each other or not), their eye contact, any questions they may ask (if any), how they direct the conversation (personal vs. product/service-driven points), how they utilize transition statements (if any), how they document their conversation (if at all), product/service knowledge, and how they end their interaction (particularly any follow-through appointments set). Remember that what you observe is for you. This is *your* assessment and no one else's. Don't use these observations for coaching just yet as well. That will come in phase 2. They're for your analysis and are inconclusive until you bring together all observations and performance reports from the team.

The endgame here is comparing all of your team members using your observations and performance reports for an overall view of your team's strengths and weaknesses, in addition, determining their level of performance, which will help guide you on how to coach and manage each team member using the Mason influential leadership model. If you manage a team with multiple departments, department managers, assistant managers, store managers, and so forth, then schedule your time wisely to give yourself time to observe each respective department or store. If you manage a single department, then it should be a little easier.

Whichever plan you begin with, the 30 percent, 20 percent, or 10 percent of your time spent pulling reports is doing just that—pulling reports. This is the time to analyze and understand how each metric affects the other. Hopefully, you'll have trainings on how to read them. This will not only help us understand our business but also form a bottom-line reference for who is performing stronger than others overall, to be used later. Analyzing reports, as you may know, is very time-consuming and can be pretty addictive, believe it or not. For many, it's like trying to solve a fun puzzle, except you can trick yourself into believing that all the pieces that don't truly fit can be found through reporting. In other words, you can fool yourself into making up useless strategies that may not be the solution.

If you're new with the company, rely on a coworker or your manager to schedule a time to meet face to face to review these reports if training isn't provided. You can either sit there all night at home, trying to see what plugs in and where, or you can get your six to eight hours of sleep and learn these reports in an hour with guidance. I hope you choose sleep. If you're already with a familiar company, on a team you're planning to flip, then your plan will be 90/10, with only 10 percent spent on pulling reports since you should already have an idea which resources you can pull from and know how to interpret them.

When you're pulling reports, be sure not to guess what's important. Ask your manager, team members, and coworkers which reports are important and why. Don't forget to ask why. A part of being a leader is understanding the whys. Know why you're reading certain reports and why particular individuals pull those particular reports. Perspective is always a plus when learning about performance records and expectations.

Pull each team member's individual performance report (if any), your team overall and any department performance report, and any other reports that reflect your team's performance compared to the area, district, market, etc. (monthly, quarterly, and annually if applicable for all reports). If you're in retail industry, look for a product detail report that breaks down the sales of product SKUs and services. When analyzing a team's performance, you want a view from the bigger picture down to a single metric. This is important for developing your strategies later on.

There *will* be some reports that will seem more useful, or useless, to your strategy than others. That's okay! That's part of growing your skill set. The important part is only analyzing what you need. Once you've learned how to interpret these reports, you can now interpret the full picture of your team's performance. Like financial reports such as the balance sheet or an income statement acting as the vitals of a business, these performance reports are vital for your team. Once you've collected the necessary reports, schedule time to analyze them within your planned time slot.

Identify MIL Performance Levels

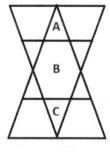 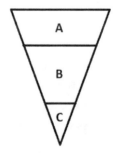

MIL Model   Performance Sub-Model

You have your observations completed and analyzed your reports. You now should have a reasonable idea of which team members would fit into their respective levels of performance. As mentioned in pillar I and referenced in our model above, you will place them into the Charlie, Bravo, or Alpha levels of performance. To assist, let's revisit the criteria as follows:

Charlie Performer—Reporting: Less than 80 percent to goal or 25 percent + behind pace.

> Behaviors: These team members typically have minimum participation during team events and meetings, tend to avoid eye contact during conversations, will seem insecure about themselves and their ability, will not have a sales process with customers or clients, consistent with only being disengaged, and/or in some cases have a negative outlook.

> Other examples of typical behaviors reflected, but are not limited to: unorganized or doesn't seem to care, consistently late, misses deadlines, easily distracted, fails to follow instructions, timid, poor tactfulness, and poor communication.

Bravo Performer—Reporting: Between 80 percent and 100 percent and/or greater than 25 percent behind pace. Hits 100 percent of goal occasionally.

> Behaviors: These team members are perfecting their craft, so what you're looking for are inconsistencies. They typically have moderate participation (more so if called upon), keep eye contact (but can still get distracted), unorganized (but open for improvement), inconsistent with behaviors (but only because of being unorganized), and/or are always willing to improve. Observe their process and their engagement skills. They may do an assessment for one customer but fail to do so

with the next, maybe not on purpose. They just don't have the behavior mastered yet to perform predictable experiences.

Other examples of typical behaviors reflected, but are not limited to, are eager to learn, engage customers with positivity, eager to take on new responsibilities, confident, impatient, easily motivated, and ambitious.

Alpha Performer—<u>Reporting</u>: Constantly at or above goal (100 percent +) or ahead of pace. Consistently over 100 percent of goal.

Behaviors: Alpha performers have perfected *their* process. These team members can be seen consistently engaged, eager to assist the next customer or client, recognized using scripts, assessments, or other resources consistently, and typically display positivity and a passion to win.

Other examples of typical behaviors reflected, but are not limited to, are self-motivated, very active, observant, detail-oriented, goal-oriented, fast talkers, expressive with body language, competitive, sometimes overconfident, and/or loyal.

With your plan in place, you'll be able to create a structured SWOT analysis from *your* point of view. When you're referencing strengths, you're looking for behaviors around which the team, as a whole, has either mastered or displayed some sort of passion that gives your team an advantage. For example, if you're in hospitality, such as the hotel business, and you witness your team members greeting each guest with a smile and a warm salutation, then you'd want to document that as a strength. The team as a whole is obviously passionate about first impressions and courtesy since they appear consistent and sincere. In the restaurant business, maybe it's recognizing your bartenders appearing to really engage with their guests, making their experience fun. I once observed at a Fuddruckers restaurant, servers dancing and singing to '80s rock-and-roll stations—even the manager. Their energy was contagious. Upon hearing them sing, I began to sing. Upon seeing them dance around, I began to rock my body to the beat. Their behavior impacted mine in a positive way. That could be a strength. If you're in the military, perhaps your unit has the best clear time in a particular exercise. Again, you're looking for existing behaviors that give the team a competitive advantage. These need to be collected from observations and reports for a stronger analysis. The minimum you should recognize is three. Sometimes, that may seem challenging to recognize but look as hard as you can. There is always a third somewhere.

Weaknesses refer to those existing behaviors that give your team a disadvantage, behaviors that could potentially, if not already, sink your team's performance and have negative impacts on customers. If you're an office manager and your team's top priority is to update personnel files monthly, but you discover multiple files are months behind, meeting deadlines could be a weakness, or anything else directly related to why those deadlines are not being met. If you're in the auto industry and you notice a potential customer searching your lot and no one rushes out the door to greet new customers, urgency could be a weakness. If you're a football coach and you notice that your wide receiver runs out of breath before running twenty yards out, endurance could be a weakness. Again, you're looking for behaviors that are or could be a disadvantage to the team's performance. Just like your strengths, weaknesses need to be collected from observations and reports for a stronger analysis. Below is an example of what your SWOT analysis can look like under Strengths and Weaknesses from the leader's perspective. The minimum you should have is three.

Day 11–25 Team's Point of View

The first ten days were spent collecting strengths and weaknesses from a leader's point of view. Now we need to collect the same data, but from the team members' perspective. As I mentioned before, this is the secret ingredient that's going to give your SWOT analysis the most impactful results for your strategy. For your reference, be sure to indicate which strength or weakness discovered is from the leader's perspective or the team members' perspective by placing a small *L* or *T* next to the line. We'll circle back around to this as to why.

Now you may be asking yourself, "Self, what does he mean, 'from the team members' perspective'?" Another great question, of course. I don't mean pretend to put yourself in their shoes and brainstorm. I also don't mean ask the team members for their input on strengths and weaknesses and then put your SWOT analysis together. I actually mean from the team members' perspective. You won't pretend here. You'll actually be in their position for next fifteen days. You can ask for their opinions on strengths and weaknesses, which can help, but you'll have to witness and experience them for yourself as well to confirm. This is where the rubber hits the road, as they say.

For fifteen days, you'll alter your scheduled time to fit similar to this routine: 70 percent of your time face to face with customers or clients just as a team member would, to recommend your products and/or services. Twenty percent of your time will be spent face to face as their leader observing as you did from days 1–10. And 10 percent of your time is pulling and analyzing reports. Notice your time spent is still 90/10. Your face time still remains the same, just observing your business from a different perspective. That is very important. The typical manager reduces their presence over time. However, you're not learning this to be typical, are you? At the very least, you want to increase your face time by day 11. For example, if you had to start on the 70/30 plan, then now is the time to start your transition into the 80/20 plan. The same if you started on the 80/20 plan—this is the time to start your transition into the 90/10 plan.

REMEMBER: During your first one hundred days, presence is crucial.

You want to maintain a consistent presence of 90 percent for the rest of your one-hundred-day training program after day 25, if you're not there already, to make you maximize your potential. That is a secret that really impacts a team to accept the culture you wish to create quickly and with less opposition—increasing face time.

Now, a typical manager's team will consist of at least three different positions. If you have more, then plan your schedule accordingly because ideally you want to put yourself in all of their shoes. The best practice here is to put each position in a repetitive rotation. As an example, you can have Mondays as a cashier, Tuesdays as a sales associate, Wednesdays as an administrator or inventory, etc. Then repeat rotation for the following days.

Keep it simple. Jumping to multiple roles in one day will cause your brain to delete some of the most important details from your observations because your attention is scattered. Additionally, spending such time under those roles will allow you to connect more closely with each team member in that respective role. You definitely want that kind of face-to-face because your team members will respond greatly to it—a great time to build trust and insight from the team members.

Even in this perspective, you can still listen actively for your team member's engagement with their customers and clients when you're not engaged yourself. For your SWOT analysis, you'll mainly focus on the process (if any) that's in place, the tools and resources available (if any) for your team, and the customer/client experience. While in the team member's role, you'll have firsthand experience with the team member's daily routine when they use tools such as call support centers, software programs, POS (point of sale) systems, etc. It's also helpful to pay close attention to cleanliness. How many tools are necessary to complete a transaction? Are they efficient or effective? How long does it take to contact the support center? Are there any gaps in service (areas absent that could provide a better customer/client experience)? Is the transaction flow smooth or not? You can't go wrong collecting as much information as possible in this stage as long as everything is relevant. Ultimately, you're gaining perspective on the strengths and weaknesses of the tools, resources, and processes each team member has to fulfill their daily routine.

As before, when you're referencing strengths in your SWOT analysis, you're looking for components in the process that give *you* and your team an advantage. For example, as a branch manager being a banker, you notice that all the tools and resources you need are located on one site, making it more efficient to find the information you need to answer questions. A single system would be an advantage as other banks use multiple systems or platforms, which slows down the clients' and team members' experience. If you're leading a distribution center as the administrator, you notice that as soon as an order was placed, you're notified immediately for delivery. That could be an advantage.

I once visited a shoe store where the manager assisting me took a picture of me from my right side, loaded it into an app he had available on his tablet, then loaded any shoe I was interested in right on my foot. I was able to view exactly how I would look in any shoe desired without trying a shoe on first, saving me lots of time and disappointment. Needless to say, I tried on half as many pairs as I normally did, and he made a quick sale. That really great technological experience impressed me greatly and didn't disappoint. If he was doing his SWOT analysis, that experience would be a huge advantage as a team member. Just like these examples, you're looking for components in the team members' process that give an advantage.

Of course, we also need to look at weaknesses exactly as before. If you manage a restaurant and your register still requires you to pull a lever to open the cash register, I'd say you have a disadvantage there. If you manage a clothing store and while receiving inventory, you notice there isn't a warehouse big enough to hold inventory, then that could be a disadvantage.

I once set an appointment for a service I needed at an auto repair shop through their website a week in advance. When I arrived fifteen minutes early, they couldn't find me in the system. Two team members told me that I didn't set an appointment, and I had to schedule an appointment two weeks out. I had the email in hand confirming. Disappointed, I asked for the manager. In his research, he found out that their website changed to a different one and he was unaware of when. Later finding out that all other locations already made the transition, they couldn't see my appointment unless they used the older program. The team members at the shop knew about the program changing on their computers, but they were not told when it would take effect or how it would have an effect on the customer level. Later finding out from calling corporate about my dissatisfaction, they indicated that all teams were notified and held a district training on how to transfer said data to the new system that managers were supposed to bring back to their teams. Unfortunately, the manager was either unorganized, had poor communication skills, or wasn't attentive during the training. I also believe he wasn't the only one. Think about how much business they lost. That broken process could reveal quite a few disadvantages. Any component in your team members' daily process that appears to be a disadvantage needs to be recorded as a weakness in your SWOT analysis.

Note to Mid to Upper Management

If you're in a midlevel to executive position or plan to promote into a role such as a district or area manager and up, then for your first ten days, you're scheduling time to follow the same observing behaviors and performance reports of your direct reporting managers. You'll be completing the same SWOT analysis, but you'll also be observing and developing your managers to utilize this guide and reflect like behaviors in your responsible stores, franchises, and so forth in phase 2. So it is especially important for you to be familiar with this guide in its entirety.

From days 11 to 25, just as the managers spend their time in their team members' shoes, you'll be spending time in your direct reporting manager's shoes. Schedule your days accordingly a day ahead to see which locations you'll visit. I recommend one a day, if possible. Two will be overwhelming, trust me. Additionally, unless there are occasional exceptions, even managers deserve the same face-to-face. Although as they develop, they don't need it daily, they still need a presence. You won't take over their role directly (particularly their decision and authority power). You will just work your day as the manager does. Your first ten days will provide you an idea of your manager's day. Just mimic what you've observed from each manager and from what you learned about their process compared to what's expected, and lead by example. You're gaining two weeks of experience in that role. If you have a fairly large area to cover, then increase however long it takes to visit all managers in *their* environment. If you're new to the company, this is a very important crash course. If you're promoted from such a position luckily, you may already have perspective, but it's even more crucial to see firsthand what behaviors are missing and be provided with a visual of what success looks like to your managers. This method and behavior are even more impactful at the mid- and upper-manager level than the team-member level because with the typical company, the higher you move up the ladder, the less you see this type of interactive training between upper and lower management. It's unfortunate, but it's the cultural truth in business. However, it doesn't mean people chose it. It just became what it is for reasons mentioned earlier about upper management disconnecting from the front lines. This is how you can make the difference, relink the gap, and increase the performance of your managers and your career.

You're executing the same behaviors described previously, but there will be a few additional behaviors and steps to complete. Other members of management may add specific observations they would like for you to perform, which is great, but you don't want to observe less than these five additional behaviors as these results heavily impact your execution in phase 2. Again, when you're observing a manager, you want to view how their behaviors reflect what you've previously learned in *this* guide and if the company's expected behaviors are reflected, *but* also the following:

1. Team inclusiveness (does your manager encourage team development through teamwork activities and/or trainings)
2. Team morale (you're basically looking for the level of passion behind the team and the manager's ability to positively impact it)
3. Do they have a process in place? A business should run like a well-oiled machine.

4. Ability to coach (if applicable) Does the manager have a skill set to coach effectively?
5. Do they know their business? (Great time to ask what are some strengths and weaknesses they are aware of about their business. Be sure to request supporting documents and reports, a "trust, but verify" technique you should never stop using.)

You can certainly add to this list, based on your experiences. As mentioned before, this is a guide to help build a foundation and to help you start your growth at a faster pace. However, never let your growth be limited to what's between a book's covers. Learn and execute these techniques, but add anything new or of value to your team.

Day 26–30 External Research

So here we are, already in the last five days of your first thirty. That means we can relax, right? No. Just checking your understanding. Remember, it's called the first one hundred days, not thirty. However, these five days will seem like a small break from your observations. That's because these crucial days will be spent to complete the rest of your SWOT analysis. So what do you have left to complete? Opportunities and threats.

If you recall, these sections are related to external factors that impact your business—in other words, variables outside your team and company that can *and* will impact your team's performance. This is where we actively explore the natural and economic conditions, the surrounding communities, and your competition, almost like taking a five-day field trip—all very important aspects of your business you can't afford not to know in this competitive market.

You can have the most influential and passionate team members on this earth, but all of their skill sets will be meaningless without having customers/clients in front of them, right? Having knowledge of your external environment helps you capture the most out of your business through learning how to capture majority of your market share.

REMEMBER: All of the time and knowledge you gain of your opportunities and threats will be wasted and useless if you don't act to maximize the information you've gathered.

The point of reviewing opportunities is to maximize any advantages. The point of reviewing threats is to plan accordingly and either minimize disadvantages or turn them into advantages. In many cases, with effective planning, you can certainly turn threats into opportunities. In retrospect, without effective planning, you can certainly turn opportunities into threats. This process is in place to learn your business and create an effective strategy that your team can effectively execute and succeed.

Natural and Economic Conditions

When I say natural and economic conditions, I mean just that. You want to know how and why your customers/clients move in and out of your business. When you're looking for natural factors, you want to look for external events like traffic patterns, travel times, environmental factors such as weather patterns or seasons, innate behaviors, etc. For example, traffic may pick up during lunch hours and after business hours because that is when most people have time to do so. If you manage a tax consulting firm, then you know that between April 1 and April 15, demand shoots through the roof because most of society tends to procrastinate (tax season). This is a natural condition. In Virginia Beach, during the summer, tourism is booming by the oceanfront because of expected beautiful weather conditions and the natural attractiveness the beach provides. All these are examples of natural opportunities because they provide opportunities for your team to grow your business and for your team to grow and excel.

Threats would be the exact opposite. Perhaps the slowest days for foot traffic may lie on the holidays. Any beach strip on the east coast during the winter will experience a major decrease in sales overall. Some businesses are located in areas with a higher risk of flooding. It's been studied in retail that when people enter stores, they naturally go right. In many cases, if you're unaware, this could be a threat. Your business may be located on a one-way street. These are all examples of natural threats because these natural events can negatively impact the performance and acceleration of your team and your business if you're not prepared.

Economic conditions are those impacted by economic factors such as the market, supply and demand, predictable events like currency value, economic disasters, business acquisitions, etc. A classic example for all of retail is the holidays. For most businesses, these times pose as big opportunities to increase sales and market share because of holiday sales. To maximize your team's performance, you may plan staff accordingly and have great sale packages available with services or products. For other businesses, their opportunities may lie right after the holidays. For example, retail stores soak up all the opportunities during holidays as the market is in its spending cycle. However, afterward, the banks soak up all the opportunities as the market now focuses on recovering through savings or refinancing. If you're a broker in real estate, you may discover the market shifting from a buyer's market to a seller's market due to low inventory. If you aren't aware, you can't prepare. All these are examples of economic opportunities.

Threats found in the economic space most certainly exist as we experienced many times in the United States as well as the world market. If a company struggled in profits and shareholders call for reducing its workforce, a layoff heavily impacts morale, which negatively impacts your team's performance. If you're managing within a technology-based business, then you should be very familiar with supply and demand reactions in the market. If a new phone comes to the market anticipating a million-plus units in sales, but the production line went on strike, only producing a half a million, that becomes an economic threat because competitors could take advantage of all those missed sales. Just as the example referencing the retailers and the banks, if you flip their seasonal opportunities, then you have threats to their businesses. Banks struggle in the fourth quarter if unprepared as well as retailers struggle in the first quarter. These are examples of economic factors that can threaten your team's performance. Again, proper planning can minimize loss under these conditions or even convert them into opportunities. Now that we have a basic understanding of what natural and economic conditions are, then we can look closer as to where to start looking—locally.

The Community

For the next five days, all your time is spent on learning about your community and your competition, but let's start with your community. This is an interesting topic for me because I find it unbelievable how many teams and businesses look past their own community to find business. I've seen hundreds of teams and businesses reach out to other zip codes, districts, and even states beyond their community to find business first. I haven't led one team that struggled to find their business right in the heart of their location. Maybe you've joined a business that doesn't cater to the community. If that's the case, a different question should be asked. I've thrived tremendously from the business provided within a two-mile radius. You would think looking this close first would be obvious, but it happens all the time. It is unfortunate for the community, but you're not the typical manager. You're becoming or continuing as a top-performing leader, so your community will be excited to have you. If you're midlevel to upper management, then the area in which your teams are within.

Regardless of how far you wish to go, learn it. You want to learn about the history, demographics, any organizations like a chamber of commerce, popular areas, attractions, organized events, etc. This data can be collected in many ways: face to face, the Internet, social media, the community, etc. Unlike other conditions, your community is a unique attribute of your business. That attribute is, if you learn about your community, it can only present opportunities for you. For example, you manage a team of salesmen and women selling a $200 vacuum and have to knock on doors just around the corner from your brick-and-mortar store to hit your monthly goal within the next twenty-four hours. You know there is a fairly big neighborhood right behind your business and decide close by is the perfect place to start. Toward the end of the day, the results were unfortunately low. Therefore, you missed your goal. After a conversation with a couple of locals, you find out that the neighborhood you sent your team into was a low-income neighborhood. Would you agree that a $200 vacuum may seem irrelevant to other needs within this community? Had you have known that, would you have made a different decision on where to earn more business? I hope so, because these situations happen all the time. To learn about your target market, you really need to learn about your community. These are people who are all potential customers or clients. What you learn and discover from your community will only be recorded under the opportunity quadrant.

REAL LIFE

I met an owner of a bakery who spent over ten thousand dollars to prepare for a grand opening on a Friday. The day of her grand opening, only a handful of people stood by the door. All weekend, she only made a little over two thousand dollars. Her baked goods were amazing, the prices were just right, and her hours were good, from nine to seven. So what could have impacted her grand opening? It turned out that there was a huge annual baking festival going on all weekend that ran from nine to five. This community prides itself on the festival. Although she only lived there for a couple of months, she didn't learn about her community. She suffered a very costly loss on her grand opening and missed a huge opportunity. If she had only learned more about her community, she could have introduced her products at the festival to gain significant exposure, make great profits, and then hold a tremendously successful grand opening the following weekend after the community had the opportunity to taste her amazing products. Her business has picked up since and is doing great now, but that is still an opportunity she regretted and can't get back.

When you get out into your communities, the opportunities you really want to look for are organizations you can join, such as community councils, your local chamber of commerce, small business network groups, etc. It is also very important to find community service organizations or nonprofits, which you can form a partnership with. I have created more opportunities and more awareness through community involvement than any other aspect of participation in the community. As we discussed about the impact on your team from community involvement just in morale and empowerment, it can also impact your community the same way. Taking care of your community will always result in your community taking care of you. I couldn't ever say enough to illustrate how important it is to help your community every chance you get.

If you're a manager in retail and you discover there is a small business chamber of commerce that meets once a month, then you would record that as an opportunity. If you lead a company located on one street and you learned about construction closing off the next street over, then this is an opportunity for you to get more business from the increased traffic. If you lead a construction company and you found out that Habitat for Humanity is looking for contractors to help them build their next home, this would be a great opportunity for you. All events within your community are important, but you certainly want to record any event you find that can impact your business as an opportunity, if any.

Every year, I've had my teams participate in multiple community events throughout the year. In some cases, they didn't know what events would be available, but they were excited and ready to participate in anything because they loved the impact it made on the community and themselves. For example, every November, we always team up with a food drive organization, set a date to hold the event, then set up a table right in the store and out (if able) so we'll be right in front of our customers and clients. Some years, we even teamed up with bigger organizations to make a massive drive in a mall parking lot. We displayed them as such to show the community that not only are we participating in assisting them, but if they would like to participate, we hope our collection will encourage them to do so. Just in the past few years, our contributions have fed over a thousand families in need. When November came close, my team got really excited to participate and started shooting ideas on what to do for the coming event. In most cases, they even challenged each other over previous years' performances, which of course led to fun competitions for the event. It was always a tremendous turnout with the help of our customers, clients, community, and team members alike.

We also held a similar event during the Christmas holiday. As a team, my team would come in after hours (a day picked by the team) in order to decorate the store and put together our center of attention for the toy drive: a beautiful holiday tree. My team would start the event off by collecting toys themselves to place at the foot of the tree. Over the month, between other participating stores and the community, the foot of the tree would overflow, completely full of presents before the 23rd. The organization we chose that year would come to pick up the toys, wrap them, and deliver them to families in need on Christmas Eve. Toys for all ages was just another moment where my team felt so fulfilled and proud to support the wonderful communities we were a part of. In addition, I would never leave it just to my team to participate. I personally would take $100 or more every year, break them into ten-dollar bills, and hang them in beautiful Christmas bags on the doorknobs of ten or more random homes throughout the surrounding communities. I did so to remind people that their community cares, a tradition I've done since I was in my younger twenties, and now my family and friends participate. The point is, you can utilize these empowerments to grow your team's performance both internally and externally. As I said previously, learning about your community can only be an opportunity because if you take care of your community, it will always take care of you.

The Competition

Have you ever dreamed of being a secret spy? This is your chance. However, keep the secret gadgets at home. All you'll need is an Internet source and your time. This is the really competitive piece of your research, as it's time to learn what threats really lie out there for your business and your team's overall performance. Although competition as a whole is a great opportunity for progress and business evolution, for your SWOT analysis, they will be recorded as a threat. After all, your competition wants to take your business, a balance to your purely opportunistic community observation. If there was any threat to document within your community, it would be your competition. A threat in this perspective means external factors that have an advantage over your business, or in other words, a disadvantage you have, which is precisely what your competition means to take advantage of.

Learning about your competition will not only help you adapt and evolve your product and/or service presentation but will also allow you to create strong value statements when customers and clients are deciding to choose your business over another. When you're compared to your competition, you need to know how to respond to those advantages and disadvantages professionally. The worst thing you can do in sales, as discussed in pillar IV, is guess. Your customers and clients alike will either know or find out. Never lie. In many cases, just knowing about your competition is a competitive advantage in itself.

Although you want to document all that you find, don't record your results on your SWOT analysis until you have completed these three steps in order to have a full picture of your competitors. When you're learning about your community, take note of any direct competitors in the area. First, be sure to gather as much information as possible, such as the business name, address, surroundings (like at the corner of a popular crossroad), phone number, manager's name (this will come in handy later in this section), and anything else you feel is important to know from observation. Second, once this basic information is gathered, do your research because you will eventually end up in their lobby. (Yup. I just said that.) Learn about their products and services offered, how often they hold sales events (if possible), how long they've been in the community, whether they participate in any community organizations or events, and any other information you feel is important to notate. The third step would be to set an appointment or a date to visit during your five days.

You know who they are. You know what they offer. The only thing left to discover is their level of service provided. Don't worry. This is the fun part. You get to be the secret spy you've always wanted to be as a kid. However, as fun as it can get, you want to be sure to get exactly what you need. Among the questions *you* want to ask, be sure to include these questions as well:

1. Were you greeted through the door? If so, how long did it take?
2. How many times were you greeted/acknowledged?
3. How are the team members dressed?
4. How is the team members' energy? (Engaged? Slacking?)
5. Did a team member ask questions to uncover your needs?
6. Did a team member ask deeper, open-ended questions to uncover any unperceived needs?
7. Did a team member offer products/services that matched your need(s)?
8. Did a team member offer multiple solutions that solve your need(s) or concern?
9. Was the team member friendly?
10. Did the team member maintain eye contact?
11. Did the team member take notes during your engagement?
12. Did you have an opportunity or were you given an opportunity to meet the manager?

The answer to these questions will help put together a great analysis on your competition. You'll be able to determine a few key traits like whether your competitor has a process, what their level of execution is, whether they're organized, whether they're motivated to perform and assist, whether they have competitive products and services, whether their management team is engaged, and whether they present a strong first impression. Furthermore, you'll also determine their weaknesses, which will certainly come into play later in this pillar. For now, you've collected enough information to make a strategic analysis about your competition. With technology these days, it wouldn't hurt for you to see also what the customers/clients are saying about your competition through surveys and reviews, if available. Sometimes, you'll find opportunities and threats just through their own webpage. Many businesses add feedback features just to appeal to the information age but don't use the feedback to their advantage. So why not use it to your advantage?

REAL LIFE

When I took over a team with an electronic retailer, the market was pretty fierce and the team was oblivious to how much market share our competition had. In addition, our customers seemed to have more knowledge than most of the associates. Imagine what those conversations would sound like when customers would try to compare us to a competitor and the associate had no knowledge of it. In the information age, when customers have more knowledge at their fingertips, companies cannot afford to *not* be in the know. While researching my SWOT analysis, I visited four brick-and-mortar competitors and an online competitor (that's right, an online direct competitor). In one day, I visited each store, looking for the same behaviors I've listed previously. For the online competitor, I answered the same questions even though I knew most answers would be no. That's the point. That was a competitive advantage I had over the online retailer. However, there were still questions that were presented to me online (minus the associate asking) that were offering or recommending additional products and services 100 percent of the time (a competitive threat). Anyhow, in addition to answering these questions with all of the retailers, I also asked about their financing options, which are pivotal in the retail world, especially electronics.

One store used clipboards with their ads on hand, and they were aggressive with referencing price matching. Another store had very informative team members about their products, but they didn't take any notes on the info I provided (that would help me save my breath in repeating myself several times). Some had associates with limited experience and knowledge about their products and services. Others provided very friendly services. Some of the stores, majority of the time, would provide some of the best prices in the industry. All these became points listed under my threats section in my SWOT analysis. Listing these points eventually helped my team evolve into the best of the best in their community and beyond, by offering more what the competition could.

In addition, by taking the time to collect these answers from each competitor and learning about the services they provide, I was able to discover a completely new advantage. I noticed during my visits, the competition didn't even know about *their* competition. That was a big opportunity point for my team. Why? Because that was something that anyone could take advantage of, but hadn't yet. My team had to be the first.

The first thing I did was collect all the weekly ads from these competitors and look solely at the financing options they provided for their top products to start. Once these were collected, I would create a side-by-side grid for comparing our bundles to our competitors'. One extra priority starting at the beginning of the week turned into providing my team with valuable knowledge of our competition. I updated the grid weekly since that was how long the industry would run their weekly sales. What started as a knowledgeable tool became a sales tool used on the sales floor to provide visual comparisons for customers, a new tool that helped close sales. When a customer would openly share that they wanted to visit another store to shop for other options, we already had the competitors' ads and their finance options on hand. This tool kept a majority of those customers from walking out the door and instead closed the sale. It looked like this:

Products	My Company	Competitor A	Competitor B	Competitor C
Product A	$99	$130	$95	$110
Product B	$298	$299	$329	$329
Product C	$840	$895	$899	$880

A couple of months after my launch, our company created a very similar grid to launch companywide. They completed the research and printout for each department, saving me more time to be on the floor, thankfully. I was excited to see my idea come to life on such a scale. This grid helped increase our sales by approximately 20 percent. Digging deeper, I wanted to see how else we could utilize this grid to increase our closed sales. Taking a survey from my team members, I found out that the biggest objection from customers about that the grid was that it was overwhelming to compare with. Although they loved the comparison available, it was rather difficult for them to determine the best offers immediately from a glance. In some instances, some prices were so close that sales were still lost even if we were a couple dollars less. Just having the number in comparison opened up those types of objections. I don't know about you, but when I'm shopping for something, I never plan to read small print, charts, or grids myself for the best deal, so I understood their objection. I preferred something more efficient to help me figure things out faster. Therefore, I had to help our customers with the same dilemma.

While sitting on the couch in our lounge, I saw an insurance commercial emphasizing how they may not always be the cheapest competitor, but you can always count on them to show you the best deal. That was it! Although we weren't always the best deal on the market (but in most cases, we were), all we wanted to do was help our customers find the best deal faster, keeping them in store longer (higher chances of closing a sale). The point was showing our customers in a glance. Thankfully, a majority of the time, we did, but we weren't doing a good job sharing that message. So I took a blue Sharpie, read over the grid, and placed a thick check mark next to the best deals in each category for each department. Reworked, the grid now looked like this:

Products	My Company	Competitor A	Competitor B	Competitor C
Product A			✓	
Product B	✓			
Product C	✓			

Ta-da! In a glance, anyone can immediately see which store had the best deal simply by looking for the big blue checkmarks under the store categories. In addition, if the deal was really a better deal at another store, we were honest enough to provide it because ultimately, we wanted what was best for our customers. In some cases, if we had a customer looking for two of the three products and we had more checkmarks than the competition, even if one product was a better deal at another location, they would still purchase with us because of how the grid impacted their perception. In other cases, we were still chosen over better competitive packages. Talk about an impact. This small change increased the team's confidence, and in sharing this information, overall sales closed over 28 percent more business. This exact result later contributed to my team becoming one of the top-performing teams in the company worldwide. The greatest point that should be taken from this example is that this all began by researching the competition for my SWOT analysis. This is only one of the millions of opportunities that could open up for your team and your career just by learning about your competition and understanding the opportunities and threats.

Your SWOT analysis is ready to complete. You've gathered internal information by observing strengths and weaknesses from the leader's perspective. Then, you've completed the secret step of observing strengths and weaknesses through the team member's perspective. For all of your opportunities and threats, you've taken time to learn about your community and your direct competitors around you. With this collected information, you now have enough knowledge to form your SWOT analysis. Study this information closely, as it will help you create a valuable strategy by maximizing your strengths, minimizing your weaknesses, taking advantage of your opportunities, and adapting to your threats. Like my example in retail and banking, having a completed SWOT analysis allowed my team to adapt to our competition and connect with our community, which ultimately contributed to creating a very powerful team of believers and achievers. Again, the SWOT analysis is not just for one industry. This tool can be used across any industry. Here is an example of a simple SWOT analysis:

Strengths (Focus)	Weaknesses (Awareness)
• The only company that offers installation	• Currently have only 2 installers
• We guarantee lowest prices	• Receive shipments only every other week
• The nearest competitor is 8 miles away	• POS systems are outdated and slow
• Two annual trade shows are coming up	• Competitor Company A have very efficient transactions
• A new apartment community is opening up 2 miles away	• Competitor B participates in multiple community events
• A new print business just had a grand opening across the street	• Competitor A runs weekly deals
Opportunities (Potential)	Threats (Motivation)

Day 31–33—Analyze to Strategize

So what now? After completing your SWOT analysis, this is where you need to take time to analyze your results and develop your strategy. During these three days, you're still at least utilizing your 70/30 rule on the floor, but I would recommend also reviewing your analysis at home. Homework? Yes, homework. Some of the best strategies come to mind outside the work environment, especially in a non-stressful environment. This time is absolutely necessary. Like Benjamin Franklin said, "By failing to prepare, you're preparing to fail." The good news is, just from your observation period, you already have an idea of what to change, evolve, and/or create. Although the foundation of my training remained the same with every team I've led, implementation was different every time. That's because of different industries, restrictions, communities, team members, etc. Every team and every company will proposition different circumstances. However, your basic principles need to remain consistent. For example, every team I've led, I've trained to greet customers/clients right through the door with a warm smile and a positive welcome, regardless if it was a department store or a stand-alone business. That's because I believe we should be thankful for every person who considered walking through our door; therefore, they should be treated as such. All my trained teams smiled and welcomed each person every time—different teams, different experiences, same behaviors. It ultimately became an infectious behavior they loved to do in their personal lives. That is a principle within my leadership and regardless of which team I led—that "Southern" courtesy and professional greeting will always be standard behavior. You have principles I'm sure you want to continue, right? If not, just adapt what you've learned here and grow from there. That's why this guide is here. That's why I am here.

The first thing you want to focus on is creating your ideal day. What I mean by an ideal day is what you'd want to experience when walking into your business. What does that experience look like if you were the customer, or a new team member, and you walked right through the door? What experience do you expect you'll have today to compare? Once you have a visual of what you should see, hear, and feel, then you have a goal. Now let's break that down by reviewing your strengths and weaknesses.

NOTE: Another fallacy behind the utilization of the SWOT analysis is that many leaders try to change everything you've documented all at once. As we discussed with organizing top priorities, no one can truly complete their priority list, and you certainly don't want to multitask top priorities. Each priority needs your focus in order to complete it effectively, efficiently, and successfully. I've never heard of a NASCAR driver playing on their phone during a pit stop, or a quarterback playing at the casino the day before a game. As easy as it may be to do those things, you *will* lose complete focus and risk losing everything you've worked to achieve. This happens all the time when lists are created.

Following what you've learned in pillar II, organize your priorities from your SWOT analysis. You might only have three strengths listed. Others may have over ten. Don't be concerned about the number you have. However, let's narrow our focus to the top three strengths and weaknesses that can dramatically impact your business. Again, this is only the start. As your team progresses, you'll have time to circle around to the next three focuses (if any).

You now have your top three strengths and your top three weaknesses, so let's grow these categories. As I said, the objective is to create your ideal day. Focusing on your top strengths first, like an Alpha priority, think of how you can maximize those behaviors. Or ask yourself, how can you help your team members maximize their strengths? For example, if a strength you've observed was product knowledge, then you could assume that your team members love to learn about the products and services they offer. So as I've done in the past with similar teams, I would bring in vendors to host small seminars, tech classes, and even some lunch-and-learns that kept them engaged. In addition, from the customers' perspective, I would try to find a creative way for them to recognize visually how knowledgeable my team *was*, similar to my assessment and competitive grid example. As another example, if one of your top strengths was transaction efficiency, then you could help each team member improve their skills with sales and efficiency by scheduling one-on-one role plays or holding competitive contests for who can score the highest on an efficiency test. These tactics help keep their strengths sharp and encourage development.

Now that you have an idea of how to capitalize on your strengths section, let's look at our top weaknesses. As I referenced earlier, don't focus on your weaknesses; however, never ignore them. That will only lead to more problems or postpone any issue(s) at hand until it's too late. The meaning of this section is simply awareness. Like forming our priority list in pillar II, the focus on developing your top weaknesses is more like Bravo priorities. We don't avoid them, nor do we make them a top priority. We plan accordingly. For example, let's say one of your top weaknesses was your team members feeling overwhelmed. You discover you should have ten positions filled, but only have seven. So one solution is to schedule a meeting with your recruiter or HR department. You'll discuss who you're looking for, what specific traits you'd like to have in a candidate, and a timeline on when to set up interviews. Afterward, schedule follow-ups. This weakness now becomes a delegated Bravo priority to someone who specializes in this field (their strength is recruiting). This will buy you time to focus on your strengths.

Furthermore, as another example, let's say another weakness may be organization. During your observations, you've noticed team members scrambling around to find resources to assist their customer/client requests or to make a simple sale. This could ultimately create an inconsistent or unpredictable experience. Although organization is a major factor in becoming efficient, it doesn't make sense for you to spend time creating a weekly class or seminar that teaches team members how to be organized. Your time is too valuable for that. Instead, you could create one seminar or training session with another member of your company who has a great system in place already. They could teach your team members how to organize their workplace. Following the training, you could set up three checkpoints for those team members: one week after the class, two weeks after the first checkpoint, and thirty days after the second checkpoint. Remember, you'll be able to see their progress daily, but the checkpoints allow team members to communicate effectively and actively respond about their progress. Having these checkpoints will allow you to focus on your top strengths with the team while developing and remaining aware of your top weaknesses.

Delegation is key in keeping those weaknesses in check so you can harbor those strengths to their maximum potential. This dynamic angle is what allows your team to learn, develop, and grow exponentially. If delegation is not available, then you can find a more creative solution, such as changing behaviors to avoid your weaknesses or expanding your strengths to minimize the impact of such weaknesses. Either way, your time is more effectively spent on growing your strengths.

So, let's jump into your opportunities and threats, or as we classified these earlier, your potentials and motivations. Just as we identified the top three strengths and weaknesses (your Focus and Awareness categories), you want to identify the top three most impactful opportunities and threats. When looking at your opportunities, I would look for those opportunities that would allow my team and my business to get the most exposure. The more exposure your team has in the community, the more business you'll inevitably bring back to your team. This area doesn't require strategy as much as it requires participation. There can be literally hundreds of organizations you can participate in within a single community. Depending on where your business is located, that could soar into the thousands, precisely why you're narrowing down to the three most impactful opportunities to start.

The key is to form a timeline of when you can get your team to participate in those community events. Nothing fancy. Just mark three upcoming events on your calendar for this current quarter or the next. Just get your team out into the community. If your community is coming in to give you their money and time, the least you can do is give you time back. Once you have dates set in your team calendar, communicate that in every way possible to your team via meetings, emails, social media, and so forth (remember to know your policies around social media for your company before posting, if any). This is something your team should feel proud of. It also helps to encourage your team members to incorporate family and friends if some events allow it. In addition, they can share their participation with their customers and clients alike. Before you reach your third event, plan the next three out. This way, your team will stay active, willing, and energized about participation. That inspiring feeling will eventually have your team bring event ideas to you. Those are the most impactful events to participate in because those are your team members' events that you fully support. That kind of support from leaders is what creates loyalty. Take advantage of it.

When reviewing your threats, you're looking for the top three biggest competitive advantages your competition practices. You'll use these as motivators to inspire you and your team to innovate new products, services, and experiences, hence referring to this category as motivations. By *experiences*, I mean the look and feel of your store, the customer service provided, and their overall experience of your customers or clients with your team. Once you've chosen your first three motivators, I recommend writing them on a board or typing and posting them in an area where only your team may view them. At the very least, print them and hand out to your team members for review during a meeting. Just like goals, these are meant to motivate your team to innovate ways to best your competition and push themselves to evolve. If your competition has a stronger first impression like cleanliness and tactfulness, then write it on the board and have an open conversation with your team on how they can provide a stronger first impression. It's very important to involve your team in how they would like to compete. This minimizes resistance and generates more passion as you're using their ideas to grow the business, not to mention that most of the best ideas are generated from your team just by listening. If your competition has a more efficient POS (point of sale) system, then write it on the board and discuss how your team can use their current systems in a more creative and efficient way to compete. At the very least, minimize the clients' negative experience from the uncontrollable issue.

REAL LIFE

I ran a team that probably had one of the most inefficient POS systems to work on, as it required the use of three platforms to make one transaction. Our competition only had one. Much more efficient, right? In addition, I'd managed teams on the competitor's side, so I had some inside knowledge on how much more efficient they truly were. However, I wasn't going to allow that to stop my performance, and I wasn't going to let it stop my team. Together, we came up with an idea that was simple yet effective, which would distract our clients from our inefficient transaction time and uncover potential opportunities in sales. My team decided during peak times to have two dedicated cashiers that would begin the transaction while the sales team showed additional demonstrations on effective accessories or new product lines while their transaction was being completed. They turned boring and inconvenient wait times into something interactive, educational, and in most cases, fun.

The amazing part of this idea was that our transaction total increased by $40 per transaction on average. That's right! We managed to make additional sales during this wait period. We turned a threat into an opportunity. We let this motivator maximize our potential.

Over time, the word about our unique experience spread and became a nationwide behavior with the company. Although our competition was more efficient with their transaction time, the experience we provided was more effective in sales and client/customer relationships. This team-generated behavior propelled our team to the top in performance, becoming the third most profitable team in the company. The top two were located in two of the biggest cities in the United States. It all started with presenting the team our competitor's advantage, encouraging a brainstorm on how to compete and provide a better service to our community. We didn't allow it to threaten us. It motivated us to become better within ourselves and to make sure we provided the best experience in the community.

With your SWOT analysis narrowed down to your top three most impactful options in each quadrant, you can see the bigger picture. Now forming your strategy should be much easier. Remember what you learned in pillar IV. If your team is missing any of those behaviors, be sure to add those trainings to your implementation strategy, especially if your competition is already reflecting them. If you work for a major company or have been with your company for quite some time, then you already have an implementation strategy that's expected for you to utilize. Just add these new behaviors and resources to your training to improve your team faster. If you're new to the company, then team up with your manager to identify the best strategy to help reflect their expectations. Again, once that is provided, add these new behaviors and resources to your strategy to improve your performance faster. Although it seems like a lot in three days, it's not. What you will learn is that following the observation period as described will develop an awareness of what to improve and a stronger idea on how to improve. If you experienced any struggle, don't worry. That only means a step was missed. Simply take another day to walk through the strategy from day 1 to day 33 and check off every step that you've completed. You'll certainly find what was missed and be able to correct it easily to get back on track. The great part about my system is that it's flexible and easy to pick up where you left off. Once completed, you're ready to begin phase 2: implementation.

REMEMBER: Like a muscle, learning this system takes time to develop through consistent study and practice. Mistakes will be made, but have no concern. That is all part of your development and growth.

Phase 2: Implementation

I'm sure you've heard a thousand times from motivational speakers, bosses, colleagues, friends, and business enthusiasts alike that it takes twenty-one days to create a habit. I've noticed that the upper management always referenced this as a challenge to their teams to hustle around a new behavior or service. Then during their follow-up twenty-five days later, they became frustrated with the results because team members hadn't memorized a certain script or behavior identically to what their expectation was. I had a manager that would consistently reference this quote and aggressively demand follow-ups on day 22 to determine if we were consistent in reflecting these behaviors in our respective departments. To his surprise (and to us), nobody was ever 100 percent, not even 50 percent. Team members were still fumbling or stuttering to remember scripts with precise greetings or rebuttals. I knew something wasn't right about this. Timing seemed off, based on these consistent results, not to mention how frustrated we were at constantly failing their expectation. So leave it to me to challenge my manager in asking who determined that it took twenty-one days. He didn't even know who said the quote. My manager was holding us accountable to something he knew nothing about.

Among my research, I found out something intriguing. Dr. Maxwell Maltz, who seemed to be a brilliant plastic surgeon back in the '50s, was the one credited for this reference in his book called *Psycho-Cybernetics*. This book sold tens of millions of copies, so it's no surprise how popular it grew in the business world. However, he was a plastic surgeon. In his book, he referenced patients who underwent his surgeries, like nose replacements and amputations, and discovered that it took approximately twenty-one days for those patients to adjust to their new life-changing condition. The interesting part is that he actually said "usually requires a minimum of about . . ." in his quote we know today about the twenty-one-day behavior change. Specifically, he said, *"It usually requires a minimum of about 21 days to effect any perceptible change in a mental image."* I don't know about you, but that whole sentence really doesn't narrow it down to twenty-one days. Obviously, the "usually requires a minimum of about . . ." part got lost in translation throughout the years. Also notice the phrasing "perceptible change in a mental image" is a completely different reference from behaviors. This was in the medical perspective on image acceptance, not new behavioral adaptation. Nonetheless, people obviously connected this theory with behaviors in general, but was there any reference to a sociological point when developing new behaviors not related to self-image?

Mind blown yet? Check this out. It turns out, in 2009, a team of researchers led by health psychologist Phillippa Lally at the University College London held a ninety-six-day study for twelve weeks. She published her results in the *European Journal of Social Psychology* discovering the best average was more like sixty-six days, not twenty-one. She had results from 18 days to projections over 250 days (those participants who didn't adapt to their new behavior within the twelve-week period). A *best* average was sixty-six days. Before I learned about this publication, I discovered that my teams learned and adapted to these behaviors between fifty and seventy days under my system. And that was with consistent coaching and development every day from open to close as this guide walks you through. I was excited to see that my results didn't differ from Lally's research and even more so to know that I wasn't crazy to challenge my manager's aggressive twenty-one-day drive.

I hope you've learned something new here to at least help you challenge the twenty-one-day myth, but back to my original point. If you haven't noticed how many days are left, take a look now. You have sixty-six days left in your first one hundred days. Coincidence? Probably so, considering that my one-hundred-day plan developed prior to Lally's publication, but what are the odds that we came up with similar results? It's fascinating actually, and I was very thankful to see such research supporting my thought process. Ever wondered why our military basic training camps last approximately seven to nine weeks (forty-nine to sixty-three days)? There are sixty-six days left in our implementation process, and these sixty-six days are reserved for the coaching and development of these new behaviors, precisely what's expected as the best average under Lally's research.

Now, Lally's research involved one behavior for each of the participants, but they also weren't in a controlled environment with consistent reinforcement, such as a work environment. In addition, the behaviors chosen weren't consistent with each participant (therefore, no team supporting reinforcement). You'll be training your team to learn a reasonable amount of behaviors in a consistent, interactive process. That means under these work conditions, team members can certainly learn within sixty-six days, especially with my model in your hand.

The more challenging question you should ask yourself is this: "Self, if the best average learned a new behavior within sixty-six days, how can multiple behaviors be taught within the same time frame?" As always, an excellent question. The secret lies in simplicity, of course, but to be more illustrative, let's refer to a previous sales strategy for example. Just like in pillar IV with the bundling strategy, you don't want to teach each particular behavior one at a time as it would obviously take too long and certainly cost a lot of money (wages and missed opportunities from team members tied up constantly in training instead of the sales floor, for example). You want to find a way to bundle smaller behaviors into a single behavior that can impact the same end result. The following section is developed to help you maximize your sixty-six days left by bundling multiple behaviors into a few. With practice each day, you'll be capable of teaching multiple skills utilizing one simple behavior, one of the most impactful ways human beings were developed to learn.

Here's an example to help. Let's say your team struggles to make a great first impression *and* with identifying additional needs. Instead of training your team to learn two different behaviors at two different time periods with two different forms of measurements for success, make it one—one single behavior that can help a team member reinforce each of those opportunities. In this example, let's require each team member to follow a three-step introduction process with every guest that walked through my doors. Here is one expected behavior I would train that would look like this:

Expected Interaction
Step 1. Formal introduction (SHINE TWICE)
Step 2. Ask three questions with every interaction.
  1. How may I assist you today?
  2. (Once a solution is found) Do you feel this solution will solve your problem? If not, why?
  3. Are there any other needs I can assist with?
Step 3. Formal salutation (SHINE TWICE)

Reading this three-step process, can you see how one behavior (Expected Interaction) supports the first impression dilemma and helping with identifying additional needs (two separate behaviors)? If you're a visual learner, here is a mathematical way of viewing this: Expected Interaction = First Impression + Identify Needs. Don't be confused with step 3 being a third behavior as we discussed in pillar IV that SHINE TWICE was about the intro and exit for the best first impression.

When we are coaching this behavior, we are no longer looking for two behaviors, but now one. We don't want to reference just a bad introduction or failure to identify additional solutions alone. We are coaching to their failure to follow the expected interaction with emphasis on which part of that behavior needs improvement. Treating multiple behaviors as one means there can't be partial credit, right? It is all or nothing just like any single behavior. Again, this is only a broad example just to illustrate how to simplify the process and increase the team members' ability to learn and adapt. Bundle behaviors where you can to help your team members, not to mention team members can now support each other, as they all have the same expectation. Peer accountability, right?

With the Mason influential leadership model, you'll know how to train each team member from each of their respective levels of performance with the same expected behavior. This model and the five pillars create the magic formula you need to maximize their potential to adapt and learn within the time given. Remember, the more you utilize this system, the more efficient and effective you'll get with execution.

The final 66-day phase is broken up into two sub-phases. The first sub-phase holds a strong reinforcement around accountability, which is crucial to your team adapting to your management skill set and your expectations. You're helping the team understand that performance is not only a priority, but also an expectation, which is also crucial for your team's success, performance in both sales and service as discussed in pillar IV. This is where you must remain most vigilant in accountability to their actions in order for your team to evolve into independent Alpha performers. This is where "bad cop" comes into play. Your team will learn your priorities through actions instead of words. Like Theodore "Teddy" Roosevelt said, "Speak softly, but carry a big stick."

In the second sub-phase, you will continue to reinforce accountability goals and behaviors, but with a fun twist. You'll introduce a strategically creative competition to fuel their newly found passion and ability to achieve. The importance here is to introduce what I call artificial competition. This is a tremendous way to measure your team's ability to adapt and apply their newly taught skills in a fast-paced environment, not to mention have fun doing it. Artificial competition is just a fancy way of saying a contest between team members. Although your team doesn't actually compete against each other in the metrics, everyone pretends they do to achieve a fun, successful atmosphere. In other words, these typically don't impact business decisions since it's technically the business playing against itself, hence the term *artificial*. So this is where a leader will use a game of sorts to have team members compete against each other for an award that impacts sales results in a particular area (department, store, region, etc.), something you see all the time, I'm sure, in one form or another.

What I call true competition is your company's business results against your competitor because both actions impact and influence the other's business (pricing, market share, service, product line, net profit, etc.). Think of it this way. True competition attempts to put you out of business. Artificial competition keeps you in business. Initiating artificial competition is the perfect way to reinforce a passion to win as a team and to help the team's self-awareness of what's possible working together in a fun environment. Just note that I said "strategically creative." That doesn't mean playing poker or blackjack for every successful sale. Strategic in the sense that it must have an emotional connection and impact on the team to fuel their desire to perform, gain 100 percent involvement, and encourage teamwork. Creative in the sense where it's something original so the experience is new for the entire team. The team's first experience at something together with positive reinforcement. Think of my Chip-Off Challenge example to illustrate a strategically creative game.

Day 34–70

Begin implementing your strategy by first scheduling one-on-ones to set expectations. All of the research you've completed helped prepare you to become an elite leader, but your team can't become Alpha performers if you don't share what you've learned. It's time to train your team effectively. Unless you already have a training packet you've developed from your experience or one provided by your company, create a training packet with at least these five pages: an engagement checklist (for each respective role), competitor checklist, community checklist, support checklist (for each respective role), and an agreement page. Expect to bring in each team member for at least an hour. Depending on the size of your team, all of your one-on-ones should only carry over a few days. This approach to introducing change is more inviting than many other strategies because you're clarifying expectations prior to accountability. As mentioned before, many team members are held accountable for actions and behaviors that they don't fully understand, a sad setup for failure through the gate. This approach will greatly impact your team members' engagement and minimize pushback. So, let's check out these checklists.

Engagement Checklist

The engagement checklist should be a training checklist consisting of every element from your ideal interaction constructed earlier for each position under your leadership—cashier, sales associate, admin, store manager, etc. Here is an example from the retail world to illustrate further:

- o Formal greeting
  - o Smile
  - o Shake
  - o Introduce
  - o Name (ask if not provided. Repeat if name is given)
  - o Eye contact
- o Identify reason for visit
- o Introduce assessment sheet
- o Ask open-ended questions
- o Identify one unperceived need
- o Introduce to manager
- o Recommend solution
- o Establish a follow-up
- o Formal salutation
  - o Thank
  - o Welcome back
  - o Initiate follow-up
  - o Closing
  - o Exit

Review with each team member each element of your ideal interaction so each has a clear understanding of what's expected. Once you've reviewed the list with your team member, lead by example through role playing, allowing the team member to act as the prospect while you perform the list in its entirety. This will provide a firsthand experience of what you expect and how the team member should reflect, increasing the chance of each team member retaining the lesson. Lastly, you want to switch roles, allowing the team member to take their proper position and reflect what they've learned as *you* play the prospect.

Have the team member use your checklist as a guide during the role play. As I'm sure you've heard before, studies have shown that it takes repeating something at least three times before your memory begins to retain information thoroughly. However, we all know that hearing the same thing over and over can really bore an audience. Repeating this behavior in three different interactions creates three different experiences while reinforcing the same lesson.

Competitive Checklist

The competitive checklist is a list you'll compile based on the information you've learned about your competition in the market, and you'll use it only to help you cover the most impactful information. As mentioned previously, this is where you want to share what you've learned. Only information that you feel is impactful to your business and what your team should be aware of should be on this list. If you'd prefer to introduce any new tools such as my comparison chart example mentioned earlier, this would be the ideal moment to introduce it. Here is an example:

- o Review direct competitors
  - o Ray's Auto Repair
  - o Don's Oil Exchange
- o Review current deals
  - o Weekly ad pricing
  - o Weekend sale
  - o Holiday specials
- o Review competitor behaviors
  - o Products/services offered (if not offered by you)
  - o Competitive advantages

This specific page is to help your team become more aware of who, as a business, they are competing against. This is the moment to generate motivation with your team, to show how they are going to be a part of something greater than their competitors. However, you also have to find out what they are after to connect the common goal. Money is never the motivator for a top performer, no matter how much they say it does. There is always an underlying goal. (For many, money helps them achieve that goal.) Climbing the ladder. Recognition. Becoming champon. Going on a European trip. Owning a new car. Buying a big house. Something. Definitely uncover what that is and help them see that by beating the competition, they'll be able to achieve their personal goals as well. Regardless of what motivates them, they have to know what you've learned. Check off each item as they have been discussed. Or you can have your team member check off the list as you discuss it. Either option is effective, just preference.

Community Checklist

For most human beings, being able to see how your help positively impacts another person is a proud and gratifying moment. Seeing your job help the community is just as impactful. This is a great connecting point too.

The community checklist is provided to help review available opportunities, upcoming events, and additional information you feel is relevant to share with your team. It's human nature to care for mankind as a whole. Paying it forward always pays back. This will help encourage team members to be prepared to participate and add additional value to what they do every day on your team. Here is a small example of what a community checklist would look like:

- o Upcoming Events
    - o Classic Car Show 07/01
    - o Middle School Car Wash 08/01
    - o Hot Rod Parade 11/01
- o Business of Interest: Nonprofits
    - o Jerry's Orphanage
    - o Donate A Car Foundation

o   Metro Children's Hospital
o   Participating Events
   o   Country parade 12/01
   o   Coat collection 10/01

This should be one of the most exciting conversations with your team members. At least, it should be. Out of all of the things to talk about, this subject has had the lowest pushback and highest excitement for it, like recess at school. You're sharing plans about getting out into the community and getting involved to help serve their needs. If it's donating or just providing your time and expertise, you're getting your team involved. Those who already are will praise you. Those who haven't yet, but wanted to, will appreciate you. And those who haven't yet, nor had time to do so, will appreciate you, all from a simple conversation to start. This seems like winning all around.

This conversation will also encourage your team members to become more aware of their communities as well. This is the basis for building a reputation in your respective area. You and your team members can be remembered throughout the community. We've all learned by now about the power of word of mouth, and as we have all witnessed and experienced, powered with social media, our actions speak louder than ever before. Encouraging your team to take care of their community is essential to your success, as your community can provide everything you need to get there. This checklist provides the grand intro into your community strategy.

Support Checklist

Next is the support checklist. This list is to help clarify how you'll play a role in their development. This is the most important checklist because without it, you'll create a misguided message that can develop negative behaviors very quickly. Without this page, there isn't an Alpha team. You will be organizing a brief list of what your team members can expect to see you perform throughout the day, week, month, or entire time they're under your leadership.

Every poor-performing team that I've inherited had a terrible communication problem with their previous manager. Everything was a surprise. Unless it's a celebration, I can't stand surprises. Those types of surprises can topple governments, let alone teams.

They're like secrets. If I stand over your shoulder and begin writing on a clipboard but stay silent and you don't know why, that creates secrets. (The secret is that you are the only one who knows why in this case.) Secrets create fear. Fear creates distrust. And if you were thinking that can lead to the dark side, Yoda would be impressed. I'm sure you know distrust destroys teams. It's the body language that can set the wrong mood if our team isn't prepared to read it. We don't want our team members thinking we are holding secrets from them about their performance. We don't want them feeling negative when you are observing for a coaching opportunity. We want them to feel calm or excited like a test they know they'll ace and if you're watching in awe. They want the recognition they know they deserve. This list helps you organize and effectively communicate what they can expect from you during their development and typical workday. Here is an example of one of my support lists with a past team in banking:

Teller
- o Two observations completed per week
- o First shift check-in per week
  - o Items required:
    - o Monthly/quarterly report
    - o Transaction logs
- o Last shift check-in per week
  - o Items required:
    - o Monthly/quarterly report
    - o Transaction logs
- o Daily expectations

Teller coordinator (supervisor)
- o Conduct at least two observations on each teller per week
- o Conduct first and last shift check ins with tellers

o   Monday performance check-in
  o   Items required:
    o   Monthly/quarterly report
    o   Transaction logs
    o   Teller binder with completed check-in reports
    o   Plan for success
o   Daily expectations

Bankers
  o   One observation completed by leader per shift
  o   Monday performance check-in
    o   Items to complete and return:
      o   Monthly/quarterly performance
      o   Completed banker check-in report
      o   Plan for success
      o   Weekly calendar access
  o   End of day reporting
    o   Items to return completed:
      o   Daily tracker
      o   Appointment log
      o   Completed assessments
  o   Daily expectations

I applied a similar structure to all the teams I've flipped. I made sure it was categorized by each position. This structures role clarity. Under each position, I underline three points. Under those points, when necessary, I referenced additional information important for the team member to expect.

First, lay out what behavior they can expect from you (the leader) or a supporting leader (if applicable, like an assistant manager or supervisor under your leadership). In this example, each member is made aware that they can certainly count on me standing close by at some point of their day to take notes on what I observe during their interaction. I emphasize this is to help their development into an Alpha performer, to help them keep consistent—no other reasons or strings attached. This conversation minimizes excuses and maximizes their effort to perform.

Second is focused on their performance meeting. Depending on where their Level of Performance lies within the Mason influential leadership model, you want to outline when their performance check-ins are and what to have prepared prior to it. For my teams, I either created or use an already existing printout that I have the team members fill out to help them set goals, monitor their current performance, analyze their past performance, and recognize behavior opportunities. You can find examples of it in the resource section at the end.

Majority of the team members I've led are surprised at what's discovered when everything is written down in front of them. The big picture is what you've help create for them. In many cases where they thought they were performing, they discover they're not (or vice versa). This is a strong resource for them to have, and it is very important for you to take your time guiding them through how to complete it.

Third, I always reiterate what behaviors I expect them to fulfill every day. This is also where I'd explain or outline additional tasks that I'd want the intended team member to complete. For instance, what you've learned in pillar II about delegation is the perfect opportunity to help team members assist you with particular tasks that complement their strengths and free up your time for other team members.

Lastly, as with any major expectations you set for your team, you should always make sure there is a clear understanding of what's expected daily, how it's expected, what happens when you meet that expectation, and/or what happens if you don't.

Team Member Agreement

The last page in your packet is a team member agreement. If you're in HR, you're probably getting excited about where this is going. The point of this page is for accountability *and* preservation. Not just for the team member, but for yourself. Sometimes they forget conversations and sometimes they "forget" conversations. You certainly could also. After all, there is a lot of information you're taking in daily and providing daily. In many cases, it will be necessary to remind team members of their expectations and hold them accountable—not always a bad thing.

When team members, or anyone for that matter, are aware that they made an agreement, they're more likely to perform to your expectations. In other words, this step encourages more willpower since they understand the consequences. In addition, should the time ever come where a team member's unwillingness to cooperate reaches HR, that documentation will be filed and supported by HR for further disciplinary action. As a matter of fact, HR *encourages* this type of documentation. So, what should this look like? Here's a simple example for you to help:

I, _____(name)_____, have reviewed the training packet in detail and reviewed the engagement checklist, competitor checklist, community checklist, and support checklist with my manager _____(your name)_____ on _____(date)_____. I understand what behaviors are expected of me with every interaction, as each customer deserves a predictable experience. I will fulfill this duty, and should I have any questions or concerns on how to develop these behaviors, I will ask for help from a team member or my manager. I accept the responsibility to help this team become its best by making sure I am at my best.

_____(Team member signature)_____   _____(your signature)_____
Printed Name   Printed Name

You're more than welcome to use this example any way it's most helpful. As I say, whatever you do, keep it simple. The first half of the example was to confirm the understanding and it may be used for documented discipline, should a moment arise. The second half is a moral promise of duty and pride—a morale tool, not a disciplinary tool. In other words, it's to help the team member feel motivated *and* obligated to provide something greater than they have before, to take responsibility for their part in the team by becoming their best. I've learned that by adding this antidote, I've created a spark in their passion by helping them become a part of something much bigger, an added bonus to their drive to show up to work on time and on point to help any customer who needs their guidance.

Once all your team members have signed, they all have a clear understanding of your expectation. More importantly, they have a clear understanding about your leadership. You'll notice that this meeting will inspire most of your team to perform and excite them to anticipate a new, exciting experience. Not all will jump immediately because some will need to learn to trust you. This meeting is supposed to be for just that. Following through is the best way to prove it. In addition, leading by example will already set you apart from previous managers. You can't just earn their trust. You also have to keep it. It's time to hold them accountable but having fun while doing it. That's right. It's possible.

Phase 3: Scrimmage

Day 70 to 100

Your final thirty days is the scrimmage, where the rubber meets the road. All the observations, research, training, and preparation now lead to seeing how the team can utilize their new skills, behaviors, and knowledge effectively and efficiently, all while following your lead. This is also where all the knowledge and behaviors you've learned from all five pillars of this leadership guide come into action.

Sometimes it could easily get overwhelming or frustrating for team members because this is where change makes the big entrance. So be sure to monitor your team members' adaptation to your new system. These thirty days will set the tone for your team's transformation into a top-performing team.

For some, it will be easy. For others, it may be more challenging. This varies based on the team members' time in their role, typically. The longer they've been there, the harder the transition. The shorter the time, the easier to adapt. It is up to you to help all team members realize their potential. To empower this transition and motivate your team to perform, you need to use your branding techniques from earlier, like rally points, and create some artificial competition.

This is the perfect opportunity to launch something fun to assist their transition. Remember that it has to be organized. It must have goals, a ranking system, and rules on how to win in order to remain fair and unbiased. Take a look at my Chip-Off Challenge example again for some inspiration. Again, you may use this idea if you want. It is *very* effective. At the end of the day, what makes the game and the learning process impactful is *you*. You must stay committed to keeping them motivated, performing, and having fun learning. The goal of this scrimmage is to show your team how to become Alpha performers, which will require the use of all your skills learned from these pillars, especially pillars II and III. Without prioritizing and holding members accountable, the only thing you've provided is knowledge. Knowledge isn't useful without action! Believe it or not, the only things that don't vary between the biggest leaders in any industry are holding members accountable and prioritizing. Why they do so is dependent on them, but what they do is all the same. You can't become a top performer without these behaviors in place.

With your contest launched, stay active and constantly reference the competitive game every chance you get, to keep the team engaged, to keep it top of mind. They love to hear updates like watching highlights from a sports channel or app. For example, using my Chip-Off Challenge, every time one of my team members did something recognizable to earn a chip, I'd openly congratulate them for reaching a mark and I would flip the chip like a coin right onto their desk. My voice grabs the others' attention to the achievement, the flip of the chip makes it fun to see and encouraging to earn (like handing over a trophy), and the sound of the chip hitting the desk makes the chance to win tangible—a great combination to instill motivation into the winning team member and those watching. They especially get excited when multiple chips are awarded. Chips just rain from the sky as in a Mardi Gras parade—fun and engaging.

Remember to keep the leaderboard you've created exposed in an area where it will have the most exposure to your team members. In some cases, it could be beneficial to have it where consumers can see it as well—up to you. As I keep saying, winners keep score. So you have to make sure the scoreboard is accessible to the team members at least. The more attention you draw to the board, the more your team members will be encouraged to keep track themselves. I referenced the board every morning or evening huddle and during every sales or award event. In addition, whatever you are using to help team members keep the score tangible, like the chips in my example, always keep them in plain sight. Like a prop, the chips are always held in my hand for other members to see, almost becoming a signature in itself—guerilla marketing at its best. When I spoke to team members, I would always position the chips in my hand, where they are always exposed, flipping them in my hand or between the fingers, just as long as my team members had it in their view. This helps their subconscious keep a mental note to earn more chips. Or in other words, perform and win—a clever reminder without saying a word. As a helpful addition, I always sent out an email every Monday with the leaderboard on it, some brief words of encouragement, and the rules at the end. You always want to reference how to win.

The game is underway. It's time to set your daily behaviors, starting with establishing your checkpoints. Using the MIL model, establish your checkpoints with each team member, based on their level of performance and be sure to add them to your calendar and priority list. It's imperative to maintain consistency with their checkpoints. For the first few meetings, they'll feel a little unprepared and unorganized, but as we mentioned about repetitive learning, your team members will adapt and become strategic by the end of the month. Just be patient. To help encourage them, you can help them prepare ten minutes before the meeting. Try asking them as a friendly reminder if they need help pulling reports or gathering their information—just a way to help open up acceptance and minimize stress prior to the checkpoint. Sometimes, team members could feel like it's more of a review at the start. Helping them prepare in this nature can really ease the tension, which can make a more productive and interactive checkpoint.

In each checkpoint, be sure to remain consistent also with the topic at hand while evaluating their performance, and it is crucial to listen.

Once you're done talking, be sure to allow them to respond. They will have much to ask and discuss during this transition, especially at the beginning, so keep the checkpoint interactive. Since the competition is underway, that may be a great icebreaker. If you have a team member refusing to prepare or cooperate in their checkpoint, refer back to pillar III about the unwilling.

With the competition active and checkpoints established, your observations should be much easier to conduct. How? Well, they know what's expected of them from the contest, and they have checkpoints scheduled to review their progress. They will have a stronger understanding for the observations and will be truly prepared for them. Unlike your observations completed in the first sixty days for identifying their performance level, these observations are now for tracking and monitoring your team's development that will continue throughout your leadership. These observations are the bread and butter of your training. The only way to know the progress of your team, identify their opportunities, and celebrate the successes is joining the front line to witness these yourself. Using the MIL model, coordinate your time to make your respective observations, starting with the Charlie performers. Remember to keep those scheduled observation times to yourself unless it calls for notifying them of it earlier. Team members expecting an observation to take place can create an inaccurate analysis of their progress and may naturally attract shortcuts. For example, team members could put on a show when they expect your observation, which may not be the same expressed behaviors if you weren't present.

REMEMBER: There will be times when it would benefit the team member to know ahead of time, and that is perfectly acceptable. For example, if one of my team members had a big appointment, I'd let them know I'd be observing during that appointment. This helps us both make sure the team member is at their highest performance. In addition, I would play a supporting role to help my team member's success rate. I would introduce myself as such to his or her clients to help uplift my team member's ability to assist their client or customer, like a wingman. Besides, no matter how

hard someone can work to convince you otherwise, sales is a *team sport*. It always was and always will be. This is an opportunity to complete an observation, to empower your team member to succeed, to aid in the success of that interaction and build upon your relationship. Now *that's* leadership. That is what you're all about, right?

When observing, stick to precisely what you or your company's ideal interaction is. Many sales companies have an observation form already in place, but if yours doesn't, by now you should have your own assembled from earlier in this pillar. Utilize the same form in every interaction and with every team member—consistency.

You'll witness other managers taking shortcuts such as jotting notes on a pad, with no follow-up, or just listening in and going off memory. What are a few issues that could arise from these shortcuts? There are many, but a few impacts consist of miscommunication, inconsistent training, failure to lead by example, and more importantly, inevitable poor performance. Always have your observation form with you or within reach when able. This strongly reinforces the team's learning curve.

Now this is where you're going to learn another huge secret of how to help team members perform faster and for you to obtain your goal more quickly. The typical observation form will consist of at least three sections (or categories). Of course, there may be multiple lines underneath each section, outlining what to observe. Almost every manager that I've worked under or beside has made the ultimate fallacy when observing or training others how to observe. They completed every section, *every* time. Some of you may be thinking, "Well, duh. That's what you're supposed to do." However, I want you to think about the last interaction you were observed on and remember everything your superior coached you on. Can you truly remember the entire coaching session? Or are you only recalling one to two things? If that. If you do, you have a stronger memory than most, which is great, but a majority of your team members don't because of all the natural distractions we face on a daily basis. But if you don't, then you can understand my point. The interaction wasn't as impactful because there was too much information trying to be absorbed. This situation makes it difficult for team members to learn and adapt efficiently. In addition, over time, it can frustrate you to wonder why team members don't seem to retain those coaching sessions. On the flip side with your manager or leader, this can ultimately put too much pressure on you, which may lead to false documentation or confusion or miscommunication of your own because of how overwhelming observations can be if completely filled 100 percent of the time, all the time. The secret is to tackle one section at a time, mastering each section one by one.

REAL LIFE

When I first took over a team in the banking industry, my manager was trained on how to complete observations and, therefore, taught me the same expectation. We were all trained to complete every observation thoroughly. As I always do during my first one hundred days, I followed protocol for my observations for the first thirty days. During that time frame, I realized how difficult it was to read the questions, listen to the conversation triggers, and write down quotes verbatim while the interactions were continuing to build momentum. Quotes eventually had to become notes, and notes became jotted phrases. I felt I must have been doing something wrong because I was having a difficult time keeping accurate information during a live interaction, not to mention how difficult it was to remain in an interaction for the entire session. Many times, I was interrupted because my time was needed someplace else that a delegated authority couldn't assist with. Or the conversation would go too fast to document on time. In addition to these small issues, if I did record the entire interaction, I would hold coaching sessions afterward, and team members had a difficult time remembering the entire conversation as I pointed out specifics recorded. It was a lot of information to take in.

I asked peers for their observations, and guess what I found? The same thing. In some cases, it was a little worse. As a matter of fact, you can always tell who the veterans were because they would have their own language written everywhere in small phrases or acronyms. Unless you knew their language, you wouldn't be able to make out what observation was made.

As I followed up, team members would make the same mistakes too often. As you can imagine, I heard, "Sorry. I forgot," quite often. I knew there was a gap here. Turns out, it was simply too much. Falling back to my "keep it simple" strategy, I decided to focus on one section only at a time until my team mastered it before moving to the next.

With this company, there were four categories with three to four instructions guiding you to listen for particular points during the interaction. I figured one category per week would create a more effective interaction and impactful coaching session by helping them focus on perfecting one section at a time. For one week, I would only focus on that one category, for example, the introduction. I would observe how they introduced themselves, if they asked for a reason for their visit, and if they properly invited them to their desk for the conversation. That's it. I was able to turn a thirty-minute to an hour observation with scrambled lingo into a ten-minute detailed observation. I freed up much more time to focus on my top priorities, and when I followed up with the team member, they recalled everything I discussed, especially using their quotes I was able to capture. Once I was able to provide my feedback, they were able to execute flawlessly on the following interactions. The following week, we moved on to the next section.

With one single focus at a time, my team members were able to retain my advice during our coaching sessions and turn around their performance much faster. After a six-day coaching focus, they mastered the section, and we continued to the next. By the end of the fourth week, my team became master conversationalists. After four weeks, I started right back where I started. Or I focused on a specific section necessary for a particular team member—whichever provided the greatest support for each team member. My peers followed swiftly after they saw the results, and upper management eventually adopted the behavior for all managers to use a similar behavior. After my results, why would you not?

Keep it simple. Start with one section weekly and let them know which section you're focusing on to help prepare them for success. Follow the MIL model to determine how many times each team member should be observed per week. For example, your Charlie performers will need daily attention and Alpha performers may need only one to two per week, unless your superior tells you otherwise. If you remain consistent with your plan, each team member will improve by the end of the week. In addition, with creating more time, you will make it easier for team members to retain information, provide you with increasingly effective coaching sessions and check-ins, and help your team begin to climb the ranks. As *should* you. Your leadership style comes a dime a dozen. You deserve to be at the top.

Remember how important it is to meet with your team member immediately after the interaction, if able. This will make the interaction more engaging and provide clearer examples while the interaction is fresh on their mind. The longer you wait, the greater the chance more important details may fade away. Besides, there is only so much you can fit on paper. Immediately after an interaction is the perfect time to motivate your team member to keep up the great successes you've observed.

Keeping within that small window after an interaction can bring in a lot of energy and excitement, especially with the contest. Think of it this way. If you won a prize, would you prefer it now, or later? You're a winner, so I know you said now. Don't let them wait to celebrate or wait to realign their behaviors. Help them win in the moment. However, when business doesn't permit an immediate follow-up, be sure to get to it as soon as you can. The first three minutes are the most impactful. I've learned that after three minutes, you'll lose much of their excitement because additional tasks or interactions took over. This makes it especially difficult for team members to remember details from their successes. If they don't remember, then it's as if it never happened. Keep them engaged and connected to fresh interactions. They may not say it, but every team member will prefer it.

You're building a routine—a routine that will help your team become its best. With the contest underway, your brand and rally points set, your observations scheduled, and your follow-ups in place, you and your team are ready to rock out your final thirty days and beyond. Holding team members accountable daily for their goals, behaviors, and contest results will only help them evolve into achieving machines. This is the most exciting time of your trial because this is the evolutionary moment when your team development begins to truly take shape. From the first thirty days you learned about your team to the final thirty days launching into the contest, your team has been preparing to spread their wings.

Every day, your team will try harder and work harder to drive their best for themselves and for you (your influential vision) because they witnessed what you've done through your first one hundred days to help develop their performance. They believe in *you*, and having that belief is the last ingredient a team needs to become Alpha performers. Once the contest is almost to a close, if you don't already have a monthly or quarterly meeting scheduled, make sure to do so. Here you will recognize and celebrate not just the contest winners, but the progress your team has made. Help them become aware of how far they've driven themselves and what they've become. Regardless if it was a little improvement, or tremendous, it's important for them to see that and for you to recognize it. Sometimes, when driven individuals are caught up in the daily routine, it's hard to notice how much time has passed and how much they've improved. This is a great time to reflect and congratulate just that on a team and individual level. By the end of this first meeting, you'll have yourself an Alpha-performing team.

From here, continue your routines daily. Plan today for what needs to be done tomorrow. Keep score. Keep records. Keep up. Keep winning. In addition, don't stop developing your new foundation by adding in new contests, behaviors, services, resources, community events, and anything else that can further prepare and strengthen your team's development, not to forget continuing to grow, learn, and evolve yourself as a leader and making sure to share that knowledge with your team. As you grow, your team will grow, and together all is possible. Remember my reference from Henry Ford earlier, saying, "Coming together is a beginning; keeping together is progress; working together is success." You're ready to climb!

CONCLUSION

WHEN THOMAS JEFFERSON said, "Do you want to know who you are? Don't ask. Act! Action will delineate and define you," he was on point. You took a huge step by picking up my guide, reading through the pillars, and learning how to strengthen your ability to create and lead top-performing teams in your business. You took this step to progress your career. Or maybe you took this step to progress your leadership skills. Either way, you acted to improve. You now have a solid foundation to flip any team out there. No matter where you are in life, you have the ability to be exactly what you need to be.

If you recall previously, we talked about the importance of having a process and that nine out of ten times, the team is failing because of the process—either a failed process or the absence of one. A process may be complex to create, but once it's part of your culture, it becomes simple. I took care of the hard part for you. Throughout my pillars, you've learned a process, right? You've learned how to analyze a team and a team member to determine their level of performance. How to develop each team member based on their specific level of performance under Alpha, Bravo, and Charlie. How to control your time and mold every day efficiently to maximize your team's development and so much more. You have the complete process in your hand now. Execution is all that is left.

REMEMBER: Reference this guide anytime you need to. Keep it on your desk. Take it with you wherever you go. Whatever you do, until you've truly mastered the process, don't let it out of your sight. Out of sight, out of mind, right?

What Now?

Time for your team to evolve and grow together. That's the point, right? Soon, completely on their own. While other coworkers will revere you, managers (positions above your own, internal and external) will be desiring your help. Through networking, relationship building, and partnerships you have or will form, more opportunities will present themselves from your successes. The secret to really unleashing the success of this guide is consistency and ability to move on to other teams. Build on your own momentum.

A moment will present itself when you have reached the peak of your performance with that team. Once that moment presents itself, then it will be time to develop one of your best to learn and, one day, take your position (if you haven't already). That will be your moment to find the next opportunity, the next team that desperately needs your leadership. It could be one year from now. It could be three years. It could be five. Whenever that moment comes, don't be afraid to say yes to that opportunity. Internal or external, know what goal you need to achieve for your career, let the recruiter or manager know, and discover where you'll be best fitted. If team members wish to follow, then you certainly want them to. This secret maneuver only aids your process and speeds up a team's learning curve.

Remember: External hires earn (most cases over 15 percent) more than internal hires because most corporate processes use your loyalty to their advantage.

So where do you go from here? Do you recall the following chart from my history at the beginning of this guide?

	LIG	WIG	TIE	MIL
Merits	-	+	-	+
Promotions	-	-	+	+

Our three groups of people here were in the Life Is Good group, the Work Is Great group, or Title Is Everything. Notice anything different from before? Remember when I said that I would reveal the mystery group later? We have been developing that this whole time. This group of achievers are team members from my system. The Mason influential leadership group, or MIL group. They are a successful group is capable of achieving merits on their path to bigger promotions because their success is much more than just a title or a position. It becomes a way of life with a purpose—a purpose set by *your* vision, a way of progress. No matter where you started when you picked this guide up, *this* is where you are now or will be.

From here, all you have to do to achieve this position on the chart is to maintain consistency with this system. Of course, always remember to evolve where it's needed. If there is anything either required to be completed by upper management or simply something new you've learned that you feel would greatly impact your team's performance, definitely add or alter this system to best fit *your* style. As before, it is important to never stop learning.

Do you recall discussing and, if you didn't have them before, making those personal goals within the next one to five years? This is where you want to revisit those goals and see not only how this new path can help you achieve your professional goals, but also how they can help you achieve your personal goals as well. Regardless if it's receiving a college degree, traveling out of the country, or buying that brand-new vehicle you've always been wanting, this guide helped you shape how you can achieve those personal goals while conquering your professional goals. Try to see how you can shape your plan to hit those personal goals.

As a standard rule, you want to complete at least twelve months with a team before deciding to move on to another, wherever that may be. This is long enough for your team to make a huge impact on their performance and to master your process. Once you have completed at least twelve successful months, you'll be ready to move forward. If you're ready to move on to another company with greater pay for a new team, then do it. If you're recruited into a higher position with higher pay, then accept it. If your company recognized your potential and provided a greater opportunity for you, then take it. As long as you have an opportunity to acquire another team that greatly needs your leadership to succeed *and* that opportunity provides you an increase in income, position, or both, you deserve that moment to say yes.

This guide is helping you strengthen your career, leadership skills, and ability to develop others into top-performing leaders of their own. Use it to its fullest to help further your ambitions as well as others. That was *my* goal—to be able to share this with *you* and help you develop into the leader that you desire to be. I hope this guide will continue to help throughout your career. With all of this being said, there is just one more thing to say:

Congratulations!

Congratulations on completing my guide. It's a lot of information to take in, but with many references to help your climb to mastery. Some of this information was new to you. Some of this information was a refresher. Some of this information may have changed your way of thinking and motivated you to continue improvement. Regardless of how this information has reached you, all this information is extremely powerful for you.

Let your leadership influence the world one team at a time. Confucius said, "He who says he can and he who says he can't are both usually right." With my guide, all you have to say is "I can!" This guide helped show you where and how to start. This is your foundation with all the pillars you need to build on it and make it yours. Now go out there and build your legacy how you want it. I wish you the best of luck!

THANK YOU!

REFERENCES

Tucker, A. (2011). *Stop Squatting With Your Spurs On*. New York: Morgan James Publishing.

Kuhnke, E. (2012). *Body Language for Dummies* 2nd Edition. West Sussex, England: John Wiley & Sons, Ltd.

Buckingham, M. (2011). *StandOut*. Nashville: Thomas Nelson.

Giles, L. (1910). *The Art of War* by Sun Tzu translated from Chinese. London, England: Luzac & Co.

Mehrabian, Albert and Winer, Morton (1967). "Decoding of Inconsistent Communications," *Journal of Personality and Social Psychology* 6(1): 109–114.

Mehrabian, Albert and Ferris, Susan R. (1967). "Inference of Attitudes from Nonverbal Communication in Two Channels," *Journal of Consulting Psychology* 31(3): 248–252.

Merriam-Webster. (n.d.). Customer. In *Merriam-Webster.com dictionary*. Retrieved July 13, 2015, from https://www.merriam-webster.com/dictionary/customer.

Niccol, A., Abraham, M., and Newman, M. (producers) and Niccol, A. (director) (2011). *In Time* [Motion Picture]. United States: Twentieth Century Fox.

Smith, W., Lassiter, J., and Zee, T. (producers), and Tennant, A. (director) (2005). *Hitch* [motion picture]. United States: Columbia Pictures.

Hughes, J. (producer), and Columbus, C. (director). (1990). *Home Alone* [motion picture]. United States: Twentieth Century Fox.

Gibson, M., Ladd Jr., A., and Davey, B. (Producers), and Gibson, M. (director) (1995). *Braveheart* [motion picture]. United States: Paramount Pictures (North America) and Twentieth Century Fox (international).

Vaughn, V. and Levy, S. (producers), and Levy, S. (director) (2013). *The Internship* [motion picture]. United States: Twentieth Century Fox.

Mazzola, A. (producer) (2013–2020). *The Profit* [television series]. United States: CNBC.

Lally, P., van Jaarsveld, C. H. M., Potts, H. W. W., and Wardle, J. (2010). "How are habits formed: Modelling habit formation in the real world," *European Journal of Social Psychology* 40: 998–1009.

Maltz, M. (1960) *Psycho-cybernetics.* NJ: Prentice-Hall.

CPSIA information can be obtained
at www.ICGtesting.com
Printed in the USA
BVHW071407100720
583431BV00001B/44

9 781984 578105